'A gripping real-life financial thriller. Joshua Oliver skilfully unravels the corruption at the heart of crypto, showing why millions of investors bought into a fiction.'

– Claer Barrett, author of *What They Don't Teach You About Money*

'Filled with surprising and infuriating details, Joshua Oliver's *Hype Machine* is a richly reported and devastating indictment of a financial bubble of unprecedented size and stupidity.'

– Zeke Faux, author of *Number Go Up*

'*Hype Machine* is the definitive history of how the crypto industry was built by a small circle of entrepreneurs who raised billions from the world's smartest money managers, then left millions of everyday people holding the bag when their empires turned out to be the largest frauds ever seen. In a riveting, often hilarious reporting journey, Oliver brings us into the room with crypto's leading figures, then deftly shows us how the crypto dream was built on little more than digital snake oil. It is a must read for anyone who thinks about money.'

– David Jeans, author of *Wonder Boy*

'The extraordinary story of FTX and its founder Sam Bankman-Fried provides critical lessons on finance, economics and human psychology. The rise and fall of this leading player in the crypto industry perfectly mirrors one of the oddest, most dangerous bubbles in recent financial history. Financial markets have always been attractive to speculative chancers. Crypto was no different. Joshua Oliver expertly weaves together deep reporting on the circus around SBF with clear explanations of the crypto bubble as a whole in this deeply reported and important book.'

– Duncan Mavin, author of *Pyramid of Lies*

HYPE MACHINE

HYPE MACHINE

HOW GREED, FRAUD AND FREE MONEY CRASHED CRYPTO

Joshua Oliver

Heligo
Books

First published in the UK in 2024 by Heligo Books
An imprint of Black & White Publishing Group
A Bonnier Books UK company
4th Floor, Victoria House, Bloomsbury Square, London, WC1B 4DA

Owned by Bonnier Books, Sveavägen 56, Stockholm, Sweden

Hardback ISBN: 978-1-7851-2096-1
Trade paperback ISBN: 978-1-7851-2097-8
eBook ISBN: 978-1-7851-2098-5
Audio ISBN: 978-1-7851-2099-2

A CIP catalogue record for this book Prelimis available from the British Library.

Cover design by Jake Cook
Typeset by IDSUK (Data Connection) Ltd
Printed and bound in Great Britain by Clays Ltd, Elcograf S.p.A

1 3 5 7 9 10 8 6 4 2

Every reasonable effort has been made to trace copyright-holders of material
reproduced in this book. If any have been inadvertently overlooked,
the publisher would be glad to hear from them.

Heligo Books is an imprint of Bonnier Books UK
www.bonnierbooks.co.uk

For Jill
My first and most important editor

'The media requires there be a new genius every season.'

Fran Lebowitz

'The purpose of democracy is to keep capitalism from destroying society.'

Michael Ignatieff

Note on Sources

This book is the product of around two years of reporting on crypto, markets and investments for the *Financial Times* starting in 2021. I conducted further research and interviews for the book during the summer and autumn of 2023 and attended SBF's trial in October. I am indebted to my colleagues at the *FT*, and at other publications, for their excellent work covering the crypto crash, and have tried to credit their work wherever it appears in this narrative. I apologise in advance if there are any oversights. I benefited from reading Zeke Faux's excellent book *Number Go Up* and Michael Lewis's *Going Infinite* before having to commit my own account of these events to paper.

I had the opportunity to meet or interview many key figures in the industry, including Sam Bankman-Fried, Changpeng Zhao and Alex Mashinsky at the height of their powers, and follow their stories as they unwound. I spoke to Arthur Hayes as part of the research for this book in the summer of 2023. I interviewed SBF over many hours, including a series of conversations over that same summer of 2023, which was interrupted when he was sent to jail ahead of his trial. I have also interviewed many former FTX staff and close associates. Outside of Gary Wang, Caroline Ellison and Nishad Singh – the three who have pleaded guilty and cooperated with prosecutors – I have had access to several of those closest to SBF. I am grateful to all these people for their time and trust. I allowed many of the people from FTX, other companies and across crypto to speak anonymously. I granted anonymity when I felt it would make it easier for people to tell you what they really think.

My research also included thousands of pages of legal documents from the various bankruptcies, lawsuits and criminal cases spawned by the crypto crash. Many of these cases are ongoing, and some of the claims made by parties have not been tested or proven in court. I have tried to make sure that my account of legal disputes is fair and balanced and that I have been clear when I am recounting allegations rather than facts. Readers should be aware that legal claims represent only one side of the story.

When I use data about the crypto market in the book, I have relied on widely accepted industry sources including CryptoCompare and CoinMarketCap. The underdeveloped nature of crypto markets, and the accusation of market manipulation and fake trading, mean that even the best data sources may at times be inaccurate or incomplete.

I have tried to be clear with the reader about what parts of the book are statements of fact and where either the people I have quoted, or I as the author, offer analysis and perspectives on events. Based on my research and experience as a reporter on this industry, I felt it was valuable to share my personal views at times. A large amount of

Note on Sources

the published material about crypto is paid for by the crypto industry itself or comes from people with economic incentives to boost digital assets. I think there is value in presenting an independent, fair and critical account. Governments and societies are having an important debate about the future role of crypto and the proper regulation of this disruptive technology, which will inform key decisions that will be taken in the years ahead. I hope this book will make a contribution to that public debate.

Relying in some cases on the memory of my sources or conflicting accounts of events in a wide-ranging and complex story that is still unfolding introduces the possibility of errors. I endeavoured to resolve inconsistencies and rely on the most credible, contemporary evidence. In addition to the editorial checks provided by my publisher, I employed a fact checker to review the manuscript. Nevertheless, any errors are mine. I have tried diligently to perform my role as a journalist, and to offer you the best available version of the truth.

Contents

Preface

Sam Bankman-Fried edged through the side door of courtroom 26A. His eyes darted around the large, dark-panelled room, seeking a friendly face in the crowd of strangers. He spotted his lawyers and moved urgently the few feet across to the defence table, where he slumped into a chair. His suit jacket, which looked two sizes too big, hunched up towards his ears.

It was hard to believe that this young man, who looked very much as if he'd borrowed his father's suit for 'take your kid to work day', was once the head of the most successful tech startup in the world – or that he was now facing the first day of his trial on charges that he orchestrated 'one of the largest financial frauds in American history'.

The list of people who Bankman-Fried has been compared to is long, and extraordinary. In three years of relentless public attention – as he became the responsible face of the cryptocurrency world, and then its arch villain – he had been variously likened to Jay Gatsby, Albert Einstein, John Pierpont Morgan, Frodo Baggins,

Michael Jordan, Bill Gates, Elon Musk, Mark Zuckerberg, Warren Buffett, Bernie Madoff and Charles Ponzi.

Bankman-Fried looked like he had lost 20 or 30 pounds in the eight weeks he had spent in Brooklyn's notorious Metropolitan Detention Centre. He had refused to break his vegan diet, and subsisted partly on peanut butter donated by sympathetic fellow inmates. Another prisoner had cut his hair for the trial. The frizzy mane that had defined Bankman-Fried's image as a celebrity CEO was pared back to a fluffy crop. He looked in every way deflated.

I had last seen Bankman-Fried in person at his parents' house in Palo Alto eight months earlier. He had still been his irrepressible self, frizzy-haired and slightly portly. He had fidgeted through our hours-long conversation – playing computer games or checking baseball scores on his laptop as we spoke, and toying with the chunky black ankle bracelet he wore at the time as a condition of his bail. His pre-trial freedom was revoked mostly because he could not stop himself from speaking to journalists like me.

Even though he was now not getting full doses of his ADHD medication, his fidgeting had stopped. The strangest thing about seeing Bankman-Fried in the courtroom was that he was finally sitting still.

The pale, shrunken Bankman-Fried sitting between his broad-backed lawyers seemed very unlike the person I had known as 'SBF' – an oddball CEO whose grand moral vision clashed with the lavish parts of his lifestyle, and the grubby way he earned his money. He had been a fascinating subject whose social awkwardness had made him utterly improbable casting for a globe-trotting celebrity businessman.

Preface

Whether he was on a private jet from his home in the Bahamas to New York, or sitting on stage with Bill Clinton, SBF – if he could help it – never wore anything more formal than shorts and a company-branded T-shirt. Now, he had asked the judge for permission to appear in a suit, rather than a prison jumpsuit. The court order, which allowed for 'four pairs of socks . . . and appropriate undergarments' was a barely noticed indignity compared to what was at stake when he finally entered the courtroom.

In court, Bankman-Fried was two people.

His defence lawyers always called him 'Sam'. To them, he was one of the great genius entrepreneurs of the millennial generation. He was a profoundly awkward young man. SBF once described how he had not quite cracked the art of smiling and other facial expressions of emotion until he was a few years out of college, working as a trader at the elite financial firm Jane Street. 'It felt unnatural. And I wasn't good at it. It didn't look right,' he said. But in spite of these challenges, he had built two multi-billion-dollar companies – a trading firm called Alameda Research and a crypto-currency exchange called FTX. He promised that both companies were engines to make money for his particular school of philanthropy. His project was nothing less than saving the world. Money was just a means to that end.

SBF had been so dedicated to this mission that he barely slept, napping on a beanbag next to his desk. He was, his lawyers said, a 'math nerd who didn't drink or party', preferring board games to bottle service. He became a billionaire – the richest person of his age in the world, with nearly a billion dollars in net worth for every year he'd been alive. He moved his business from his native

California to Hong Kong and then to the Bahamas, where he bought a $30 million penthouse for his friends to live in – but still drove himself around in a Toyota Corolla and wore cargo shorts to business meetings.

In the rush of success, he had neglected the details. As customers of FTX entrusted billions upon billions to his care, he failed to build the infrastructure needed to keep it safe. To be honest, SBF thought having a bunch of boring grown-ups with titles like 'chief risk officer' around would slow down his race to save the world. And, yes, perhaps he had attended one Super Bowl party too many. He had lost control of spending and risk. When the crypto market crashed in 2022, he went bankrupt.

'Sam' was ready, eager, falling over himself to admit that it was all his fault. He knew he had made unforgivable mistakes. But he didn't think he was guilty. He was in court on that clear October morning because the US government – embarrassed by its failure to intervene in the crypto market before millions of Americans lost money in the crash – had decided to make an example of the most famous crypto executive they could lay their hands on.

Prosecutors told the court about a very different person. The whole story of 'Sam', they said, was 'built on lies'. Bankman-Fried – the government lawyers called him the 'defendant' – was a master manipulator. From the beginning, his $40 billion-dollar crypto empire had not been what it appeared. He bought the silence of those who challenged his reckless handling of other people's money, and paid off anyone who came close to discovering the secrets known only to his tight inner circle. He used the aura of philanthropy and the baffling complexity of cryptocurrency to conceal the truth.

Preface

FTX sucked in billions from customers with promises of a better financial future, and passed it secretly to Alameda, which became a slush fund for spending in SBF's maniacal pursuit of wealth and influence. He deceived the world's most sophisticated investors. He bought respect in Washington, and meetings at the White House. He threw millions of dollars at celebrities to obtain a parade of endorsements from Tom Brady, Larry David and dozens more A-listers. He charmed the media. Only the crypto market crash exposed the truth. The 'defendant' had stolen at least $8 billion from several million people.

If he was guilty, the 'defendant' would probably spend decades in prison. If he was acquitted, 'Sam', like any other thirty-something whose life had fallen apart, would be heading back home to live with his parents.

*

SBF's parents, Stanford University law professors Joe Bankman and Barbara Fried, sat on the wooden pews a few rows behind and to the right of their son. In another life, with a different child, it might have been a wedding.

Out of the windows, the sunlight sparkled on a sweeping view of New York's downtown skyline and the river beyond. The Brooklyn Bridge was almost in view. Although they were obviously focused on the ceremony that was about to unfold, some part of their mind must have been wondering quite how they were going to pay for it all. The panel of lawyers flanking their son would be billing the family tens of thousands of dollars an hour.

Bankman and Fried watched as the people closest to their son, one by one, walked down the aisle to the front of the room and said their piece about SBF. Gary Wang had first met SBF at a high school summer programme for gifted maths students and became his right-hand man at FTX. He said SBF had ordered him to give their private trading firm Alameda unlimited access to the customer money stored in FTX's vaults. 'I trusted his judgement,' Gary said.

Adam Yedidia was SBF's best friend from college at MIT, who had got him on to veganism in the first place. They had shared games of padel tennis in the grounds of the penthouse, and many board game nights together with their fellow room-mates. Adam said that when he finally learned the truth about what SBF had done, he quit his job at FTX and left the Bahamas at once.

Nishad Singh had probably known SBF the longest. He was a childhood friend of the Bankman-Frieds' younger son, Gabe – and they had attended the same elite Bay Area high school. 'Sam is a formidable character, brilliant, so I had a lot of admiration and respect for him,' Nishad said. 'Over time I think a lot of that eroded, and I grew distrustful.' Nishad's girlfriend and family sat a few rows behind the Bankman-Fried parents. They did not acknowledge each other in the courtroom.

The person who everyone had been waiting for to walk down the aisle between the courtroom pews was Caroline Ellison. On paper, she and Bankman-Fried were a perfect match. Their lives had followed eerily parallel lines. As Bankman-Fried was growing up on the fringes of the Stanford campus, Caroline was raised near MIT – also the child of a pair of academics. For college, they swapped places. Ellison studied at Stanford, Bankman-Fried at MIT. Their paths finally crossed as traders on Wall Street. They shared philosophical interests. Both loved the *Harry Potter* series as children, although Bankman-Fried became dismissive of literature as he grew up. Ellison remained interested in fantasy, sometimes creating live-action role play games, where her friends could dress up to act out different adventures. It seemed inevitable they would come together. Caroline joined SBF's first startup. They began a tumultuous romance.

Caroline gave the court the clearest picture of Sam's heart. He just didn't think rules like 'don't lie and don't steal' were justified. His own moral code – the greatest good for the greatest number – was more important. And if he had the slightest edge in probability, he would take any risk regardless of the consequences. She portrayed a person who would see nothing wrong in gambling with other people's money if he had a 50.1 per cent chance of never getting caught and doing something useful with the winnings.

The lawless world of crypto gave SBF the perfect opportunity to ignore society's rules. Now, he was in the grip of the US justice system. Caroline, Nishad and Gary had pleaded guilty to multiple crimes as part of a vast, fraudulent conspiracy. They had come to court to testify that Bankman-Fried was the mastermind. Adam had received immunity so he could speak in court. He was worried, he said, that he had 'unwittingly . . . contributed to the commission of a crime'.

SBF sat impassively through the days of testimony, tapping on the laptop in front of him or whispering into this lawyer's ear. Once or twice, he shook his head at the testimony he heard from his former friends. He would have his chance to tell his side of the story.

*

The stories these five friends told, of the millions and billions they had toyed with like so much Monopoly money on a penthouse board game night, seemed utterly fanciful – as if the group of friends had been playing a years-long 'live-action role play' of running a cryptocurrency empire, which had somehow turned into a horrible reality.

The jury panel of twelve members and six back-ups, who sat in three rows of leather armchairs with their backs to the spectacular views out of the courtroom windows, included a nurse, a special education teacher, two conductors from the Metro North commuter trains and a man who described himself quite precisely as 'a tool and parts clerk' for vehicle maintenance at the US Postal Service.

Another young man with mock diamond earrings in the back row, who held his baseball cap in his hand as he entered and left the courtroom, initially seemed quite reasonably less concerned with the case on trial than with the fact that he had been ordered to serve on the jury each day, even though he worked a night shift at a Midtown hotel.

In a day and a half of jury selection, the judge had grown increasingly exasperated with the reasons and excuses offered by the potential jurors hoping to get sent home. A woman who had plane tickets booked to attend her husband's co-worker's wedding somehow got off. So did a stylish young woman who was due to travel to El Salvador as operations manager for the Ms. Universe pageant. The judge spent several minutes arguing back and forth with a teaching assistant in the back row about whether her absence from work would mean that the disabled students she assisted would not be able to ride the school bus. He heard from a man whose ex-wife had died

Preface

two weeks earlier and who was due to fly out to help his daughter with the paperwork. As the hours rolled by the judge became less patient. He insisted a dignified lady had to reschedule an MRI, for which she had waited months, so that she could help decide SBF's fate.

All the back and forth seemed like a calculated reminder of how far SBF's reality of billion-dollar gambles and plans to save humankind had diverged from the real lives of a random cross-section of humanity from the streets of New York, hauled to court on a Tuesday morning.

The witness who seemed to make the best impression on the jury was Adam. After earning tens of millions in 18 months' work for FTX, and then losing almost all of it when the company collapsed, Adam had come back from the tropical island of untold crypto riches to become a high-school maths teacher. He had rejoined the real world.

Gary, Caroline and Nishad could not do the same. At least, not yet. They were too closely tied to the wreckage of FTX to simply return to civilian life. For all three, cooperation in the trial was the key to avoiding a prison sentence. They were now ready to condemn the implausible and reckless crypto-financial dealings, which – during the heady days of the crypto bubble one year earlier – each had seemed to think were perfectly fine. Their testimony might be enough to buy their freedom. The opportunity to live a normal life was the prize held out in front of them for turning on SBF.

As his friends had fled the scene of the crime, SBF had remained on the island. He believed, and I think still believes, that if he'd been given a bit more time and flexibility in the lawless world of crypto he could have made everything right again.

The US government has tried hard to yank him back to reality. They plucked him from the Bahamas and placed him in jail. One night in December he was photographed, racoon-eyed in the glare of spotlights on the tarmac at Nassau airport, as federal agents marched him to a jet bound for America. He wore handcuffs and a smooth white dress shirt with wide cuffs, like an old-fashioned mobster. But the government could not convince him to say that he was guilty of fraud, or that he was wrong about the reality of the crypto phenomenon. His position had become ever more isolated. He entered the courtroom as the sole bad guy of the drama. 'They'd have you think he was quite the villain,' said his defence lawyer, Mark Cohen. 'Or, more precisely, almost a cartoon of a villain.'

Could it be true that this unprepossessing, badly dressed young man was, alone, to blame for the $2 trillion implosion in cryptocurrencies that prosecutors were now – in a broad sense – trying to avenge?

Of course not. SBF's rise had been supported and enabled by the vast global cryptocurrency industry, by Wall Street and Silicon Valley, and by a collective financial delusion on a historic scale. His trial looked at this vast canvas through the pinhole of one individual's guilt or innocence.

In his journey to fame and fortune, whether by luck or calculation, SBF had tapped into powerful realities in 21st-century capitalism. What you can promise is more important than what you can do. A good story is worth more than the truth. And if you want to separate people from their money, tell them that they can get rich by changing the world.

Introduction

Next year, my mother will retire after 20 years as a public-school teacher in Toronto, Canada. She taught grade six and was a school librarian, before switching over to kindergarten and eventually becoming principal of a suburban elementary school. Her pension fund, the Ontario Teachers' Pension Plan, is one of the largest investors in the world, managing nearly $250 billion on behalf of 336,000 current and former teachers in the Canadian province where I grew up. In late 2021 and early 2022, Ontario Teachers invested $95 million in Sam Bankman-Fried's cryptocurrency empire.

Maybe because it was in some small part my mum's money, the Ontario Teachers investment in FTX always stuck in my mind. Even at the time, it seemed weird. At a conference hosted by FTX in Nassau, Bahamas in the spring of 2022, I sat near an executive from Ontario Teachers at a dinner in a Mediterranean restaurant overlooking the pool and gently ribbed them about how they'd better not lose my mother's money betting on Sam. What was at that time a nagging doubt that something didn't quite add up should, in retrospect, have been a deafening alarm bell. Because SBF was not only surprisingly young and inexperienced to be the chief executive of a multi-billion-dollar company; he was also lying. He took the money from Ontario Teachers and dozens of the world's most sophisticated professional investors, alongside billions more in deposits from customers of the exchange, and handed billion after billion in free loans to his own trading firm Alameda Research. His companies spent money like water, splashing out on luxury condos, political donations, massive celebrity marketing campaigns and investments in bizarre cryptocurrencies and startups. Seven months after the Bahamas conference where I had dinner with the Ontario Teachers exec, and SBF had dinner with Katy Perry and Orlando Bloom, the collapse of Alameda's crypto investments cascaded into the failure of FTX. Shortly after the company went bankrupt, Ontario Teachers decided it wasn't getting its money back and wrote down the value of its $95 million investment in FTX to zero.

All of what I have just described should be completely impossible. When Ontario Teachers invested, FTX was a two-year-old company. SBF was its 29-year-old chief executive. Most of his key lieutenants were even younger, his childhood friends, college roommates and romantic partners. The company had recently moved its headquarters to the Bahamas. FTX was a crypto exchange, which means it let its customers buy, sell and trade different cryptocurrencies. Its speciality was trading in derivatives, financial contracts that allow users to bet on the future prices of assets – usually with

Introduction

borrowed money. And underlying all this were cryptocurrencies, assets that are conjured from thin air and cryptography, the value of which is based on nothing more than what the next person will buy them for.

So, we arrive at the question: how did my mother's pension fund come to lose $95 million investing in a crooked 29-year-old dork in the Bahamas running a company that facilitated trading in leveraged financial contracts based on assets that don't really exist?

*

The collapse of FTX was the most dramatic episode in the crash of cryptocurrencies in 2022. In just a few months, a $3 trillion-dollar bubble in digital assets went up in smoke. Ontario Teachers, and the other investors who trusted FTX, got into crypto at the peak of that bubble. To really understand what happened, you have to look at how SBF capitalised on this extraordinary financial delusion – and go back to try to understand where the bubble came from.

You can chart what happened by following one pretty simple number, adding together the US dollar value ascribed to all the cryptocurrency tokens in the world. This is called the total crypto market capitalisation. The number started at zero on 3 January 2009 when Satoshi Nakamoto (not a real name, or necessarily a real person) mined the so-called 'genesis block', the first link in the Bitcoin blockchain that has continued to clink forward ever since. Crypto was born.

Crypto's founding impulse is a pretty reasonable one. Looking around at the wreckage of a global financial crash, people said to themselves, 'Surely we can do better.' It's hard to argue with that logic. In the previous decades, the internet had caught on and revolutionised information and communication technology with innovations like Wikipedia and social media. For all the faults of the internet revolution, there was still a genuine spirit of optimism that technology could be applied to improve the world of money. The original crypto project, what you might call 'Crypto 1.0', was about using technology to create a better financial system. It was like Occupy Wall Street for hackers.

Vitalik Buterin, the Russian–Canadian founder of Ethereum, the second largest cryptocurrency project, could be the poster child for first-wave crypto. Buterin's Ethereum ecosystem includes a cryptocurrency, Ether. It also adds a whole range of interesting technologies for creating automatic contracts and decentralised organisations. Sallow and emaciated, with piercing eyes and a Lego-man haircut, Buterin is out of central casting for a whizz-kid computer programmer. He looks like he has been stored in a cool, dark place. And despite creating a cryptocurrency that is still (even after the crash) worth around $200 billion, he and his gang of followers retain the DIY air of a university hacker collective.

During its first decade, crypto's popularity grew gradually. It was a big hit with criminals moving money around the dark web, but otherwise remained a niche interest. Total crypto market cap built from a few million dollars into the low billions. This sounds like a lot of money, and by human standards it is. But it's a drop in the ocean of big-time finance. Hundreds of individual companies are worth more on their own. In 2017, things started to change. Ethereum gave people the ability to create new tokens with incredible ease. New tokens were popping up everywhere, and people were making money from selling them. Values kept shooting up. By the peak of the first boom in 2018, the total crypto market cap broke above $800 billion.

$800 billion is an amount of money that will really get people to sit up and take notice. Equally striking was the speed at which that value had appeared. In a single year, crypto's total value grew 45 times. That rapid growth was fuelled by rampant and often bizarre speculation. Those values were obviously not sustainable, and they quickly crashed back to earth. But the spectacle of all that fast-moving money drew attention, not only from the media and the public, but from the people who became the architects of the crypto world we see today.

The idealists, libertarians and techno-utopians who brought crypto from its infancy in 2008 to the doorstep of mainstream attention in 2017 were no match for the group of people who take centre stage for the next act of the story. SBF, whose background was at a Wall Street trading firm, was one of the people who arrived in the industry around this time – attracted by the vast amount of money sloshing around and the obvious opportunities to speculate, trade and scam your way to easy profits. He wasn't alone.

SBF was in the vanguard of a takeover of crypto by people who came from traditional finance and Big Tech. The new arrivals kept crypto's promises of a fairer, more open and decentralised financial system. They abandoned almost everything else. Bit by bit, these new arrivals started re-engineering the financial system using dig-ital assets.

*

'Decentralisation', the cornerstone of the original crypto vision, all but disappeared from the scene. For Bitcoin to work as a decentralised currency without any middlemen, each and every user had to hold their own wealth independently with their own digital wallet. If I sent you $100 worth of Bitcoin, that transfer would move from me to you through a decentralised tech system without trusting any central institution to manage the payment. That cuts out one of the main jobs that our banking system performs, shuffling money from me to you. The design neglects another important job that banks, along with the government, do for us. You can lose your ID, forget your passwords or misplace your bank cards and eventually – after a probably painful faff – various institutions will allow you to re-verify your identity and reclaim your money. Crypto, in its original design, doesn't work like that. If you lose access to your digital wallet, you lose your money. Forever. No mercy.

We have all at some point had to call our bank's customer service line or go into a branch to resolve some kind of issue with accessing the funds in our account. Imagine if that meant losing the money forever. So far, we have not reached a point where a substantial chunk of the population – or even a large proportion of crypto users – are prepared to take that kind of risk. I am not sure we will ever reach that point, or if that would even be a desirable future. The original vision for crypto neglected the fact that people like to have trusted institutions to bail them out. Bitcoin was a brilliant piece of tech undone by its failure to account for a boring, obvious reality about human fallibility.

The idealised crypto vision goes something like: Step One: invent a very clever system to make banks irrelevant, which requires people to use some fairly complicated tech (Bitcoin, that is). Step Two: get a large number of people comfortable with using that complicated tech so that it becomes commonplace for people to hold and spend their money in a decentralised system and we really don't need banks any more. Steps Three to Infinity: build on top of that decentralised system to make a whole new economy that's better for everyone!

The problem is that crypto got stuck at Step Two. Decentralised wealth and payments have still not caught on. Most of crypto-land has ignored that fact and moved on to Steps Three through Infinity – creating an immensely complicated new financial system that talks a lot about decentralisation but isn't very decentralised. Only a small subset of the crypto world actually operates decentralised tech systems (and even within 'decentralised finance' there are questions about how truly decentralised they are, given that a relatively small number of coders and founders often have effective control). To take crypto trading, for example, the volume of trading on decentralised exchanges has rarely been more than 15 per cent of the amount traded on centralised exchanges like FTX. And here we are talking about the appetite for 'decentralisation' among people who are *already* in crypto.

*

It turned out that only dedicated crypto hobbyists and criminals looking for secretive ways of moving money would really put up with the inconvenience of using crypto for payments. Instead, trading has become the main thing that crypto is for.

FTX was one of many multi-billion-dollar businesses created by profiting off this trade. Binance, the largest crypto exchange, founded by Changpeng 'CZ' Zhao, who insists that the company isn't based in any country and has no headquarters, made more than $1 billion a month from crypto trading at the peak. These crypto-financial conglomerates muddled together the services that in traditional finance are provided by stock exchanges, brokers, custodians and banks. Instead of creating a financial system without central institutions, crypto created a generation of offshore hyper-banks, which demanded that customers trust them almost blindly.

What made these exchanges so popular was a financial innovation pioneered, in 2016, by a man named Arthur Hayes. A son of auto workers in Buffalo, New York, Hayes's prodigious talent in everything from bodybuilding and ballroom dancing to high-stakes trading took him from upstate New York to big bank trading floors in Hong Kong. He popularised a simplified, supercharged crypto version of the derivatives contracts that he had traded in traditional markets. By letting traders borrow money to place their bets, derivatives created a market that was faster, more volatile and much more exciting. The number one thing for which crypto is now used is to speculate on its own price movements using derivatives. Even after the crash, the scale of that trading is still more than $2 trillion a month.

The millions of people who joined in this trading were generally clear-eyed about what they were doing. The most common reason people in the UK gave for getting into crypto was 'as a gamble'. A large share said they were expecting to 'make money quickly' (whereas only 10 per cent wanted to make payments).

Introduction

But there was a second significant group of crypto recruits, who saw digital assets as an 'investment', a way of 'saving for retirement', or an alternative to traditional financial services. What these people wanted was a safe place to put the money that they didn't need right away, and for that money to grow over time. Tina Fey, in her TV series *30 Rock,* described investing as 'that thing that rich people do where they turn money into more money'. For many years, banks had paid savers bugger all interest rates for the money deposited in their accounts while making plenty of profits themselves. People who could save a few thousand dollars in the bank got nothing for it. The richer you were, the better chance you had of successfully accessing the increasingly sophisticated and risky investments that would actually grow your wealth. Crypto promised to break down these barriers, and let anyone turn their money into more money.

An array of crypto companies – some of which grew into multi-billion-dollar operations – took in deposits from millions of customers on the promise of paying much higher interest rates than you'd ever get from the bank. Then, like banks, they lumped that money together and used it to make loans in crypto. Loans to whom? Mostly to big crypto traders who wanted to make even larger gambles on where the market would go. One of the biggest was SBF. With the growth of digital asset lenders, crypto had fully reinvented the bank. But unlike banks, these companies were essentially unsupervised. At Celsius, one of the largest lenders, chief executive Alex Mashinsky operated a scheme that one of his own employees called 'very Ponzi-like'. He faces trial for fraud in the US and has denied wrongdoing. Crypto lending made an interesting study of what

9

would happen if you had a deregulated banking system. The answer was almost immediate disaster.

*

From 2017 until early 2020, these different components of the new crypto-financial system – exchanges, derivatives traders and lenders – were built up in relative obscurity. Crypto is known as a boom-and-bust business. The hungry entrepreneurs who dived into crypto in the 2017 boom, sharks from the world of traditional finance, knew that at some point a new wave of enthusiasm for crypto would push the minnows into their jaws.

When the wave came, it was a tsunami set off by an unexpected earthquake. The global economic crisis following Covid-19 forced governments to open the taps of free money like never before in history. After the first shocks of Covid had passed, most people in Western economies actually had more money in their pockets. We were locked down. We were bored. The economic future was uncertain. And the interest rates in traditional finance were as low as they could go. It was the perfect moment for crypto.

The total value of crypto expanded from around $250 billion in early 2020 to a peak of nearly $3 trillion by late 2021. The value of all those assets was still for the most part based on nothing. You still couldn't look at a Bitcoin and tell me what it 'should be' worth, except for the price that the next person would pay to buy it. When more people bought crypto, prices went up. As the prices went up, even more people thought, 'I don't want to get left behind by this crypto thing.'

Introduction

In the US, the portion of the population that had ever moved money into crypto rose from 3 per cent in 2020 to 13 per cent by June 2022. By that summer, 5 million people in the UK owned crypto, nearly a tenth of all adults, half of whom had made their purchase in the previous year.

On top of Covid and macro-economics, the hype machine that drove the crypto bubble was fuelled by a lot of good old-fashioned marketing. Companies splashed hundreds of millions on celebrity endorsements, social media influencers, sports sponsorships and advertising campaigns to tell the world that crypto was something new and different. Crypto ads were on the side of double-decker buses in London and played at the Super Bowl. Mashinsky told people to 'unbank themselves' with Celsius. CZ promoted Binance as a 'decentralised' company. SBF said he would give his riches to charity, and build FTX into a model financial institution. The message they pushed was clear: crypto was an antidote to the ills of the old financial system.

The reason the crypto industry spent so lavishly on marketing is that the entire operation of the crypto machine depended on a steady influx of new customers and new money. Enthusiasm, emotion, atmosphere – what people now call 'vibes' – play a role in all financial markets. But in crypto, the level of hype is the only predictor of where prices will go. Crypto is a vibes-based financial market. And in 2021, the vibes were great.

More buyers increased prices, which encouraged more buyers. The more people bought and traded crypto, the more money exchanges made from fees. More crypto depositors meant more business for the lenders, and more assets that they could lend out to the big traders. Having lots of new traders in the market meant that big, professional trading firms could make more money by screwing over the amateurs. Carol Alexander, a professor of finance at the University of Sussex, said big exchanges use promotions and offers to reel in more DIY traders. 'This way, they feed these little ordinary fish to the professional sharks which dominate their trading platforms,' she said.

Each cog in the crypto machine lifted money out of the pockets of ordinary people and handed it to a small crypto-financial elite. And for a short period, the crypto elite made out like bandits. CZ was briefly reckoned to be one of the world's richest people. SBF became a billionaire many times over, one of the youngest people ever to make so much money. Apparent profits were easy to come by and the spectacle of wealth creation was magnetic.

It couldn't last. Jeremy Allaire, chief executive of the company Circle and a major figure in the crypto industry, said: 'An inordinate amount of the "value created" during the past bull market was almost entirely speculative in nature.'

Still, for a while, lots of people thought that they were rich. It is easy to see crypto assets as sort of ethereal, and to conclude that because they don't make sense they must not be real. But for as long as the crypto bubble remained inflated, digital assets were as real as any other. People could, and did, cash them in for dollars and buy Lamborghinis, houses, yachts and pizzas. Luxury cars became a sort of icon of the newly crypto-rich. 'Buying a Lambo' was a cultural totem for striking it rich, even if SBF burnished his image as the acceptable face of crypto by driving his Toyota Corolla. In all the excitement, people seemed to think the orgy of easy money might last forever. Then, in just a few months in 2022, a couple of trillion dollars that crypto's temporary winners thought was theirs to keep evaporated as quickly as it had appeared.

*

The crash that unfolded from the spring of 2022 was eerily similar to 2008. Looking back on it later, Arthur Hayes told me: 'The reason why people went bust in 2008 is the same reason why people went bust in crypto in 2022. It's just too much leverage, an assumption about the direction of prices, a business model predicated on numbers only going up. When numbers started going down, then their business fell apart. You could cut and paste every single Wall Street firm that went under with a similar crypto firm.'

Although the parallels around excessive borrowing, complexity and overconfidence are strong, crypto added an extra ingredient. For centuries, the business of creating new assets has been an oligopoly. When it comes to currency, the main job of central banks and their armies of boffins is to decide how much money there should be, in order to optimise the economy. For other financial assets, like stocks and bonds, only a small number of institutions are empowered to create them, through carefully controlled processes. Crypto smashed all these controls. 'You could, in a weekend, write a smart contract, throw up a website, list a token and generate millions. It was a little bit like the 2000s IPO mania but on steroids,' said one crypto entrepreneur I met. The mania for initial public offerings in tech during the dot com bubble was at least limited by the rules around getting these things listed on the stock market.

In crypto, anyone with a little bit of technical ability could create an infinite number of new tokens whenever they wanted. In the hyped-up world of the crypto bubble, people were liable to believe that these ephemeral new assets had some value.

'Look at what happened in 2008. We had a proliferation of financial assets that you could borrow against; leverage went through the roof; complexity went through the roof. You could take a house, create a CDO, put a derivative on it and have a synthetic CDO squared. But somewhere – very tenuously – there was a house. What crypto does is that it gets rid of the need for the house,' said Hilary Allen, a law professor at the American University Washington College of Law, who worked on the congressional commission appointed to study the causes of the financial crisis.

Allen, a long-time crypto sceptic, was one of the experts called to testify before Congress in the aftermath of the crypto crash. She told me: 'My concern about crypto has always been what the traditional financial system would do with it. If traditional finance sees that you can just make up financial assets, they are going to get in on that.'

The crypto phenomenon is to some degree an extension of how parts of mainstream finance have 'become too financialised, too untethered and that are not serving the economy,' she argued.

'If crypto does one thing right, it is to diagnose the problem. Unfortunately, they just replicate or exacerbate problems from traditional finance. People's acceptance of assets that were totally made up may reflect the fact that things had become a bit too made up already. To some degree it's an indictment of our financial system that people can't tell the difference between a stock or bond and crypto.'

Introduction

Unconstrained asset creation became a scam artist's dream, and it supercharged the bubble in the crypto financial system. The whole edifice was built on self-belief. The crash happened, in no small part, because everyone suddenly looked around and asked, 'Why are these tokens that you just made up worth anything at all?'

*

So far the story is one you might read in an economics textbook. Economists know that super-low interest rates, meaning nearly free borrowing, isn't really natural. There's no such thing as money for nothing. The drip of easy money is like lacing the financial water supply with small amounts of cocaine. It does tend to stimulate economic activity, but it also leads people to do things that they will later regret. When interest rates are low and money is plentiful, people do increasingly bananas things until financial excess starts to collapse under its own weight.

The financial world is divided into two types of money. You and I, dear reader, we are the 'dumb money' – normal people who will invest our hard-earned cash based on fallible emotions like greed, exuberance or the 'fear of missing out'. Dumb money investors are expected to follow financial fads. We charge into the latest trendy investment when the going looks good. We buy when prices are highest and sell when prices are lowest. As much as film, music or clothing, investments sold to the general public go through fashion trends. And when these trends get big enough and silly enough, we call them bubbles. By early 2022, crypto was, if not the biggest, then certainly the silliest bubble of all time. The first people to get hurt when a bubble pops are always the dumb money. Regular investors who believed the hype were wiped out in their millions by the second crypto bubble. People lost their houses, their kids' college funds; the fallout destroyed relationships and wrecked marriages. For people who follow financial bubbles through history, these losses are distressing but they are also factored in. It is what you would expect to happen.

But one thing happened that wasn't supposed to happen. The other class of money is 'smart money' – sophisticated professional investors who are not supposed to make dumb mistakes. These are investment institutions like, for instance, my mother's pension fund. What made the 2022 crypto crash special is that a whole bunch of professional investors got taken to the cleaners too. The executive from Ontario Teachers was not the only representative of 'smart money' around the dinner table in the Bahamas, with the other hangers-on at the court of SBF. They were joined by investors from Singapore's sovereign wealth fund and executives from Goldman Sachs. People in the 'smart money' camp have a harder time admitting that they can also get caught up in bubbles. But they did. The top institutions in global finance gave crypto not just billions in investment, but also their implicit endorsement. Their backing gave the crypto bubble its final push, giving even more ordinary people the confidence that this thing was legit.

The billions that professional investors lost in crypto leave them with awkward questions. How were they taken in by a fraudster? How did they not spot the rot at the core of SBF's empire? And how did they not see that crypto was a bubble set to burst? Investors leant too far into a style of investing that seeks not growing cash flows but

Introduction

radical geniuses. On the hunt for new companies that would make them as rich as the early investors in internet giants like Amazon or Facebook, they thought SBF was the next Jeff Bezos or Mark Zuckerberg. The model of investing that seeks out the next big idea and believes in the unique power of superman founders to make it real can, apparently, make professional investors just as vulnerable to hype as the person on the street.

What you'll often hear people say about the big investors who fell for SBF is that they 'didn't do their due diligence', which is the term for the rigorous analysis and digging you are supposed to do before investing your money into a company to make sure that it checks out. The fact that investors didn't do *adequate* due diligence on FTX is, I would argue, self-evident. The company they invested in stole all their money, and a bunch of other people's money, and then lost it all. But as a factual matter, it's not true that investors didn't do *any* due diligence. Some of them spent months on it. It makes the story all the more remarkable that the world's top financiers did a lot of homework to make sure FTX was a good bet without managing to spot that they were running a really simple con: get money from depositors and investors. Lend that money to yourself. Borrow even more money based on assets you made up. Spend like nobody's business, partly on burnishing your own reputation to attract more money from more lenders, depositors and investors. Repeat.

One of my favourite summaries of the FTX debacle is a one-liner from a crypto analyst, Niklas Polk, who I spoke to on a video call from Brazil a few weeks after the company blew up. He summed up how the crypto industry had viewed SBF and his associates. 'We

17

knew or kinda guessed that they were doing some shady things. But we all thought they were very successful at it,' he said. 'Many people in the [crypto] space thought they were evil, but thought that they were evil geniuses.'

That's a pretty good joke for a crypto analyst. It's also a troubling idea. The implication is that the crypto industry was perfectly happy to ignore suspicions about SBF, as long as he was successful. The problem was not that he was up to no good. The problem was that he got caught. As long as FTX was printing money for everyone around it, they were ready to see its fatal flaws as keys to its success. Its lack of professional staff, structure and safeguards were viewed as hallmarks of a lean and efficient startup. Its offshore location in the Bahamas was seen as a canny tactic, necessary to avoid strangling and behind-the-times regulations in the United States. And SBF's strange habits, his social awkwardness and insular leadership were seen as hallmarks of a visionary genius on the scale of Zuckerberg or Elon Musk. Some of the professional investors who pumped billions into his empire are perhaps the guiltiest of falling into these traps.

Their defence has mostly been to point the finger at SBF. They were the victims of a fraud, not participants in inflating a bubble. The crypto industry has joined in this tactic: 'Every industry has its shady characters. It isn't crypto's fault.' SBF is undoubtedly at fault. But the sidestep of implicitly blaming one 30-year-old for everything that went wrong in crypto is plainly bogus. He was far from being the one 'bad apple' in a generally good industry. It's more accurate to say that there were some good apples in a digital asset industry that had become mainly a

Introduction

noxious offshore casino, powered by hype, borrowed money and screwing over everyday investors.

Crytpo currently finds itself at a somewhat ironic juncture. The original idea was to use technology to make the financial system more democratic and less exploitative. Instead, the crypto industry took many of the worst features of modern finance – speculation, fraud, greed, excessive borrowing, an obsession with moonshots over sensible ideas and the conviction that maladjusted young men are the most likely harbingers of profit – and turned them all up to 11. The story is an indictment of what one FTX insider described to me as the 'economic and social ecosystem that allows a 28-year-old to become a billionaire'. It was as if the citizens of a frontier town in the American Old West got fed up with the ineptness of their sheriff and decided to take matters into their own hands, only to find that their vigilante posse was quickly co-opted by the very same bandits they were trying to stamp out.

*

As a journalist for the *Financial Times,* I met many of the key players in the 2022 crypto crash at the height of their powers and followed their stories through decline to fall. I spent dozens of hours interviewing SBF before, during and after his fall from grace – from a beachfront terrace in Nassau to his parents' living room when he was out on bail. And I spoke to former employees and insiders across the crypto industry, including senior ex-FTX executives – some of who, to my knowledge, have not spoken to any other journalist.

Hype Machine

I came to write about crypto, and really about finance, somewhat in spite of myself. I studied history, not programming or economics, and I have explored the cryptosphere in large part in a state of total bewilderment. Compared to many of my colleagues in the mainstream press, I started off as more of a moderate. I was not reflexively convinced that crypto was a bad thing. I thought many of its ideas were interesting, even if they had flaws that seemed obvious. The more I have learned about how the crypto machine really works, the more critical I have become.

Crypto critics have three main lines of attack. One, crypto is a godsend for criminals, helping drug lords and human traffickers, and creating a well-stocked hunting ground for scams, big and small. Two, crypto is an environmental disaster, burning huge amounts of electricity for no obvious benefit. Three, crypto has become a high-tech shadow financial system where a small elite have tried to rewrite or ignore the rules of global finance for their own benefit. I have been most fascinated by the bits of crypto that did the best job pretending to be an alternative to mainstream finance, and which came closest to being accepted as the future of money.

Many of the dozens of bankruptcies, lawsuits, regulatory actions and criminal prosecutions spawned by the crypto crash are still live. We will be learning more about what happened in 2022 for years to come. I have tried to reflect on the events that I reported on, and go back over the evidence, to present a comprehensible account of how something as absurd as the crypto bubble and the collapse of FTX could really have happened. Along the way, I hope you'll feel you've learned something about what crypto really is, and how the crypto machine really operates – rather than the promises of what crypto might have been, or could become.

The thing people most often say to me about crypto is that it 'doesn't make sense'. They have a point. No part of this story – the crypto bubble, the rise and fall of FTX, the investors who were ensnared – is sensible. The mind boggles looking back at all the outrageous things people in crypto took for granted. FTX, a two-year-old company, was given a valuation higher than Germany's 153-year-old Deutsche Bank, the largest lender in the fourth largest economy in the world. The crypto token Dogecoin, which was literally created as a joke (and disavowed by its inventor as a joke gone too far), was valued at its peak at $73 billion. The nation of El Salvador adopted Bitcoin as a legal tender and promised to build a volcano-powered crypto city.

Over time, though, I have started to see the difference between something that 'doesn't make sense' and something that is inexplicable. While I agree that the crypto bubble of 2022 does not 'make sense', I do think that it can be explained. This book is an effort to do so. The first thing you should do if you want to understand crypto, and especially the 2022 bubble, is to stop looking for explanations that 'make sense'. The signature feature of this episode in financial history is that the legend of crypto created a sort of reality distortion field, in which things that were obviously silly were taken seriously, things that were impossible were treated as real, and things that were unsustainable were accepted as the new way of the world. Why? Because crypto.

A Bunch of Dorks

In 2017, a 25-year-old Wall Street trader named Sam Bankman-Fried quit his job because he wanted to change the world. He succeeded. But not perhaps in the way that he had anticipated.

As SBF later told the story, he had become increasingly disillusioned with his job at Jane Street, one of the high-speed trading firms that sit in the background of the stock market shuffling tens of trillions of dollars across its books every year in lightning-fast trades that smooth the functioning of financial markets. The firm is an unconventional player in global finance, better known as a home for T-shirt-wearing maths specialists than bombastic traders in shirtsleeves and gold watches shouting down the phone.

Even in this nerdy atmosphere, SBF stood out as an unusual thinker. His mind works through a stylised set of equations and thought experiments. In conversation, he will throw out premises, set up hypotheticals and lay out his theoretical reasoning. Except that with SBF, unlike other people, he will actually follow his abstract conclusions in the way he lives his life. The calculation that was troubling him at Jane Street was about his generous Wall Street salary. Thinking about the value of income, he reasoned, the first $20,000 is by far the most important. It buys food, shelter, the necessities of life. The next $20,000 makes a huge difference to economic security and quality of life. But as you keep adding $20,000 tranches of income, each one matters less. By $120,000 a year, he reckoned, each additional boost in income matters very little. 'There is just this classic decreasing marginal utility of money to people, which, maybe it's logarithmic, whatever. Certainly, the more money you have, the less the marginal dollar matters,' he said.

This indifference to boosting his wealth made SBF unusual casting for a Wall Street trader. His doubts stemmed from a revolution in his thinking that came about in college, at the Massachusetts Institute of Technology (MIT). SBF had joined a co-ed fraternity called Epsilon Theta, which he described as being short on beer pong and long on board games. This was not a place for wild parties. He once told me that he had 'tried to get drunk once to see what it was like, and I failed'.

SBF was introduced to Will MacAskill, one of the founders of a philosophical movement called Effective Altruism. EA, as disciples call it, encouraged SBF to think about the value of his income not just for himself, but for others. It prescribes that people need to think more rigorously about how to maximise the amount of good they do in the world. One of the best ways to make a difference, EA holds, is to earn as much as you can and give away the vast majority of what you make to the causes that, on a mathematical basis, do the most good. They favour interventions like buying mosquito nets to prevent malaria, which for the smallest amounts of money do the most to save or improve people's lives. The school of thought has a utilitarian bent, advocating the greatest good for the greatest number. It fit the ideals of SBF's family. His mother, Barbara Fried, was quoted once as saying that her husband and two sons were 'take-no-prisoners utilitarians', and that she had been 'inching toward' that worldview over time.

SBF gave up on his half-baked plans to follow his parents into academia and become a physics professor. Scholarship had not seriously appealed to him, and he thought the most exciting physics work had been done in the last century. He looked instead for a way to put his faith in EA into practice by making serious money. He followed a common path for elite maths graduates, and became first an intern and then a trader at Jane Street. The company impressed him as being less formal and structured than the other Wall Street firms who were recruiting Ivy League mathletes. In one of his interviews, a co-founder of the company dropped by to chat about politics and baseball.

His Jane Street superiors were impressed with SBF's prowess as a trader, and they admired his ascetic EA values. SBF is a devout vegan, with a lifelong interest in animal welfare. Brett Harrison, who taught him in a coding class at the firm and later followed SBF to FTX, before becoming a fierce critic, recalled SBF at Jane Street. 'He seemed like a sensitive and intellectually curious person who cared about animals, and that endeared him to me.'

Jane Street is notoriously obsessed with calculating probabilities and risks, being early to spot the danger of the Covid-19 pandemic when other financial players were still blasé. The firm turned

SBF's ability in maths into a passion for trading, and reinforced the mathematical way he thought about the world. It drills its recruits on a concept called 'expected value'. The idea is to think about the possible outcomes of your decision, to calculate how big a gain or a loss they would represent, and then work out the probability of each eventuality. By tabulating the weighted average of all the outcomes, you get a number that lets you compare the potential value of this choice against other courses of action. The concept is also popular within Effective Altruism. One of the consequences of this way of thinking is that a very, very large potential pay-off – even if it's quite unlikely – can tilt the average strongly in favour of a particular option.

It was this idea that, by 2017, was giving SBF serious doubts about his path in life. If he kept on trucking at Jane Street and earning his handsome Wall Street salary, it was almost certain he could keep on delivering a good, steady income to his EA causes. But was he playing it too safe? Was there not a bigger, bolder way that he could try to make a difference? SBF's affluent background meant he was in no danger of being destitute if he tried something and failed. The more he chatted with his friends involved in EA, he said, 'it made me ask myself some hard questions about expected values and about, if I really think I should be trying to maximise expected values, that probably implies substantially riskier strategies than what seems intuitively right.' So he quit his job and moved back to California in search of something new.

This story, as SBF told it to FTX's in-house podcast in 2020, is one of many examples of how he created his own legend. SBF in his own telling is special, not just smarter but also more ethical than the crowd. He is indifferent to wealth, downplays his own success, and is preoccupied by how to do good in the world. The stray references to 'marginal utility', 'logarithmic' scales and 'expected value' easily leave the audience thinking that this guy is operating on a higher level.

There is, of course, a simpler way of telling this story. A socially awkward teenager with a prodigious passion for maths, and a philosophical bent influenced by his law professor parents, arrives at MIT. He finally finds a like-minded community where he fits in, among the thetans and EA enthusiasts. He looks up to MacAskill, six years older and the leader of the EA movement, and takes his advice about what to do with his life. Many of his peers are recruited into trading, and he follows the easiest path to make big money. But after a few years, rounding 25, he is slightly bored. His groovy EA friends make him feel guilty about his safe and conventional Wall Street job. So like a thousand affluent twenty-somethings before and since, he quits to figure out what he really wants to do with his life and heads to California.

SBF had a knack for making his own story, and his ideas, seem rather more remarkable than they were. His fusion of ethical calculations with a trader's logic could be deceptive. There are huge hand-wavy gaps in the apparently logical chains of reasoning. When you take mathematical concepts beyond the realm of trading statistical probabilities for a cash outcome, and try to use them to run your life – and other people's – you reach scenarios that cannot be tabulated. The insight he reached about the marginal utility of extra earnings is not really much more complicated than the idea that money can't buy happiness. In what sense could he actually calculate the likely future value of leaving his Jane Street pay cheque for totally uncertain alternatives? When he talked about the probability and value of different life outcomes, SBF was really just pulling numbers out of the air.

The same often applied to his ethics. At the peak of his wealth I asked SBF how he reconciled his morals to living in a multi-million-dollar penthouse in a gated community in the Bahamas, a nation with glaring wealth disparity. 'If my personal consumption is less than 1 per cent of what I make, I'm just not going to worry about it,' he replied. But who makes that rule? What ethical calculation backs up 1 per cent as the standard? Why didn't he instead decide to put himself on the average per capita income of Bahamians, or the average global income?

Of course, it's easy to mock Effective Altruist ideals. They set such high moral standards that they inevitably look hypocritical. Lots of EA adherents do an admirable amount of good. But the danger lay in the way that SBF combined their ideals with what he learned in Wall Street, in order to attach a veneer of mathematical legitimacy to arbitrary judgements. The fact that he could portray with absolute certainty his own intoxicating moral universe played a big role in how his story unfolded.

*

When SBF landed back in San Francisco in the autumn of 2017, cryptocurrencies were already a hot topic of conversation in a city obsessed with profiting from inventing the future.

At the start of the year, the price of Bitcoin had broken $1,000 for the first time. And, by September, it was nearly $5,000 on its rapid ascent to an all-time high above $19,000 by the end of the year. The boom in prices attracted attention. Speculators were offering thousands of new tokens to avid investors in 'initial coin offerings', a phenomenon that became known as the 'ICO bubble'. Stock market investors, too, were taking an interest. A beverage company that said it would change its name from Long Island Iced Tea Corp. to Long Blockchain Corp. was rewarded with a 380 per cent rise in its shares. It didn't matter that there was no obvious way for the drinks maker to actually become a tech pioneer. The intention behind the name change was enough. The chief executive gave a short, 93-word statement that the company planned 'to pivot our business strategy in order to pursue opportunities' in the blockchain technology that underpins cryptocurrencies.

Behind the financial excess, there were the beginnings of serious interest from Wall Street. Jane Street, the firm SBF had just quit, made its first moves into crypto that year. Max Boonen, an ex-Goldman Sachs trader who became an early and prominent crypto financier, explained in one interview that, before 2017, there hadn't been much interest in crypto because 'there wasn't that much money to share'.

'In late 2017, a lot of big [high frequency] traders came into the market because they saw that there was a huge pie that they wanted to capture. Everyone in crypto in 2017 made a ton of money. It was obscene. It was not challenging to make money.'

SBF was just in time to join the party. He had taken a job at the Centre for Effective Altruism, a group promoting EA ideas, but he was increasingly fascinated by crypto markets. He told me that he spent the nights trading crypto and the days dozing at his desk.

He said the first trade he made exploited a 10 per cent gap in the price of a crypto token called Stellar on two different exchanges. By buying at the lower price and selling at the higher one, SBF made easy money. This type of trade is called arbitrage. Stunningly, he was able to execute it by just clicking through the websites of each exchange, buying, selling and transferring manually. Even more enticing price gaps beckoned. Crypto platforms in Japan and South Korea, isolated from other markets, offered pricing that was vastly different from the US. For a former Jane Street trader, these seemed like the kind of trades that should be impossible.

Jane Street and similar firms on Wall Street have vast robotic armies of algorithms ready to spot and execute trades like this in fractions of a second. Arbitrage trades are so attractive and so apparently simple that they have become hyper-competitive. The challenge is to build systems that can spy and exploit pricing gaps faster than the next guy. In crypto, the market was so young and had so few sophisticated players that opportunities which would be hoovered up in an instant by the Wall Street machine were just lying around. Bringing a fraction of Jane Street's systems and discipline to crypto would be a massive money-making opportunity. SBF set out to capture it. The company he founded was called Alameda Research.

With little backing or reputation, SBF recruited key employees from his personal network. Perhaps the most important was Gary Wang. The pair first met at maths camp, but became close as roommates and fellow thetans at MIT. Wang had landed a coveted job at Google, working in their office back in Cambridge, Massachusetts, helping to build the software behind Google Flights. Gary is the stereotypical computer genius. He has had the same rectangular, utilitarian glasses and bowl haircut since his high school yearbook photo. Colleagues said he often worked nocturnally, from 5:00pm to 4:00am. For charm and social skills, he makes SBF look like George Clooney. Their subordinates describe the bond between SBF and Gary as mysterious, but obviously ironclad. To my knowledge, Gary has never given an interview. People who worked with them thought Gary trusted SBF implicitly. 'If you ever hear Sam and Gary talk to each other, it is the weirdest thing. Somehow Sam just understands him,' said one colleague. Another was more blunt. 'Gary doesn't speak to humans,' they said.

Gary quit his Big Tech job and flew out to California to join his old friend. Gary commanded respect and affection among his colleagues as a true computer programming genius. He was, Nishad once said, 'brilliant beyond belief'. He had few interests outside work, although he was an avid fan of the TV show *Breaking Bad* and later found love with an FTX employee. The pair were engaged to be married. 'Gary is super interesting because he's very much an enigma,' said another co-worker. SBF relied on him heavily for technical work. Gary trusted SBF to manage the big picture. 'Sam is ultimately more of the businessman. He is not God's strongest coder,' the co-worker said.

Next to the reclusive Gary, SBF's second key hire was 'relatively more normal', the co-worker said. Like SBF, Caroline Ellison was the child of professors. Her father taught economics and inculcated her with maths from an early age. She also loved fantasy. Her parents read the first *Harry Potter* to her out loud. When the second book came out, Caroline, aged five, wouldn't wait and insisted on reading it herself. To unwind from her job at Alameda she wrote the scenarios for live-action role play games, where groups of friends – sometimes in costume – act out fantasy adventures.

Growing up, she threw herself into maths competitions. 'I just loved the math[s] team community. It was a great community to hang out with,' she said. Major trading firms would sponsor the competitions and recruited heavily from the maths programme at Stanford, where Caroline studied. But she was put off by the stereotype of Wall Street culture as somewhere 'really competitive and intense and everyone is yelling at each other,' she said. She was small and mousy, with a slow, almost drawling style of speech punctuated by nervous laughter. But with not much idea of what else to do, she found a job at Jane Street and there she met SBF. Shortly after he left, Caroline was on a visit to the west coast. They arranged to meet for coffee, but SBF kept rescheduling the date. When they finally met, he was evasive about his new project. He quickly capitulated, and told Caroline about his months-old crypto trading outfit. 'It seemed like too cool an opportunity to pass up,' she said.

Alameda began its operations out of a rented three-bedroom home in Berkeley, California. The handful of staff worked 18 or 20 hours a day in the cramped living room before catching a few hours' sleep. Dozens of people came and went. One of the visitors was Nishad Singh. 'At that time it was really chaotic. It was unclear who was there part-time and who was there full-time,' he said. Nishad knew the Bankman-Fried family from high school, and was closer in age to Sam's younger brother, Gabe. He was awed by his friend's older brother. 'I watched Sam execute a sequence of trades. I knew nothing about trading at the time. But even then it was sort of understandable that [the] sequence of trades was super profitable and easy to understand and that there were lots of them available,' he said. 'There was all this operational flurry around getting Alameda into a state where it could really take advantage of these trades. It was really fun. It was really chaotic. And it was clear that it could possibly be onto something that could be pretty big.'

No one who worked with Nishad had a bad word to say about him. The youngster of the founding team, he's remembered as sweet, upbeat and energetic. He also showed incredible tenacity. When he was 16, Nishad ran 100 consecutive miles. Asthmatic and 'unathletic', with a self-confessed weakness for Oreos, he started running seriously because his mother was training for a marathon. For Nishad, running became an exercise in just putting one foot in front of another and never giving up. 'The game for long-distance running is definitely a mental one, at least the way I approached it,' he said.

Nishad was working at a 'dream job' on artificial intelligence research for Facebook, his first role out of college at the University of California, Berkeley. He started coming by the Alameda office to hang out and work at nights and weekends. SBF lobbied him about the ethical imperative to join full-time and maximise his chances of making really big money . . . for charity. Nishad agonised about the decision to quit Facebook for Alameda. 'It was hard and it wasn't really obvious until I was sort of careful about the math[s] in thinking about the upside scenarios,' Nishad later said. 'A big part of what convinced me was talking with Sam about what those upside scenarios looked like. Crypto trading was better than any trading environment that he'd ever seen.' Nishad became an essential number two to Gary, someone who could handle the tech but also manage the tech teams and relate to the rest of the company.

Hype Machine

The one key recruit who did not quite conform to the Alameda template for hyper-idealists was Sam Trabucco. Trabucco also knew SBF from maths camp and MIT, and had been a trader at Susquehanna, a major rival to Jane Street. Trabucco is less well known than the other early team members because he stepped down from Alameda just a few months before it collapsed and has not been prosecuted. However, right up until 2022, as one of Alameda's original traders, he was seen as having a strong hand in its strategy. Trabucco shared the rest of the group's intense intellect and love of games and puzzles. He wrote crosswords for the *New York Times* and played competitive Scrabble. But he was more cynical and aggressive. He has a round face and a smile that tends to look more sinister than cheerful. Compared to his self-effacing colleagues, he showed more ego. 'Outside of Sam probably I am the best at fast thinking on the team, that makes it so that on the 1 per cent of days when things are craziest I probably add a disproportionate amount of value,' he once said. He honed his trading skills as a poker player, although he also enjoyed the fantasy game 'Magic: the Gathering'. He was not an EA devotee. When they had all struck it rich, and SBF was giving sermons to *Vogue* magazine about his moral philanthropy, Trabucco bought a boat and named it 'Soak My Deck'.

Trabucco was already making money for himself in crypto. Thousands of new tokens were being created in 2017, and when one was selected to be listed for sale for trading by a major exchange, opening it up to masses of buyers, its price would almost always soar. Trabucco built a bot that monitored the website at a major crypto exchange. The automated system would catch the announcement of a new listing a fraction of a second early, and buy the token before the price skyrocketed. 'Something simple like that was a quite profitable strategy that I was able to make from a lap-top. Given that, it's sort of a no-brainer to drop what you're doing and do this full-time,' he said.

Alameda presented the opportunity to go beyond this small-time scalping and be part of something bigger. Trabucco moved next door to the Alameda house in Berkeley. The hours were intense. 'The first six months were sort of absurd. Almost every sleeping hour was in the office. Let alone every waking one,' Nishad said. 'It wasn't like we were forced to do it. It was that we were all really motivated by this and really excited by it. And that was a really fun growth period for me and probably a lot of people.'

Together, the small group of old friends and colleagues formed the core of the new trading firm trying to make its fortune in the Wild West of the early crypto markets. Young and maniacally hardworking, they had the drive to succeed and very little to lose. The company was all-consuming. It was a social life and a belief system – bound together by EA. Alameda employees developed their own distinctive vocabulary, full of references to 'expected value'. When they decided not to do something, they'd often say it was because they weren't 'excited' about it. The focus was on the upside. The atmosphere in the Berkeley headquarters was much more like a college dorm than a trading floor. As Nishad described it: 'When we were running just Alameda, we were just a bunch of dorks in basketball shorts and long socks.'

*

By the time SBF launched Alameda in 2017, crypto was approaching the end of its first decade. It traces its origins to the moment, in January 2009, when an anonymous persona called Satoshi Nakamoto made the first entry on the Bitcoin blockchain. At its most basic, a blockchain is just a database. Compared to a simple spreadsheet storing a series of data points, there are a few crucial differences. First, records kept on the blockchain are distributed, stored in multiple copies on different computers. Two, anyone can't just jump online and change the shared file. There is a strict procedure for how new entries are approved and agreed by everyone who holds a copy of the ledger. And finally, most importantly, you can never go back. Once you enter data on the blockchain, it cannot be changed. With the first link of the Bitcoin blockchain, its creator Nakamoto included an indelible message: 'Chancellor on brink of second bailout for banks'.

The phrase, borrowed from a headline in *The Times* newspaper, links Bitcoin from the very beginning to the legacy of the 2008 financial crisis, when excessive risk-taking by the big banks in complex and obscure financial products based on mortgages forced governments to spend billions of taxpayer dollars on a bailout to prevent an even worse economic calamity. The idea that 2008 demanded a radical response and a rethink of the economic order is a powerful one. The grievous failings of the conventional financial system, both at the time and since, have given cryptocurrencies an ideal foil. Every time banks and governments stumble, you'll find people on the internet talking about how crypto is the solution.

Satoshi Nakamoto, whoever they are, made the argument against conventional institutions clear. In some sense, it was a regressive position. Financial institutions had failed and it was time to stash electronic coins under the mattress. Transactions should be made directly between individuals. But crypto ideology also has a forward-looking techno-utopian strain. Building on the heady success of the internet, could technology solve the inherent problems of human institutions by making them redundant?

'The root problem with conventional currency is all the trust that's required to make it work. The central bank must be trusted not to debase the currency, but the history of fiat currencies is full of breaches of that trust. Banks must be trusted to hold our money and transfer it electronically, but they lend it out in waves of credit bubbles with barely a fraction in reserve. We have to trust them with our privacy, trust them not to let identity thieves drain our accounts,' Nakamoto wrote in an early message about Bitcoin. The ideological flavour of the invention was clear. 'It's very attractive to the libertarian viewpoint if we can explain it properly.'

The impressive thing about Bitcoin is that it is basically functional. The system, which involves miners doing complex maths to validate new entries into the unchangeable blockchain record and a limit on the total supply of coins at 21 million, has endured. At its peak, Bitcoin was worth north of a trillion dollars. The prize for hacking it was enormous. And nobody did. It is a remarkable technical achievement.

As for the rest of the Bitcoin vision, it has to be judged a failure. It simply never caught on as a currency, or anything like it. Even in El Salvador, where the government made Bitcoin a legal tender, required businesses to accept it as payment and gave citizens financial incentives to use the digital currency, the uptake has been feeble. Bitcoin has wandered the internet for more than 15 years in search of a purpose. Over the years, Bitcoin has been a sort of financial Rorschach test. People have gazed at the interesting apparition and tried to figure out what it is. The conventional definition of a currency has three parts: a means of exchange, you pay for things with it; a unit of account, you use it to record the value of things; and a store of value, which does what it says on the tin.

Bitcoin has at best a marginal use as a way to pay for things. Buying drugs on the dark web, and occasional stunt purchases involving pizzas, are more of an embarrassment to crypto boosters than a mark of success. When it comes to accounting, Bitcoin's value has mostly come to be quoted in terms of the conversion rate to US dollars – which is a strong hint to its failure as a currency. The only time most people think about the conversion rate of our local currency is when we're going on holiday abroad. Within the UK, a pound is worth a pound. Whereas the value of Bitcoin is really only relevant if you know how many dollars it is worth, because you can use dollars to buy stuff.

The best case for Bitcoin's purpose is as a store of value. The theory that Bitcoin is 'digital gold' holds a reasonable amount of water. Gold's value as the ultimate safe asset is basically arbitrary. Its uses for making wedding rings and in various fiddly technical applications are secondary to the fact that people have, for dozens of centuries, believed in gold as a valuable thing. In a digital form, Bitcoin shares gold's characteristics as something that is distinctive and in limited supply. The difference, which is a pretty big difference, is that Bitcoin doesn't have thousands of years of history on its side.

A Bunch of Dorks

Thinking of Bitcoin as digital gold also conveys the reality that it's a highly impractical way to pay for stuff. SBF used this analogy in one of our interviews. Paying with Bitcoin, he said, is like lugging gold bars around with you to the shops. Visa and Mastercard can process thousands of transactions per second, while Bitcoin's network can only cope with a mid-single digit number. The energy required to create new blocks makes it a very clunky, wasteful and impractical payment system.

The 'digital gold' idea works to some extent in theory. It still does a bad job of explaining how Bitcoin behaves in the real world. Gold is a safe haven asset. When bad stuff happens, people buy gold. It is also an inflation hedge. If regular currencies are losing their value through inflation, gold's value tends to hold up. For a while, people thought Bitcoin would mirror these functions. That notion was effectively killed off during Covid. When the virus struck and people scrambled for financial safe havens, Bitcoin's price dropped like a sack of rocks. And the sharp rise in inflation in 2021 was immediately followed by the collapse of crypto asset values.

Bitcoin's price is also very volatile, which is a bad trait for a safe haven asset. The way it trades in the market tends to mirror stocks, especially tech stocks, in an exaggerated form. The explanation usually offered for this is that investors buy both Bitcoin and tech stocks when they're feeling optimistic, and dump them both when they're feeling nervous. Since people mostly think Bitcoin is a riskier bet than owning a bit of Netflix or Facebook, it gets more of a boost on the way up and a bigger hit on the way down.

Fifteen years into its life, we know a lot of things that Bitcoin isn't. It's not a currency, a safe haven asset or an inflation hedge.

The best you could say is that it's a version of digital gold that for some reason trades like a tech stock on steroids. It's a mess.

*

Thousands of other cryptocurrencies have followed Bitcoin. By far the most important of these began in 2015. The big idea behind Ethereum is the smart contract. Buterin and his collaborators created a system where both the terms of the contract and the actual execution of it are tied together in an unbreakable technological deal. If you agree to send one Bitcoin to your buddy for $12,000 at noon tomorrow, those terms are written into the smart contract. Once you've agreed to it, the contract will inexorably carry out the transaction at noon tomorrow. The catchphrase associated with this breakthrough is 'code is law'.

Ethereum is its own blockchain, separate from Bitcoin, which has the technical capacity to encode these smart contracts. It also comes with its own cryptocurrency, Ether, which is recorded on the Ethereum blockchain and used for payments within the ecosystem. Ethereum is different from Bitcoin in that it doesn't just do one thing. It's more like a little experimental crypto economy, in which coders are invited to come and build stuff. Many parts of the crypto world that you might have heard of are built on top of Ethereum. You can create decentralised autonomous organisations or build protocols for trading and lending. Most non-fungible tokens (NFTs) are based on Ethereum, as are thousands of smaller cryptocurrencies. To do all of this stuff, you need Ether. So the demand for Ether, and its value, is based in some sense on the amount of activity within the Ethereum ecosystem and on the level of excitement about its future. Over the years, other networks have sprung up to compete with Ethereum. Each offers different design and functionality to lure coders to play in their sandbox.

This flurry of new ideas and technical tinkering is what people call 'Web 3'. Web 1 gave us the early building blocks of the internet like IP addresses, and simple services like email, that might be a bit clunky but are freely accessible to everyone. Web 2 created super-slick apps like Instagram and Google Maps at the cost of handing control of these services – and the personal data that goes with them – to a handful of Big Tech companies. Like other tech buzzwords, Web 3 is a bit tricky to pin down. It generally seems to refer to a bright future for the internet where we get to keep the nifty services we're used to from Web 2, but where they are run in an open, decentralised way – more similar to Web 1 – that is based on blockchains and tokens.

If you want to divide cryptocurrencies into some simple categories, Bitcoin sits in a class by itself. Ethereum, all its imitators and all the Web 3 dreams built on top of them fall into a second sweeping category. Generally speaking, this group includes tokens that, like Ether, trade in the open market and have a value based on a project, like Ethereum, that is trying to create some sort of new technology, application or business – be it smart contracts, decentralised lending, metaverse gaming or trading NFT pictures of monkeys. This category of tokens has one conspicuous difference from Bitcoin. The key to Bitcoin's value is that the total supply is limited. There can never be more than 21 million Bitcoin. In contrast, many of these other tokens can be created at will. In many cases, whoever controls the token can just print more.

People often talk about this broad slice of the cryptosphere as similar to startups or tech companies. If you believe in the product that they are working to create, you can buy the token as an investment in its future. This is a decent analogy, but not a precise one.

Unfortunately, people often carry the 'crypto as tech stock' analogy to a high degree of abstraction. Buying Ether because you believe in Ethereum is one thing. It's more common, in my experience, to hear people say that they are buying Bitcoin because they 'believe in blockchain'. That's like buying Netflix shares because you believe in film. There is *some* connection between the two. If people watch lots of movies, there's a good chance Netflix will benefit. But equally, it could suffer a technical failure, produce a series of flops or simply lose popularity over time to Amazon Prime, Disney Plus and HBO Max. It's entirely possible that movies are the entertainment of the future and that Netflix will sink into obscurity. Social media is doing great. Snapchat, not so much. Short video content has become our favourite content, thanks to TikTok. Does that mean profits for the owners of Vine? It is quite important that the thing you claim to believe in is actually linked to the thing you're investing your money into.

This relates to one of the major criticisms levelled at crypto. You may have heard financial experts warn people away from digital assets by saying that crypto has no 'fundamental value'. The simplest way to value an asset is that something is worth what someone else will pay for it. That is its market value. The idea of fundamental or intrinsic value is about trying to calculate objectively what that value *should* be. In other words, are you being stupid if you pay more than this amount?

A Bunch of Dorks

Analysts look to calculate the value of a stock based on the income that the company will pay to shareholders, or the value of a bond based on the interest rate bondholders are paid and the risk of them not getting their money back. There's lots of room to disagree about these calculations, but there is at least some way of measuring whether the current market price makes sense. Markets often deviate from these fundamentals. Lots of people think tech stocks have been overvalued because investors buy them based on airy promises of future profit, rather than actual income today. If people are feeling iffy about the UK economy after Brexit, foreign investors might 'undervalue' British companies. The tides of emotion in the market pull in different directions, but 'fundamentals' provide the anchor.

This kind of analysis generally fails when it comes to crypto. How are you supposed to know if you are overpaying for Bitcoin? Bitcoin doesn't pay any income to its holders. It doesn't give you the right to ownership of any underlying asset. It just is what it is. The market price for Bitcoin is the only price for Bitcoin. It's a similar story for swathes of crypto assets. The fundamental basis for their value is either vague or non-existent. Without that fundamental anchor, crypto prices are at the mercy of investors' feelings.

Talking about feelings or emotions can make markets sound not quite scientific enough. Financial professionals prefer the more technical-sounding word 'sentiment'. Younger people would call this 'vibes'. Vibes are very important in crypto. When the vibes are good (sentiment is positive), more money floods in to buy crypto assets and demand pushes prices up. When the vibes are bad (sentiment is negative), people rush for the exits, and the flood of money out of crypto brings prices back down.

Hype Machine

The central importance of vibes to crypto price movement has created an extraordinary financial incentive for people who already own lots of crypto or run big crypto companies to keep the hype machine going. From influencers to corporate Twitter accounts and podcasts, there is a never-ending torrent of pro-crypto media that tries to keep the enthusiasm on the boil as much as possible. Crypto is not just a set of assets or a category of technology, it is also a subculture – one that verges on the cultish.

Many of the tropes of crypto culture seem to encourage blind faith over rational action. One meme is 'HODL', a misspelling of Hold that stands for 'hold on for dear life'. Variations on the meme range from Yoda – 'In Bitcoin, I trust. HODL, I must' – to Gerard Butler as King Leonidas in the film *300* telling the Spartans to 'HODL' the line in the face of the Persian onslaught. One particularly on-the-nose image just shows the sinking Titanic, with the caption 'HODL'. The message is: 'No matter what's happening, don't sell your crypto.' Another favourite line is 'Have fun staying poor'. Crypto critics can be as smug as they like – they aren't getting rich. An even more lethal concept is 'FUD', which stands for 'fear, uncertainty and doubt'. This phrase serves the same purpose in crypto as Donald Trump's 'fake news' does in politics. Negative information about crypto is FUD. Whatever the criticism, you can label it as FUD and dismiss it. Ignore the details. It is against the movement and therefore wrong. Fake news.

Vibes have eclipsed technological progress as the key predictor of crypto price movements. Blockchain technology is vaguely in the background, acting as a bulwark to the validity of crypto. Since at least 2017, people have been telling me that it is '1993' for blockchain. The reference is to the year that the internet was poised to explode into the mainstream and change every aspect of our lives. The fact that it's been 1993 for at least seven years now reflects the reality that blockchain remains poised to change the world, but hasn't actually done it.

The problem may be that blockchain has been overhyped. The technological history of the internet goes back at least to the 1960s. It was developed largely in obscurity for decades by the military and academics before reaching mass commercial applications. Maybe it's not 1993 for blockchain, but 1963 or 1978 or 1989? There might be some great idea stewing in the blockchain mix that will in 40 years or four years change the world. At the moment, the most promising practical applications are extremely unglamorous ones, in areas like supply chain management and settling trades in the bowels of the financial system. And there is no necessary connection between the success of some of the ideas, or some future breakthrough, and the value of the crypto assets we have today.

Blockchain's curse is that it came into the popular consciousness tied to a tradable financial asset, Bitcoin. That has meant that the technology has been under the public gaze almost from minute one and inextricably tied to the boom and bust of crypto speculation and all sorts of financial games. The Alameda founders are, by their own admission, among the huge number of people who got into crypto not because of the technology but because it looked like a big financial playground with almost no rules where you could make real profits with fake money.

Nathaniel Whittemore, a popular crypto podcaster who led marketing for FTX, put it this way. 'Almost everyone comes in [to crypto] in moments of "number go up" or from some kind of FOMO reason or because they have got a friend who says it's the future.' He gave the boom of the prices in NFTs as an example. 'A ton of people came in because these fucking pictures were worth, like, your house. And like, that is unignorable. Of course it's unignorable. Come on, we're only people. You're going to pay attention to that.'

For Whittemore, speaking in a 2022 interview, the reason people stay in crypto is that after following the big numbers into the cryptosphere they will find some interesting piece of technology or promising application that appeals to them. In his own case, he says he became preoccupied with how crypto payments could help refugees. But he acknowledged that he got hooked, back in 2017, partly because prices were booming. 'For sure the reason that it was so in my craw and all around was this sort of explosion of numbers and everyone going home for Thanksgiving in 2017 and seeing Bitcoin race up a thousand bucks every day. That pulls people in.'

I don't want to discount the fact that there are some genuinely idealistic people working in the cryptosphere who see opportunities for technology to make a difference in the world. I've met many of them. But the inrush of people when prices are rising, and the stampede for the exits when they fall, suggest that the motive force is not technology but the magnetic appeal of big piles of cash.

*

Another challenge to making sense of the crypto market is the accusation that large parts of it are fake. Creating fake trading activity is a great way to hype up assets. If people think something is getting popular, they are more likely to hop on the bandwagon. An easy way to fake activity is by trading with yourself, which is called wash trading. It's like giving people money to come and shop in your own store to make it look popular. A study, published by the National Bureau of Economic Research, looked at trading data from 2019 and found that the majority of trading on unregulated crypto exchanges looked fake. The scale of fake trading ran into trillions of dollars.

There are also substantial accusations that crypto prices are heavily manipulated by big players in the market. There are a bunch of ways of twisting the market to your advantage. One of the most prominent cases in crypto history emerged during the huge surge in crypto prices in 2017 that drew Alameda and so many others into the market. A paper by academics John M. Griffin and Amin Shams advanced evidence agree a massive scheme to inflate the price of Bitcoin involving Bitfinex, one of the largest crypto exchanges at the time.

The people who run Bitfinex also control Tether, the largest stablecoin. Stablecoins are a third big category of cryptocurrency. They are intended to match the value of a real-world asset, usually the US dollar. Mostly, they do this by promising to hold $1 worth of real-world assets – either hard currency or other financial instruments – to back each $1 stablecoin they issue. The logic is similar to currencies on the gold standard that hold ingots to back up the value of paper money. The job of Tether is to serve as a proxy for the US dollar in the crypto world, and to smooth the flow of money between dollars and crypto. The popularity of stablecoins is another piece of evidence of the enduring appeal of the dollar, and the failure of Bitcoin as a currency. Even people trading crypto often prefer to convert their profits into crypto-dollars because it's a more reliable place to store wealth. Those based outside the US might have trouble getting dollar bank accounts. And every time you have to move money between the traditional financial system and crypto it is a huge and very expensive palaver. So keeping money in Tether's crypto-dollar is a neat solution. These borderless, largely anonymous crypto-dollars also have a clear appeal to people looking to move money for less than legitimate reasons. From being worth just $4 billion at the start of 2020, the total value of Tether stablecoins in circulation has catapulted to more than $80 billion.

The crew running Tether and Bitfinex are an unusual bunch of characters. Tether was founded in 2014 by Brock Pierce, a former child actor known for the 'Mighty Ducks' films. Jean-Louis van der Velde, the current chief executive, is Dutch but studied in Taiwan and ran a small electronics company in Shenzhen, China in the early 2000s. 'JL', as he's called, is a ghost. He has no public profile. Even some prominent crypto executives say they rarely if ever interact with him. Tether maintains that he does in fact run the company. The man many people think is actually in charge is the titular chief financial officer, Giancarlo Devasini. Devasini, who has at times gone by the alias 'Merlin', was a plastic surgeon before abandoning medicine and, like JL, becoming an electronics entrepreneur, in his native Italy. One of his businesses collapsed after a fire destroyed its premises in 2008. Today, the unlikely pair run what is effectively the reserve bank of crypto, controlling the asset that underpins most of the crypto financial system.

The basis for that asset's value has at times looked pretty shaky. Tether has been consistently attacked for misleading people about what assets it uses to back its digital dollars. At first, it claimed to hold real dollars on a one-for-one basis for each Tether coin. Later, it changed the story to say it holds a basket of various assets. In 2021, Tether paid $41 million to settle a complaint from US federal regulators that it had misled investors about having enough dollars to back its stablecoin. Tether said these were historic issues that have been resolved. The same year, it paid $18.5 million to end a long-running probe by the New York State Attorney General. 'Tether's claims that its virtual currency was fully backed by US dollars at all times was a lie,' Attorney General Letitia James said at the time. Tether admitted no wrongdoing.

The basic outline of the market manipulation allegations, raised in 2018, is that Tether created unbacked digital dollars and used them to buy Bitcoin through Bitfinex to push up the price. The researchers noted patterns of particularly intense activity when Bitcoin dropped below round-number thresholds of 1,000 or 500, which are of psychological importance to crypto traders. They estimated that the scheme might have accounted for as much as half of Bitcoin's price rise in 2017. The following year, it was reported that US authorities had launched a criminal investigation of the allegations. Nothing has come of the probe so far. Tether and Bitfinex called the research 'flawed' and inaccurate.

The most amazing thing about Tether is that none of these accusations, regulatory complaints or settlements has remotely dented the crypto market's willingness to treat the stablecoin as being as good as a dollar. The key promise that Tether made to its early users was that one real dollar was there to back every Tether. No less an authority than New York's Attorney General has said this was a lie.

Tether did not endorse her statement, but it did pay her $18.5 million to leave them alone, and change its own story about what backs its coins. And this is one of many, many scrapes it has got into over the years. As Bloomberg columnist Matt Levine put it: 'They probably have the money, more or less, but they seem to be going out of their way to seem untrustworthy.' Crypto traders' reaction has been a big collective shrug. Cryptoland has blithely continued to act as if one Tether is worth one dollar. If you need an example of how value works in crypto, here it is. It works as long as people believe. Why do they believe? Because Tether is useful for people who are trying to get rich in crypto. They need a way of porting the dollar into cryptoland. And as long as everyone doesn't stop believing in Tether at the same time, then it does that job just fine.

*

Against the onslaught of criticism that crypto is a speculative market, based on nothing, that is cynically overhyped, manipulated and falsified for financial gain – and its failure to gain truly widespread buy-in – the digital asset phenomenon has been amazingly resilient. A large part of this persistence has to come down to the fact that many of the ideas and technology wrapped up in crypto are really cool, even if they often don't quite work as advertised.

One of the crucial ideas is the democratisation of finance. Before the internet, publishing information was by and large restricted to a handful of institutions. An oligarchy of newspapers, book publishers, TV stations and other big organisations had control of mass publishing. The internet and social media shattered that control.

A Bunch of Dorks

Now, anyone can publish in countless different forms, for free on the internet. What if the same thing happened to finance?

Financial activity like sending payments, issuing loans and creating financial assets is controlled by a fairly small number of regulated institutions in our financial system. Crypto promises to make these activities a free-for-all. To take a company public in an IPO and list its shares for the public to invest in is a substantial bureaucratic ordeal. You have to get banks to support you and hire expensive lawyers and produce thousands of pages of documents that almost nobody reads. In crypto, anyone with some basic technical skills can create a tradable financial asset out of nowhere in minutes.

It is a revolutionary idea. But is it a good one? In publishing, we value greater freedom to publish and express yourself as an important good in society. Because we are committed to freedom of expression, regulation of the press and publishing has been relatively limited. Finance has evolved a lot of regulation and constraints designed – however imperfectly – to prevent people being ripped off by fraud and stop excessive risk-taking threatening economic stability.

The internet revolution in publishing has hardly been free from downsides. It has left us with immense challenges around disinformation, the business models for rigorous journalism and the very future of truth in our societies. What does all that look like when applied to the realm of money? The early years of the crypto financial system give us some indication of what happens when the ability to lend, borrow, trade and create assets is stripped of all controls. It is not a pretty story.

The first big experiment with the democratised creation of assets, the 2017–18 ICO boom, did not last long. From spring 2017 to the autumn of 2018, thousands of new coins launched on the market and collectively raised nearly $20 billion. 'In 2017, stuff didn't even have to work. You just had to have a white paper, pay a consultant to get it listed somewhere . . . you could have an ICO where they claimed that they'd had a crowd sale but one guy just bought all the coins,' said Su Zhu, a prominent crypto trader who would come to play a big role in the 2022 crash.

A lot of that money disappeared. A study in April 2018 suggested that eight in ten ICOs were 'scams'. Others made wild promises to bring in money, failed to deliver and sank into obscurity. There is no accepted single answer to why the ICO phenomenon petered out. The weight of all these scams and flops certainly contributed to the public losing enthusiasm for throwing their money at these ephemeral tokens. Crypto prices slipped into reverse from early 2018, with Bitcoin falling 75 per cent by the end of the year.

The Securities and Exchange Commission (SEC), the US regulator mainly responsible for controlling the pipeline of new investment products being offered to the American public, did its best to inject bad vibes into the market for random crypto tokens. Among other cases, it went after two companies that raised some of the largest ICOs. Block.one agreed to pay a $24 million fine to settle a case involving its $4 billion ICO. The SEC went further with Telegram. The messaging app, still popular in crypto circles, was forced to give back the $1.2 billion it raised in coin sales and pay an $18.5 million fine.

The 2018 slump in crypto markets was bad news for the young Alameda Research. SBF had been relatively late to the crypto phenomenon and launched the company almost at the peak of the boom. The market had turned from 'bull' (good) to 'bear' (bad), and pickings were slimmer. 'The bear market was a hard thing to sort of swallow. Before the bear market, dumb trades were everywhere. And by dumb, I mean obviously incredibly good trades were everywhere. And so we had this hilarious phenomenon where so long as we really just focused on getting the good trades done correctly, it was the right decision not to worry too much about our mistakes,' Nishad said, recalling this period. 'Patching up our mistakes wasn't worth the effort when we could sort of throw everything at getting the trades done perfectly or done as well as we could.'

Alameda's 'trade now and ask questions never' approach didn't work as well in downbeat markets. Nishad, Caroline and the other early employees all recall a massive effort to upgrade the speed of their trading systems so that they could make enough money in the downturn. 'In the bear market, a lot of the obviously good trades dried up. And so we had to really tighten up our operation,' Nishad said.

The lack of crypto enthusiasm also made it hard to recruit new talent to Alameda, an obscure firm trading in a market that looked to be dying. The founders had to work even harder to keep afloat. In a later interview, Trabucco said: 'It became pretty unappealing to join a crypto firm. In 2017, when [Bitcoin] was hitting 20k for the first time it was a decent amount more appealing.' The interviewer asked why he stayed, when the market had gone sour. In cryptoland, questions about why you stuck with digital assets through a market downturn are supposed to elicit lofty answers about your deep belief in crypto and commitment to 'HODL'. 'The conviction was largely monetary,' Trabucco said flatly.

Alameda could still scalp enough percentages here and there to make some money.

SBF, however, had his eyes on a more lucrative prize. The biggest companies in crypto are exchanges, the venues where people come to trade. Many of the opportunities that Alameda exploited to make money existed because the big exchanges that dominated trading in 2018 were clunky and sometimes dysfunctional. What if, instead of trading around those failings, Alameda could build an exchange of its own? SBF was confident in his tiny team of ex-Wall Streeters and Silicon Valley coders to create something better.

The biggest challenge was not technological. It was social. Exchange businesses are a bit like social media platforms. You need a lot of people to use your platform before it really works. Alameda had been a reclusive company, holed up in Berkeley. 'We didn't have any customers. And we didn't know how to get customers. We didn't know anyone,' SBF said.

SBF started trying to change that. Alameda began to offer private trading services to big clients and to seek new investors. A marketing document for the firm produced in the autumn of 2018 says: 'Plain and simple, we have better trading, engineering and operational talent than any other cryptocurrency trading firm. We have decades of experience from the best trading firms on Wall Street . . . and the best technology companies in Silicon Valley.'

Alameda advertised its 'market neutral' strategy, meaning it didn't bet on whether crypto would go up or down. It promised to make trades that were fast, technical and low risk. The document claimed Alameda had $55 million in capital and traded $150–300 million per day. 'Up until now, we've maintained a low profile, and are emerging to seek funding,' it said. Investors were invited to loan the firm money for a promised 15 per cent annual return. That is a big number in the investment world. More striking was Alameda's guarantee to pay back all its loans. There was, it said, 'no downside'.

SBF's most important move was to leave the US. The centre of the crypto markets was in Asia, especially China. So SBF left Berkeley and headed to Hong Kong. The whole company eventually followed. 'Gary and Sam basically took off to Hong Kong . . . and built the exchange in a couple of months, the first version of it,' Nishad recalled. He stayed behind in Berkeley running the tech for Alameda. 'The 15–20-hour days didn't hurt. It definitely helps you improve quickly.'

'[I] kinda was enamoured of the craziness and just how much energy there was,' said Nate Parke, who joined Alameda's tech team in mid-2018 and took over as the trading firm's tech chief when Nishad left for Hong Kong to join the team working on the exchange. Still, SBF remained a peripheral figure in crypto, hanging around the edges of crypto conferences looking for investment. One veteran investor described him, at that time, as 'one weirdo among many'.

*

Absent from the scene when SBF sought new investors was the name of one of Alameda's co-founders. Tara Mac Aulay trained as a pharmacist in Australia and worked as an international aid worker for the Australian Red Cross. Like SBF, she had been drawn to the EA movement and ended up as chief executive at the Centre for Effective Altruism, where SBF briefly worked. She helped launch Alameda as a money-spinner, exploiting crypto riches to raise money for charity. Mac Aulay brought in key early investors who gave Alameda the money to get started, recruiting them from her EA network.

The partnership with SBF didn't go well. Reports, notably by *Time* magazine and the *Wall Street Journal*, detail the growing anxiety about SBF's leadership from some of Alameda's early staff. Employees said he had made risky trades that defied their promise of a safe 'market neutral' strategy, and lost money. SBF resisted the idea of implementing normal bookkeeping and financial controls, even though Alameda didn't have a clear sense of its financial position and which trades were profitable (SBF said he later fixed these issues). Staff were also concerned about SBF's 'inappropriate romantic relationships with subordinates', *Time* reported. And he backed out of a plan to share ownership of the firm.

Mac Aulay and a group of supporters tried to oust SBF as chief executive, offering to pay him to step down. In a document prepared before the attempted 'intervention' to get rid of SBF, reported by *Time* journalist Charlotte Alter, his employees claimed he was 'misreporting numbers', 'failing to update investors on poor performance', 'negligent' and 'unethical'. 'Sam will lie, and distort the truth for his own gain,' it read. Employees 'didn't trust Sam to be in investor meetings alone'.

SBF listened in silence and refused to quit. Instead, it was the dissident employees, around half of Alameda's staff, who were left with no choice but to go. 'I and a group of others all quit, in part due to concerns over risk management and business ethics,' Mac Aulay later said.

A Bunch of Dorks

The remainder of Alameda's team erased Mac Aulay from the company's history. The diminished Alameda leadership moved to Hong Kong and set its sights on launching a new exchange. In one interview about the firm's early days, SBF made a rare and veiled reference to a schism among Alameda employees. He portrayed it as an 'internal fracture', a 'disagreement over what path to take'. 'It was a really hard and gruelling period for the company,' he said. He never mentioned Mac Aulay.

The lesson SBF said he drew from the disagreement was singular. In an interview just two months before his empire collapsed, he alluded to the early split at Alameda as the most difficult problem he'd ever faced. Rather than thinking twice about risk-taking or management, he concluded that he should have shown the dissenting employees the door much earlier. 'Frankly, if this is a sticking point for you, if you can't get yourself comfortable with being at a place that has made this decision, then maybe this isn't the company for you,' he said. It was a lesson he clearly took to heart. People who challenged SBF did not last long at his court.

In retrospect, this episode was a turning point. If SBF had been ousted from Alameda in disgrace, or been forced to submit to some semblance of the normal rules that should apply when you're managing other people's money, then much of the rest of this story would never have been written. Instead, SBF's critics stayed silent and his star continued to rise.

The clash with Mac Aulay suggests another interpretation of SBF's origin story. Maybe he wasn't brilliant and ethical, or awkward and directionless. Perhaps all the talk of EA and 'expected value' was a smokescreen for his true motivations: influence, fame, power and, above all, money. A Wall Street trader's income might have seemed like a big prize to the undergraduate SBF. But life as a worker bee at a low-profile trading shop was nothing compared to crypto, which presented a bigger and faster route to a far greater prize.

In the aftermath of SBF's undoing, Mac Aulay wrote: 'I am shocked, appalled, and frankly, angry. [Bitcoin] was birthed from the trauma of 2008. Sam's actions are a perversion of everything crypto stands for. My heart goes out to all of the victims whose trust was betrayed, savings lost, and livelihoods destroyed.' Her words could apply not just to SBF but to many of the crypto financiers who trace their story back to the boom times of 2017–18. It was then that many people realised that crypto was a brilliant place for an unscrupulous person to make an obscene amount of money.

Pirate Ship

The world's largest crypto company celebrated its second anniversary atop Shanghai's 58-storey International Finance Centre, with sweeping views over the river and glittering skyline in the heart of China's largest city. The dress code for the event, in July 2019, at the Ritz Carlton hotel, was black and gold, the company colours. 'What about just wearing a company T-shirt?' one employee cheekily asked. 'No,' came the reply. It wasn't just that the bosses wanted their scruffy crypto coders to dress up for the Ritz. Revellers must not show the company logo anywhere. It would be 'against security policy'.

The company, Binance, had good reasons to celebrate. In its first two years, it had become one of the biggest names in crypto, with millions of customers and a vast following on social media. It also had reasons to be discreet. The secrecy surrounding its glitzy birthday party attested to the strange character of the organisation. Binance warned its staff not to post pictures on social media, identify themselves as Binance employees on LinkedIn, or share their location online.

Binance said the secrecy was intended to protect employees' personal safety. It also served to protect the company. Binance's founder, Changpeng Zhao, known universally as 'CZ', had an audacious vision to grow the business into a dominant global financial force. In public, CZ denied that Binance had a head-quarters anywhere. The radically disruptive crypto giant rejected everything a normal financial company would do to secure legit-imacy. Establishing a prestigious HQ, seeking approval from top-tier government agencies and courting the mainstream media were not for CZ. The location of its operations and even the chief executive's physical whereabouts were often shrouded in secrecy. It was, he said, a decentralised company. Employees worked around the world, and the company was based wherever CZ happened to be. 'Wherever I sit, is going to be the Binance office,' he once said.

By being everywhere and nowhere, Binance ensured that no one government would have control over its global operation. When China cracked down on crypto a few months after the company was founded in 2017, Binance melted into the background – ultimately reappearing in Japan. It was the first of many shifts in its centre of gravity as Binance slipped away from regulatory pressure in dozens of countries. But a few months after Binance toasted its success at the Ritz in Shanghai, its footloose strategy faced its toughest test yet. Crypto news website The Block broke the news that Binance's Shanghai office had been hastily abandoned. Employees had fled after a 'raid' by Chinese authorities.

Pirate Ship

CZ fired back on Twitter. The report was 'fake headline news of the non-existent "police raid", which damaged our reputation . . . We will be suing.' He said Binance hadn't had an office in Shanghai for two years. So how could it be raided? The Block retreated as far as changing the word 'raid' to the rather demure-sounding 'visit', but maintained that the office was real.

Years later, in an interview in 2023, CZ casually admitted that the office had been real all along. 'Some government official visited the office,' he told Bloomberg. 'You can write two very different narratives as a journalist, right?' CZ said. 'You can say, "This guy escaped into a restaurant," or you can say, "The guy walks slowly into the restaurant and enjoys the sunshine view."'

CZ has never been afraid to use threats and play games with the truth in his relentless drive to grow his crypto empire. His offhand admission of how far he had misled people about the Shanghai office back in 2019 spoke to his limits as crypto's most high-profile chief executive. From one angle, CZ is the apex predator of the crypto industry, a ruthless entrepreneur feared by his enemies in business. In his dealings with SBF, CZ was always the senior partner. When their relationship turned to rivalry, CZ emerged victorious. He grew an obscure startup into the world's biggest crypto exchange, likely becoming one of the world's richest people. But at other times he seemed like a man who is out of his depth, not quite able to pull off his Machiavellian persona.

Binance's defiance of national boundaries, as it shifted around the world and operated from the international waters of the internet, was audacious. CZ relentlessly pushed the company to prioritise growth, even if it meant letting billions in dark money flow around the world. It was a delicate game that CZ played without enough finesse. Binance clashed with authorities from the UK to Japan. CZ himself moved from China to Japan, then on to Singapore and Dubai – as each jurisdiction clamped down on crypto. As the crackdown intensified, CZ seemed to detect the way the wind was blowing. He said Binance had made mistakes in its early years and was ready to clean up its act, becoming a fully regulated financial institution. It was too late.

*

The narrative CZ tried to craft around Binance being hustled out of China back in 2017 drew on his own family's flight from the country decades before. 'The irony that I was once again forced to leave China – approximately thirty years after my parents fled with my sister and me – was not lost on me,' he once wrote.

Born in Jiangsu province, north of Shanghai, to a teacher and an academic, CZ was living with his parents on the campus of the University of Science and Technology in Hefei when China was rocked by the 1989 Tiananmen Square massacre. Two months later, the family obtained visas and moved to Canada. 'I remember the line outside the Canadian embassy was three days long. We had to take shifts at night to keep our position in the queue. It changed my life forever and opened up endless possibilities for me,' he wrote.

CZ became a Canadian citizen. In recent years, he has called out journalists and critics who he accuses of deliberately emphasising his background in China as a way to cast Binance as a sinister foreign operation. The broad strokes of CZ's early life fit the pattern of thousands of first generation immigrants who arrived from overseas, became Canadians and forged impressive lives. He fondly recalls teenage years in Vancouver, when he first learned to code. His humble part-time jobs at McDonald's and working at a petrol station have become part of his legend. 'The Former McDonald's Cook Who Made $1 Billion,' ran one headline. He studied computer science at McGill University in Montreal and dived into the world of trading, with early jobs at the Tokyo Stock Exchange and Bloomberg. He bounced through different cities around the world – Tokyo, New York, Singapore and Hong Kong – working in trading tech. In the early 2000s, he moved back to China as a self-described 'expat' and entrepreneur.

Like SBF and other crypto luminaries, CZ's conversion to digital assets has been mythologised. The story begins with a first conversation over a poker game and then to devout reading of the Bitcoin white paper, followed by CZ selling his apartment in Shanghai to buy Bitcoin and jumping into jobs at crypto ventures. In a 2021 *New York Times* interview, CZ also credited a chance encounter with Ethereum founder Buterin, at a conference in 2013, with helping convince him to go crypto. But in his early roles in crypto, it was not just his faith in Bitcoin that made CZ stand out, but also his ability to bring the heft of traditional markets to bear.

During a brief spell as chief technology officer at the exchange Okcoin, now OKX – one of the largest crypto exchanges – CZ was quoted as saying: 'I am excited that I can leverage my Wall Street experience directly at Okcoin, and I see many opportunities for the company to fill gaps and shortfalls within the Bitcoin trading ecosystem.' In reality, his ambitions were already becoming even larger. He wanted to fill those gaps and shortfalls in the crypto trading world with a company that he could lead. Amid the wild enthusiasm for initial coin offerings in mid-2017, CZ sold $15 million worth of his own new cryptocurrency 'Binance Coin' – now called BNB – to raise the funds to start his own exchange, with the clear goal of being the biggest and the best.

Just eight months after its launch, it looked like he had already succeeded. A *Forbes* profile described the company as the world's biggest crypto exchange with 6 million users and credited CZ as a billionaire. The reporter likened him to 'some cross between Mark Zuckerberg and Steve Jobs' thanks to the black hoodie he wore. It's difficult to judge exactly how fast and how big Binance grew. But no one contests that the answer to these questions is *very* fast and *very* big. Binance says it has 150 million customers worldwide.

CZ's priority was growth at any cost. 'Their strong suit is on-the-ground marketing in China and the Chinese diaspora around Asia and Central Europe. That's where they're very, very strong. And he's built a very, very good business,' said the former CEO of a rival exchange who knew CZ well. (Binance said it does not operate in China and its mission is 'to grow the market overall so that it leads to increased adoption of digital assets'.)

Although SBF enjoyed greater fame and influence, FTX was a minnow compared to the Binance whale. When SBF and his Alameda garage band decided to start building a sophisticated crypto trading platform back in 2018, they initially pitched the idea to CZ. SBF imagined their new platform could become a specialised unit within Binance. He told me the pitch to CZ was a 'five-minute Zoom call' that 'went nowhere'. Binance built up its services for pro traders in-house. But when FTX launched as an independent company the following year, Binance came on board as an early investor – owning a fifth of SBF's new company.

SBF was the master communicator, leaning into his unconventional persona and making it one of his greatest strengths. CZ appears to fancy himself as an ice-cold financier. He also occasionally flirts with the role of business coach or self-help writer. In 2022, he penned a 6,000-word blog post on his management principles. The guide runs to 15 points with sub-headings and covers everything from when to sleep to the best way of writing text messages, as well as a bid to seem relatable ('I chill just like most other people . . . I love snowboarding. I watch some movies'). He said 'controlled chaos' can be a good thing. 'In a strongly structured organization, there is less organic innovation, less internal competition (or pressure to improve constantly),' he wrote.

Binance's ultimate ownership is concealed in a maze of offshore entities, but it is generally accepted by regulators, former employees and business partners that CZ is the primary owner and calls the shots, with a small circle of long-time associates. Former executives told *Forbes* that Heina Chen, one of CZ's closest associates, was effectively CFO of Binance although she didn't formally hold the title. (Binance denies this.) Outside this sanctum, people describe rival power centres. 'There is a very, very tight group that basically decides everything. And then they have these competing groups going after different opportunities. I think they just give full autonomy for people to run off and do something,' one former business partner said.

Within his inner circle, the links are not only professional. CZ has had a year-long romantic entanglement with one of his top lieutenants, Yi He, who runs a vast and eclectic portfolio of Binance departments including its venture capital investments and deciding which tokens get listed on the platform. Once a popular travel host on Chinese TV, Yi He described, in a rare interview with Bloomberg, how she first recruited CZ as chief technology officer for Okcoin, and he in turn recruited her to Binance. The pair have children together – for many years an open secret in crypto circles. As far as we can judge from their public comments, the current status of the relationship is best described as 'it's complicated'.

In person, CZ is a chilly figure. He eschews introductory meetings and said he doesn't bother 'maintaining many relationships'. He tries to portray an almost monk-like devotion to his mission of crypto world conquest. 'Remove distractions from your life. For me, I don't have many hobbies. I exercise for 30 min[utes] each day. I don't have many physical possessions that need to be maintained. The time cost is high,' he wrote.

When he came to meet a panel of journalists at the *FT* office, he arrived in a small motorcade of a black Range Rover and a gleaming Mercedes van with a bodyguard and a couple of aides. Dressed in a blue suit with an open collar, he cut a professional figure, deftly parrying an onslaught of questions. But he was charmless and awkward. Like SBF, he was manifestly uncomfortable with small talk. Worse, he lacked the FTX founder's enthralling manner and gift for storytelling.

It's tricky to tell what makes CZ tick. CZ's allies say his first love is the tech. It's an account of his motivation that tallies with the decades of his career that he spent knee-deep in the plumbing of high-tech financial systems. But the image of a techie at heart, driven by a passion for innovation, doesn't match with CZ's drive for world domination. Rivals, some of them very bitter ones, told me not to look for a complex psychological profile. CZ is a man who wants money and power. One said CZ's mission is simple: 'To be the biggest exchange, I think. The most dominant.' (Binance said CZ is motivated by the company's 'mission', not money.)

If wealth is what he's after, he has already been phenomenally successful, although it's quite difficult to say just how rich he is. When you think about the list of questions that would allow you to figure out CZ's fortune – What percentage of Binance does he own? How much is the company worth? How much crypto does CZ personally hold? What property or other assets does he own? – The answer to every one of them is 'not sure' or 'don't know'. The best we can say is that he is probably very rich, but that his wealth is also hugely volatile depending on the massive ups and downs of the crypto market. Bloomberg added him to their billionaires list in 2022 with a fortune of $96 billion. Eighteen months later, it was two-thirds less.

*

In its rise to dominate crypto trading, Binance has defined an entire category of organisation: the crypto exchange. The basic job of a crypto exchange is the same as the function of a stock exchange, which – at risk of stating the very obvious – is where people come to buy and sell stocks. In the past, stock traders crowded on to the famous trading floors in Wall Street and the City of London and yelled buy and sell orders at each other from the opening bell until the end of the trading day, in the hope of finding a deal. These days, the deal-making process is a more sophisticated electronic one, and many stock exchanges – including London's – no longer have a trading floor.

Crypto exchanges do the same thing. At their heart is a piece of technology called a 'matching engine', which does what the name suggests: matching up willing buyers and sellers of digital assets to complete deals. But even calling crypto exchanges 'exchanges' gets traditional finance experts a bit hot under the collar, because the giant companies that dominate crypto trading break all the neatly defined boundaries of how trading works in traditional finance.

The most important difference is that crypto exchanges do something that traditional exchanges would not go within a mile of: they hold your assets. To trade on an exchange like Binance you would usually deposit your cash or crypto into wallets at the exchange, meaning that Binance has control of the assets – and all you have is the right to ask for them back. Actually handling other people's money is a dangerous business. You need to make sure it doesn't get lost or stolen, and it introduces something called 'counterparty risk', which is finance speak for the risk that someone will not pay up when they are supposed to. Traditional exchanges rely on a network of other institutions including custodians who look after the assets and brokers, like Vanguard or Robinhood, who take orders from clients and go to the exchange to make the deal. Their roles are separate from the exchange, which is supposed to be a neutral forum for buying and selling.

Pirate Ship

The lines between exchange, broker and custodian are not the only carefully guarded distinctions in traditional finance that crypto exchanges blur or break. In late 2023, Binance held an estimated $60 billion on behalf of customers. These are not just short-term pledges from people looking to trade. In crypto, plenty of customers use exchanges as a convenient place to store their crypto wealth. To stop that money just sitting around, some exchanges will offer you an interest rate if you let them lend your dormant crypto out to other people. Verging into the business of taking deposits, making loans and paying interest starts to make crypto exchanges look less like 'exchanges' at all, and much more like what, in traditional finance, you'd call a bank.

The last, and most egregious, piece of line blurring is when crypto exchanges also have their own in-house traders. FTX and Alameda were not the only exchange and trading firm to have an uncomfortably close relationship. US regulators have alleged that trading firms and accounts controlled by CZ engaged in manipulative trading on Binance (which they deny). Reporting by my *FT* colleague Nikou Asgari revealed an in-house trading team at another major exchange, Crypto.com.

At this point, traditional finance wonks are holding their heads in their hands. One can argue about the niceties of market structure and the proper role of exchanges, brokers, custodians; whether all these middlemen deserve the fees they take; and more technical functions like clearing and settling. But having an exchange and a trading operation in the same hands creates a huge temptation to favour your own traders over other people, giving them an edge in speed or insider information at the expense of other customers.

Equally, having the same organisation verging into the realm of banking, with all the risks involved in lending, adds another massive source of potential trouble.

Senior figures on traditional finance have been agitating about how risky it is to have crypto exchanges operating as catch-all financial institutions. They have tended not to phrase their warnings in the most hair-raising terms. Jon Cunliffe, Deputy Governor of the Bank of England, gave a speech along these lines in 2022:

'FTX, along with a number of other centralised crypto trading platforms, operate as conglomerates, bundling products and functions within one firm. In conventional finance these functions are either separated into different entities or managed with tight controls and ring-fences.

'To prevent conflicts of interest, regulation imposes requirements and constraints on the connections between a financial firm and its affiliates . . . For financial market infrastructure firms, such as a central counterparty, an exchange or a custodian, the regulatory system and international standards in place aim to stop these important pieces of financial market infrastructure from taking on credit liquidity and market risk beyond what is absolutely necessary to discharge their core functions.'

Right . . .

The casual listener would be forgiven for not quite catching the key message: 'what these crypto jokers are doing is extremely dangerous'. Cunliffe does deserve credit for tackling these subjects directly, even if he uses the staid tones of a central banker. His key points were twofold. Crypto exchanges lack the balance of different institutions performing different roles, and they lack the checks from independent supervisors that everyone is behaving properly.

Banks, stock exchanges, brokers and custodians each have their own hefty rule book, and regulators who check and double-check that the rules are being followed. This is not at all to say that the regulated system is foolproof. Far from it. To take one of my favourite recent examples, in 2023 a warehouse linked to the London Metals Exchange found that bags that were supposed to contain nickel were actually full of rocks.

When you trade in traditional finance you are placing your trust in a system where a number of independent institutions manage different steps in the process, and check each other's homework – with democratically accountable regulators breathing down their necks. This system can very reasonably be criticised for its many historic failings, and for including a lot of expensive middlemen and gatekeepers. But when you trade with an unregulated crypto exchange, everything is being handled by one institution which has no real oversight and no obligation to be transparent about how it handles your money – and which might execute your trade with its right hand, while trading, possibly against you, with its left. To trade on Binance, you have to trust Binance, which means trusting one guy – CZ.

*

Eagle-eyed readers will have noticed something odd about the above description. The battle between traditional finance and crypto is supposed to be that 'tradfi' is too centralised with power in the hands of a few institutions, while crypto is a decentralised system that doesn't require the user to trust any institutions at all. When you look at companies like Binance, clearly something has gone slightly awry.

Alesia Haas, chief financial officer of Coinbase – the leading American exchange – boasted in congressional testimony in late 2021 that her company securely stores 12 per cent of global crypto assets. Those figures have shifted around since then as the crypto market gyrated. Looking at Binance, in 2023, it appeared to hold somewhere around 5 per cent of all the crypto in the world. To give a back-of-the-envelope comparison, the world's largest bank by assets, the International & Commercial Bank of China, holds around $5.5 trillion, which is less than 1 per cent of the global net worth of $630 trillion according to McKinsey's estimate. So in terms of the share of wealth concentrated in any one institution, crypto is many times more centralised than traditional finance. Not to mention the fact that some of the biggest crypto 'banks' are not accountable to share-holders, politicians, voters or anyone else. Trading in the supposedly decentralised crypto market takes place mostly within a handful of hyper-centralised financial conglomerates that require almost blind trust in their honesty and effectiveness.

Exchanges are extremely powerful. They have control over which tokens are available for traders to buy, and charge hefty fees to those who want to have their token listed for sale. For smaller cryptocurrencies, this is the power of life and death. Exchanges also make a lot of money by taking a tiny percentage of the value of the trades. Those percentages quickly add up to big money if, like Binance in 2021, you process $34 trillion of deals in a year.

Pirate Ship

The crypto community is aware of the rather glaring practical and ideological problem posed by the exchanges' dominant, central role. Crypto purists are some of the harshest critics of what they'd call 'centralised exchanges', like Binance. In fairness, there is some variation among exchanges. Coinbase is a public company. That doesn't make it perfect. It has fought many battles with US authorities over the limits of crypto regulation. However, it does mean that it is subject to more oversight and stricter transparency requirements than its offshore peers like Binance. There are also some traditional finance players that have set up their own crypto exchanges following the established, regulated model.

But for crypto diehards, all of these approaches only make matters worse. These solutions try to make crypto more trustworthy by making it more like traditional finance. Crypto believers prefer decentralised exchanges, the best-known example of which is called Uniswap. Decentralised exchanges operate using smart contracts to automate all the functions of a traditional exchange. The only thing, in theory at least, between the buyer and the seller is a decentralised, technological system. These projects are a much more comfortable fit with the original vision of crypto.

The problem is that decentralised exchanges have also not exactly caught on. The scale of centralised trading absolutely dwarfs the amount of decentralised trading, and the vast majority of centralised crypto exchange volume takes place on offshore, unregulated exchanges. Centralised exchanges are, simply, much easier to use. They have slick websites and integrated credit card payments. Decentralised exchanges are more complicated, often more expensive to use and they require their users to look after their own crypto assets.

*

Keeping your assets entirely in your own hands is the ideal imagined by crypto's pioneers. It's also really tricky. One sunny afternoon in a coffee shop near London's Somerset House, a senior crypto executive – just by way of small talk – told me a story that illustrates why. My contact, who lived in London, had recently been on holiday. This was in the hinterland of the Covid-19 lockdowns when 'staycations' were all the rage. He was just driving a few hours out into the countryside with his family for a change of scene.

We all know the sinking feeling of setting off on holiday and realising with a jolt that we've forgotten our passport in the sock drawer. A few hours into his drive, this chap had the same feeling. Except that he hadn't forgotten his passport. He had forgotten his bank account. This executive was one of the more sophisticated and committed crypto believers who genuinely kept the 'vast majority' of his personal wealth using a small physical device called a 'hardware wallet'. These products mostly look like little USB sticks, with a couple of buttons on them or maybe a tiny screen. Inside, they store the cryptographic information you need to unlock and control your wealth on the blockchain.

If you have heard any stories about crypto, they are probably the tales – equally hilarious and heart-wrenching – of people desperately searching through rubbish dumps looking for lost hardware wallets, or else racking their brains to remember a password they set five years ago when crypto was worth peanuts but that now holds the key to millions of dollars. For my contact, the dilemma was not quite so dire. He just had to decide whether to turn the car around.

The thing about so-called 'self-custody' of your assets is that it is utterly unforgiving. If you lose your little matchbox-sized device, or forget your complicated password, the money is gone. Forever. So I wonder: if two or three hours into a long car journey, you realised that you had left your bank account home alone, what would you do? Because if the house burns down, or gets burgled, it's not a matter of turning up to the bank with your passport and reclaiming your accounts. It's not a matter of going through the faff of even replacing your passport at the drab office by Victoria railway station in London. Your money is just gone.

He turned around. For my associate, the extra several hours on the motorway were more than worth the peace of mind. I'm sure I would have done the same. But for me, the prospect of ever being in that position is simply terrifying. It's been more than a decade since I lost my wallet, but it does happen. I like to be able to reset my passwords. And I suspect most people would agree with me.

People know that we are fallible. And we like to have institutions that can bail us out. This is the fundamental, very basic reason why decentralised systems have stayed in the realm of crypto hobbyists and centralised exchanges have grown. To some extent, CZ agrees with me. He has said that, for now at least, only 1 per cent of people are prepared to handle self-custody of their crypto assets. 'For most people, for 99 per cent of people today, asking them to hold crypto on their own, they will end up losing it,' he said.

*

The growing popularity of exchanges in crypto's first decade represented the gradual selling out of its founding ideals. The rise of exchanges is the clearest sign of the transition from Crypto 1.0, with its focus eliminating trusted middlemen, to Crypto 2.0. Step by step, starting from the idea of replacing financial institutions with self-custody, the crypto world has reinvented the bank.

What the early exchanges did was make it much easier to buy and sell Bitcoin. Before, the only option was to personally go out and find another cryptonaut to trade with. Over time, exchanges increasingly also offered the 'on ramps and off ramps' to swap between crypto and fiat currency (although the on ramps are notoriously smoother than getting money out). Exchanges also established a commonly accepted price for Bitcoin against the dollar. Previously, there was no way to judge a standard price from the scattered, private deals.

The easier exchanges became to use, the more they grew and lowered the barrier for people without technical skills to gain access to crypto. By late 2013, the dominant early exchange, Mt. Gox, hit 1 million customers. Its peculiar name came from a time before Bitcoin, when a forerunner of the exchange was used to trade cards in the popular fantasy game 'Magic: the Gathering'. (Mt. Gox is, brilliantly, short for 'Magic the Gathering Online eXchange'.) At its peak, it was handling 80 per cent of Bitcoin transactions.

Pirate Ship

The success was short-lived. Mt. Gox suffered a massive hack and the theft of hundreds of millions of its clients' crypto assets, forcing it into bankruptcy. A *Wall Street Journal* report at the time blamed the disaster on the company's security measures failing to keep pace with the huge scale of the riches it was guarding. The newspaper described Mt. Gox's French CEO Mark Karpeles as 'a geek – fascinated with trading cards and anime – who fell into his central role in the burgeoning bitcoin world but was unable to cope with the ballooning size and importance of his company'.

The history of crypto is punctuated by exchange disasters, usually involving hacking or theft. In 2018, Gerald Cotten, the CEO of Canadian crypto exchange Quadriga, died in mysterious circumstances in India. He took with him the keys to unlock around $200 million worth of other people's crypto, reportedly stored on his laptop at his home in Fall River, Nova Scotia – a town of around 2,500 people that doesn't even have a bank branch (although there are a couple of ATMs near the mall, by the Dairy Queen). Investigations revealed that most of the clients' money wasn't even in the locked wallets. Cotten had 'spent, traded and used those assets at will' in the year before his death, an investigation by Canadian authorities concluded. 'In effect . . . Quadriga operated like a Ponzi scheme.'

The case neatly illustrates the incredible temptation and potential for bad behaviour that unregulated crypto 'banks' represent. That big pile of other people's money is just sitting there, ripe for the taking. Despite repeated scandals, exchanges have continued to grow because customers apparently are still keen to find an institution that they can rely on to look after their crypto-money.

In musings on the subject, CZ wrote: 'Between being decentralized and potentially losing your coins, or using a centralized service that keeps your coins, most people today still choose to use a centralized exchange. That's why [centralised exchanges] are more popular today.'

This is an ideologically awkward statement for someone who claims to be a big believer in decentralisation. The Bitcoin white paper itself, crypto's founding text, says: 'the main benefits are lost if a trusted third party is still required'. When you look at Binance and other centralised exchanges, it's hard to escape the conclusion that the main benefits *have* been lost.

CZ wriggles out of this ideological bind with a manoeuvre that has always reminded me of some mediaeval Catholic theologian trying to reconcile apparently contradictory doctrine. 'Centralized exchanges provide an incremental step for users to access crypto,' he wrote. '[They] act as a bridge between centralized and decentralized systems.' If we go along with CZ and assume that only 1 per cent of people can handle decentralisation today, 15 years after Bitcoin was invented, even if the speed at which people are catching up increases a lot, this bridge is going to be a very long one indeed. And bridges in the style of Binance look like quite a centralised way of crossing the river. Even if you assume that we are on the bridge to decentralisation, and I personally am very sceptical, in the meantime it will be important to make sure that centralised crypto institutions behave themselves. The story of FTX, and indeed the accusations against Binance, suggest that they have not.

*

Pirate Ship

In January of 2023, I was temporarily based in the New York office of the *Financial Times*. On a chilly Wednesday morning, we got word from the Washington bureau: the US Department of Justice would make a major announcement later in the day. Officials didn't give much of a teaser. It was a major cryptocurrency case, with an international angle.

I don't think I was the only crypto journalist who felt a bit of a tingle down their spine. There was one major, international crypto case that everyone had been waiting for: the case against Binance. There had already been many credible media reports that CZ's exchange was under investigation. Might the Feds be ready to take a crack at Binance?

When Deputy Attorney General Lisa Monaco stepped up to the Justice Department podium, the news was a let-down. The US charged the Russian founder of a Hong Kong crypto exchange with funnelling $700 million in illicit payments, breaking US law. I had never even heard of the company involved, Bitzlato. I was not alone, at least to judge from the extensive Twitter mockery of the DOJ's supposedly 'major' announcement. The eye rolling was probably unjustified, as my colleague Scott Chipolina argued a few days later in the *FT*. The hundreds of millions in payments had flowed to the Hydra Market, a massive dark web supermarket for drugs and other illegal products, where buyers could even give sellers an Airbnb-style rating out of five stars. It was a significant win for the DOJ.

Still, the crypto world would have to wait for the case it had been holding its breath for. Binance had fought plenty of small battles with regulators in dozens of countries, from Japan to Germany.

It had faced a string of issues about its marketing, and undisclosed payments to influencers and sports stars hyping up crypto. Even the powerful UK regulator had not, however, really succeeded in denting the Binance juggernaut. Only the US government, or possibly China, really had the muscle to take Binance on.

In the first half of 2023, it seemed increasingly clear that Binance knew something was coming. Binance started talking a lot about how it had made mistakes in its early years and was ready to pay the price. In an interview in February, the company's chief strategy officer and spin doctor Patrick Hillmann told the *Wall Street Journal* that Binance was ready to pay money to settle historical issues with US regulators. 'There were some gaps in our compliance system in the first two years,' he told Bloomberg around the same time.

I saw Hillmann, a big, jovial, smooth-talking man – who has since left Binance – at a dinner in London a few months later. He was all talk about sorting out and 'remediating' past issues and moving on. He introduced me to the company's new chief compliance officer, Noah Perlman, a former US prosecutor who had worked at Morgan Stanley. As we were chatting, a stranger joined the circle to introduce herself. Learning that Perlman had just taken the top compliance job at Binance, she laughed and said he was 'brave'. He looked green. And with good reason.

Compliance is one of those finance words that does itself no favours. It sounds like a drag. What compliance means is the function of making sure bad stuff doesn't happen. Notably, it means knowing who your customers are, and making sure that baddies aren't funnelling money through your platform. For most of its history, Binance wasn't so much sloppy or lax about compliance as it was actively hostile to it.

CZ once described his company to a new senior hire as a 'pirate ship'. The core money machine is Binance.com, the exchange website that can be accessed around the world and which mints billions upon billions of dollars. The closest thing Binance has to an official home base is the Cayman Islands, where some key corporate entities are registered. But it has a vast network of companies in dozens of countries. CZ himself, and the Binance centre of gravity, has bounced from China to Japan and to Singapore. At one point, Binance flirted with establishing a base in Malta. Dubai, where CZ settled, became its de facto headquarters. (Binance said: 'We would not refer to it as our HQ.') In France, where CZ was welcomed in a personal meeting with President Emmanuel Macron, the company has a large office. In several of these countries, Binance has had different forms of regulation or oversight for its local units. But the Binance.com pirate ship doesn't dock in any of these ports. It stays safely floating in international waters.

CZ explained in a 2019 internal conversation how Binance does business through various units in different jurisdictions to 'keep countries clean [of violations of law]' by 'not landing [Binance]. com anywhere. This is the main reason .com does not land anywhere.' Samuel Lim, then Binance's chief compliance officer, put it even more bluntly in 2020. 'Because we do not want .com to be regulated ever, we created local entities to be registered with the regulators, and ring-fence accordingly.'

When regulators cut off a head in one country, Binance can grow another one. Jeremy Allaire, the prominent crypto chief executive who runs the company Circle said: 'The offshore regulatory arbitrage has spawned global hydra companies without a known base, who often act with impunity.'

A senior official at a major regulator told me: 'Binance basically gets kicked out of countries every second week, and they are just using a different entity to service the clients. Even if you prohibit a firm to be active, effectively, it is very hard to enforce it. If someone wants to deposit at Binance, it is very hard to stop them.'

*

CZ's strategy was an amped-up version of a playbook borrowed from Silicon Valley. I remember when Uber first arrived in my home town, Toronto, in 2012, seeing footage of taxi drivers jumping on to the bonnets of cars in angry protest at how the ride-sharing app was undercutting the licensed taxi drivers. I was quite sympathetic to the taxi drivers, and for some time refused to take Ubers until the constant inconvenience and faint ridiculousness of my stance wore me down.

Then, as now, the taxi drivers had a point. The city had rules to govern the business of being paid to drive people around. Uber arrived and because it had a cool app basically decided that it didn't have to follow the rules, making it much more competitive than the taxi drivers who often had to pay a small fortune for their city licence. This is not fair. Over time, Uber has fought out these issues in cities and jurisdictions around the world – being thrown out of some and reaching a compromise in many. Uber drivers in Toronto now need a city licence, but ride-sharing services have their own permit system separate from taxis.

Uber was in a better position to fight these skirmishes because it asked for forgiveness rather than permission. By growing quickly, it established market share and cemented a level of popularity that put pressure on politicians to reach an accommodation – rather than simply shutting it down.

Watching Binance dance around global financial regulation has been immensely frustrating for its rivals, and for the watchdogs who are supposed to police it. 'The challenge is about economics,' said Julian Sawyer, former CEO of the exchange Bitstamp. 'Regulation, compliance, KYC, anti-money-laundering, all that stuff costs money. Bad actors can spend more on marketing and make more profit. So you are up against that competition. That's the most important thing.' I remember meeting the CEO of a small UK investing startup, who was trying to build a company offering relatively safe, conventional investments in a way that would appeal to younger audiences and people who hadn't traditionally seen themselves as 'investors'. He recounted an enquiry the company received from the Financial Conduct Authority, the UK regulator, querying the precise wording of one of the small-print footnotes on his website, and whether this fully followed the regulator's rules. I remember his understandable frustration at the fact that companies like Binance could offer much riskier products to the same UK consumers without anything like the same scrutiny. It's a win-win for Binance and other offshore players, and a lose-lose for its more responsible competitors, with another big loss for its customers. 'The FCA can sanction Binance in the UK. It doesn't do anything. It's irrelevant,' said a senior UK crypto industry executive.

But the game CZ played was extraordinarily risky. In many countries, Binance made use of a legal concept called reverse solicitation, which means that if a citizen happens to go online of their own accord and opens a Binance account, the national regulator is not empowered to police them. The US does not take this relatively laid-back approach to financial regulation. If Americans are using your services, then the US government generally considers you very much within their reach. The US also does not give you a pass just because you're a whizzy new crypto company. If it looks and smells like regulated financial activity involving Americans, the US watchdog expects you to sign up for oversight. Flouting Toronto taxi rules is one thing. Thumbing your nose at the Securities and Exchange Commission and the Justice Department is entirely another.

*

Early in Binance's life, the danger of having US customers impressed itself on the exchange's senior leadership. In a 2018 internal chat, Lim stated the problem clearly: 'We are operating as a fking unlicensed securities exchange in the USA bro.' He was also clearly aware of a second danger. Binance was letting American customers trade with people in countries like Iran that were under US economic sanctions. In 2018, Lim wrote privately that 'there is no fking way in hell I am signing off as the [chief compliance officer] for the [sanctions] shit.' He worried that Binance's customer service teams were effectively 'teaching ppl how to circumvent sanctions'. In a message to CZ, he said: 'Are we going to proceed to block sanction countries ip addresses (we currently have users from sanction countries on [Binance].com)'. CZ too was aware of the risk. When we met in 2022, he said: 'The [US] sanctions are not a joke . . . If you don't do this well, you end up in jail.'

CZ took advice on the problem of US jurisdiction from a consultant. The consultants' presentation, in 2018, has become one of the most controversial documents in Binance's history. It presented three options. Number one: do nothing. To simply carry on as an unregulated US satellite was possible, but judged 'high risk'. Number two: throw yourself on the mercy of US regulators. In practice this meant doing what Hillmann claimed Binance was doing as late as 2023, proactively talking to US regulators and being prepared to pay up to settle historic breaches of the rules. This option did not appeal. The cost might be high, and being cut off from the US market would be painful. The third option was called the 'Tai Chi' plan, named for the martial art known for its evasion techniques. Binance, the consultant suggested, could create a so-called 'Tai Chi entity' in the US that would 'reveal, retard, and resolve built-up enforcement tensions', and '[i]nsulate Binance from legacy and future liabilities'.

CZ initially demurred, citing more 'conservative' advice from US lawyers. When *Forbes* first reported on the Tai Chi plan in 2020, Binance filed a defamation lawsuit against the magazine but backed out three months later. In reality, Binance had implemented the thrust of the Tai Chi plan. CZ later wrote in a private chat: 'If we blocked US users from day 1, Binance will be not [*sic*] as big as we are today. We would also not have had any US revenue we had for the last 2 years.' He said it was 'better to ask for forgiveness than permission' and to operate in the 'grey zone'.

The entity Binance created as its American decoy, called Binance.US, was in theory an independent company that paid fees to license branding and technology from Binance international. In reality, the walls between the entities were never more than paper-thin, with international executives exerting control and even moving US customer money without US executives even knowing about it.

CZ ordered a systematic effort to make sure Binance didn't lose clients through the transition. Staff drew up lists of VIP American customers and contacted them with less than subtle hints about how to use VPNs or overseas corporate entities to maintain their access to Binance. In a discussion about blocking US IP addresses, CZ commented that the pop-up message on the website should be coded to hint at how people could still access the international platform. 'I'll have a look at it myself,' CZ wrote. 'We need to word it very carefully so that we let people know what they need to do, including using a VPN, without explicitly stating it.'

In early 2020, a confused employee messaged Lim to ask if it was still a 'hard requirement' to block US customers. The response was a straightforward explanation of Binance's evasive manoeuvres. 'Yes, it still is. Because if US users get on .com we become subject to following US regulators . . . But as best we can we try to ask our US users to use VPN or ask them to provide . . . non-US documents. On the surface, we cannot be seen to have US users but in reality we should get them through other creative means.' In a conversation later in the year, he suggested the drive to grow the business by skirting the rules came from the top. As they discussed a workaround to getting a big US client on to Binance, he said:

'CZ will definitely agree to this lol . . . I have been briefed by top management to always find a way to support biz.'

Binance knew that the ability to operate in the 'grey zone' was important to its customers. Until August 2021, you could have an account on Binance with no identity checks as long as you didn't withdraw more than two Bitcoin per day. At some points that year, two Bitcoin was worth more than $100,000, which is a lot of money to be potentially moving through anonymous hands daily. In an internal chat, discussing some Binance customers, Lim said: 'Like come on. They are here for crime.'

This opportunity to move large sums around the world covertly was exploited by exactly the people you might expect. In February 2019, Lim as compliance chief was notified of 'HAMAS trans-actions', referring to the Palestinian group officially labelled ter-rorists by the US government. Lim explained to colleagues that terrorists normally send 'small sums' whereas 'large sums constitute money laundering'. Around the same time, a compliance employee joked that Binance should put up an advertising banner saying: 'Is washing drug money too hard these days – come to binance; we got cake for you.'

*

The case against Binance finally arrived in three parts. In March 2023, the Commodity Futures Trading Commission (CFTC), a US regulator that oversees large parts of the crypto market, brought a case against CZ, Lim and several Binance entities. In June, the SEC revealed 13 charges against CZ and Binance for a string of alleged misdeeds, including evading US regulation and using CZ's personal trading firms to fake trading volume and funnel some customers' money through a web of entities in complex and obscure transactions that raised a serious risk of funds going astray.

The SEC claimed that for several years, two companies owned by CZ – Sigma Chain and Merit Peak – were important traders on Binance and faked trading volume through 'wash trading'. CZ used his trading shops in a 'strategic pattern' to boost the apparent popularity of Binance around the launch of new products, crucially, as he was trying to raise millions from venture capital investors in the exchange's US arm, the SEC alleged.

Binance said it would fight the cases. After months of tense negotiations, in November, the Justice Department finally delivered the hammer blow. CZ flew in secret to the United States and appeared in a Seattle federal court to plead guilty to violating money laundering and sanctions laws. He agreed to pay $50 million and step down as chief executive. His lawyers hope he can avoid a prison sentence. Binance, the company, pleaded guilty and agreed to pay a record $4.3 billion settlement.

Treasury Secretary Janet Yellen and Attorney General Merrick Garland both appeared at a triumphant press conference. Through hundreds of thousands of illicit transitions, Yellen said, Binance had facilitated drug trafficking, child sexual abuse and terrorism – including payments associated with Hamas, Al Qaeda and ISIS – and more than 1.5 million crypto trades that violated US sanctions.

Even in defeat, CZ had been canny. For months, he had remained in the United Arab Emirates, which has no extradition treaty with the US. He avoided touching down anywhere that US authorities could lay their hands on him and whisk him stateside to face charges. His evasiveness gave him leverage in negotiations with the US. Announcing the deal on Twitter, CZ made it sound almost like a welcome vacation. 'What's next for me?' he wrote. 'I will take a break first. I have not had a single day of real (phone off) break for the last 6 and a half years.' He also asked for a pat on the back for the misdeeds that he had not committed. 'I am proud to point out that in our resolutions with the US agencies they do not allege that Binance misappropriated any user funds, and do not allege that Binance engaged in any market manipulation,' CZ wrote. Even then, his comment was only half true. The SEC lawsuit, which did allege 'manipulative trading', was not included in the November settlement.

*

If SBF ever wanted revenge against CZ for the role that he played in FTX's downfall, it's certain that SBF's fall accelerated the US case against Binance. Over the years, the two crypto tycoons had swung back and forth between alliance and rivalry. When SBF launched FTX in 2019, he was a new arrival in a market that already had several well-established players. He moved to Hong Kong, and later to the Bahamas, in part because it would have been very difficult (and probably illegal) to operate FTX from the US.

At first, SBF was very much the junior to CZ, courting his favour and endorsement to win financial backing and legitimacy in crypto circles. But swiftly after its 2019 launch, FTX's rapid growth started to make SBF look like a potential rival to CZ. They were utterly contrasting characters. FTX was scrappy and optimistic. SBF was always on TV, selling his philanthropic ideals and vision of bringing together crypto, Wall Street and financial regulation to create the future of finance. CZ was forever clashing with the press and skirmishing with regulators.

Binance's position as an investor in a fast-rising competitor started to become tense. SBF began to feel that having Binance on board made it harder to present a positive face to regulators. To buy out Binance's investment was a major financial effort, even for SBF. But by mid-2021 it seemed essential to FTX's growth. He raised more than $2 billion to repay CZ and sever their financial link.

Both the addition to his debt pile and the simmering hostilities with CZ would come back to haunt SBF a year later, when his company was teetering on the brink. Long before the Feds came knocking for CZ, his revenge for years of rivalry with SBF had already been delivered, and it was decisive.

Casino

Arthur Hayes took the stage in a darkened auditorium in Taipei to the irrepressible strains of the horn line from the theme tune to the movie *Rocky*. Although not a boxer, Hayes is an impressive athlete. A towering, muscular man, he strode onstage in the glare of a crisp circular spotlight wearing an immaculate white T-shirt and blue jeans. When his opponent followed Hayes onstage, in his own spotlight, it was clear that, if this had been a boxing match, it would be over seconds into the first round. But in the battle of wits that was to follow, Nouriel Roubini was a dangerous opponent. Standing as tall as Hayes's shoulder, Roubini looks every inch what he is, an economics professor. The professor arrived at the Taipei event in a rumpled suit, looking like he had been put through a tumble dryer head first and was pissed off about it.

The economist, nicknamed 'Doctor Doom' for his early warnings about the 2008 financial crisis and his generally glowering attitude, seemed to be in an even worse mood than usual. Maybe it was the company. Roubini is also well known for his visceral attacks on crypto. So the pro-crypto audience packed into the Taipei Marriott ballroom for the Asia Blockchain Summit was going to be a tough crowd. The event, in July 2019, had been organised as a stunt, a verbal bout pitting the ultra-crypto-sceptic professor Roubini against Hayes, at the time one of the industry's leading CEOs. Taking their seats side by side in white leather armchairs, Roubini seemed thoroughly disgusted to be so near to Hayes. 'I am your referee for this morning,' intoned Andrew Neil, the veteran British journalist who had been signed up to host. 'We've had the Rumble in the Jungle, we've had the Thrilla in Manila and we've now got the Tangle in Taipei.'

Roubini did not mince his words. 'I'll make it honestly personal,' he said. By the end of his three-minute opening statement, the professor had talked about 'shady behaviour . . . con men, criminals, scammers, snake oil salesmen'. He said Hayes's company, BitMEX, had been built to profit from 'retail suckers' and 'screws' its customers, thousands of whom had ended up in 'financial ruin'.

'You make money by people going into financial ruin,' he spat at Hayes. 'It is an example of everything that is sick and rotten in this particular industry.'

Hayes seemed a little knocked off balance, caught between remaining the 'nice guy' and wanting to respond in kind to Roubini's broadside. 'I am not trying to force anyone to use BitMEX. We just have a website . . . Somehow, a few hundred thousand people have found our little oasis and started trading,' he countered. 'People saw that this was a phenomenon. There is something happening here. There was real value to what was being created in this system. And they decided that they wanted to speculate. Well, people speculate in everything. I'm sure if we put some chickens on the stage here, I put up a QR code, and I let you bet on which chicken was going to win, we would have probably a million dollars traded in the next five minutes. Human beings love to speculate. And we are just going to give them an opportunity to do it in a very safe manner.'

Neil jumped in to stir the pot. 'Are you saying he's a crook?' he asked Roubini. Hayes laughed at the question. The professor took a long pause. Every country, including the US, has laws to protect small investors, he explained, by limiting 'highly speculative, highly risky' investments. BitMEX, formally based in the Seychelles, gets around them. 'These people,' Roubini's voice rose almost to a yell as he gestured at Hayes, 'don't give a shit. They don't give a shit about anything. They are just like drug pushers, right, they get you addicted to something and if you are then royally screwed, so be it. I make money out of you.'

Hayes tried an awkward joke about swapping crypto for the opioids business. Neil pushed him on the question of regulation. 'Why are you in the Seychelles? It can't be for the weather,' he said. 'Is it because there are no financial regulations?'

'There definitely are regulations. We are regulated by the financial services authority in the Seychelles,' Hayes responded. 'Maybe to a US-centric Roubini who thinks maybe the New York [regulators] and the New York [Attorney General] is the only game in town, and we need to bow down and take an ass-fucking from the US government just because it's "regulated".' Hayes delivered the line with air quotes and a big smile. 'Now, that is really not my game. I didn't really want to sit on bottom bunk with Bubba all day. So I got out of that situation. Um, so, I don't think that just because the US does something that everybody else needs to follow.'

Neil ignored the vulgar analogy and kept to his line of questioning. Surely BitMEX has an easier time with the Seychelles regulator than with the heavies in New York, London or Frankfurt?

'It just costs more to bribe them,' said Hayes.

'Costs more to bribe them!?' Neil feigned incredulity.

'Yah,' Hayes shrugged.

'But that's not really an answer is it,' said Neil.

'It is an answer,' said Hayes.

'So how much are you paying to bribe the Seychelles authorities?' Neil asked, getting a laugh from the audience.

Hayes replied with another grin: 'A coconut.'

That exchange – an offhand comment in the heat of the moment in Taipei – now looks like the point when one of the inventors of the modern crypto industry overplayed his hand. Hayes played a relatively small role in crypto's most recent boom and bust, except as an observer. That's because he spent those years battling the US government and serving a six-month sentence in home confinement. Nonetheless, his role in creating the crypto markets as we know them today is fundamental.

'Arthur helped invent the plumbing of the current crypto trading infrastructure,' his friend Andrew Goodwin wrote. Launched in 2014, Hayes's company BitMEX had grown by 2019 into one of the leading crypto exchanges, handling tens of billions in transactions every day. Hayes was hailed as one of the youngest Black billionaires in history. The secret to BitMEX's success was a set of new financial products, souped-up versions of the derivatives that

Hayes had traded earlier in his career when he worked for major banks. By translating these ways of trading from Wall Street into digital assets, BitMEX revolutionised crypto, creating a market that was even more volatile, more exciting and where it was much easier for amateur traders to take wild bets. The result, as Roubini suggested, has been vast riches for the winners, a hugely lucrative revenue stream for the trading platforms, and agonising losses for many optimistic speculators who found themselves on the wrong side of the trade.

Hayes is cast by some as a crypto martyr. It is not lost on anyone that crypto's most prominent Black entrepreneur suffered one of the earliest and most aggressive pursuits by US authorities. For the next generation of crypto tycoons – including CZ and SBF – battling to control the trading market that Hayes did much to create, Hayes's story was clearly a cautionary tale. Hayes has said that his comments at the Tangle in Taipei debate were a joke. It turns out the US government doesn't have much of a sense of humour.

*

The story of Arthur Hayes's early life reads like a postcard version of the American dream. Born in Buffalo, New York, he grew up between the upstate border city and Detroit, Michigan. His parents worked for General Motors, one of the triumvirate of US car companies that practically ran 'Motor City'. Hayes excelled academically, attending an elite Buffalo high school with the help of a scholarship. When he applied for a college scholarship, his record detailed a marathon of advanced classes from calculus and economics to Russian literature.

It seemed there was nothing he couldn't do. 'A-grade trumpet player in the school orchestra; co-founder of the chess club; writer for the school newspaper; annual mock trial participant; weekly volunteer tutor in a disadvantaged neighbourhood in Buffalo; Varsity tennis player; ski racer; JV soccer player; lettered in Varsity bowling; Varsity cross-country runner who held school records and earned college prospect status; and a volunteer who served meals at the City Mission,' read one account of his schooldays.

When I interviewed Hayes – still an imposing figure but now with a dash of salt and pepper in his hair – he explained why he worked so hard. 'I generally just disliked [Buffalo] and knew from a very early age that I didn't want to live there. And so I was very focused on doing well in school and being able to leave. That was sort of my, like, motivating factor in high school, like, okay, get good grades and get the fuck out of here,' he said.

He won the college scholarship and went on to study at Wharton, at the University of Pennsylvania, one of America's top business schools. Again, his achievements were prodigious. He studied Chinese and competed in every arena from ballroom dancing to bodybuilding. Hayes had his eyes firmly set on a career in finance. 'From junior year, I basically cold emailed every single investment bank and I got one interview at Deutsche Bank. And then I was able to convince them to give me a job,' he said. His home-town paper carried the news that he'd got the job in a column on 'Hires, Promotions and Honours' alongside new appointments to the board of the Buffalo Zoological Gardens. In a sign of how far Hayes had come from where he grew up, the newspaper twice misspelled the name of Germany's largest bank as 'Deutsch Bank'.

A few days later, the paper carried a full profile of Hayes (this time getting the bank's name right). He talked about his dream of getting into finance. 'For me it's the only place to work,' he said. 'You get responsibility at a very young age. From day one, on the desk as a first-year analyst, they throw you into the mix. They expect [you] to begin generating revenue as soon as possible, and they'll not hold you back. They give you as much as you can handle, as fast as you can handle it.' The most compelling reason for his career choice, queried the journalist? 'If you're good at what you do, they compensate you generously,' Hayes said.

He told me that he'd been turned off the thought of possibly becoming a lawyer after realising the limits of what you could earn. 'Being a lawyer is great but you only have 24 hours in a day and you make your money billing. That sort of got me off of being a lawyer because you really can't make that much money, 'cause you leverage your time. So I thought finance is the easiest way to make a lot of money so that's kind of where I applied myself.'

Hayes had read Ben Mezrich's 2004 book *Ugly Americans*, a lightly fictionalised account of freewheeling traders in 1990s Japan. He was intoxicated by the idea of playing this high stakes, money-making game on the other side of the world. But he decided Japan was yesterday's economy. He wanted to go to China, and moved with Deutsche to Hong Kong. The city's character, a financial frontier town powered by hard-driving capitalism, appealed to him. 'Its financial system is allowed to be freer and more experimental,' he later wrote. 'Hong Kong is a "can do" kind of place. The energy and hustle of its residents is intoxicating – it's why I knew from my very first night of bar hopping in Lan Kwai Fong that it would be my home.' Hayes had found the place he'd dreamed of in Buffalo: the dynamic, commercial centre of the action.

Hayes was praised by his boss at Deutsche as 'the most likely to succeed' in his graduate class and for having 'the truest "out of the box" attitude'. His room-mate during the early days in Hong Kong said Hayes was a generous friend with a 'pathological' inability to do the dishes, who used to schlep huge quantities of protein powder around the trading floor. Like many young traders, Hayes burned the candle at both ends. He and his close circle of friends – they called themselves 'the Fam' – revelled in the city's nightlife. Hayes later reminisced about the set of six 'bottle rules' they devised to make sure no one wriggled out of paying their share of the drinks bill. 'There is one member of the Fam whose ego always gets ahead of his willingness to pay on various occasions. One time a few years ago at 1 Oak in Tokyo, he got the maths wrong and thought a train of six bottles of Dom P could be had for the price of one. He ordered the train, felt like a baller and then – after realising his maths error when presented with the bill – tried to charge the entire group for his folly,' Hayes recalled. The rules were clear. 'If you order champagne, you pay for that entirely by yourself.' The friend paid up.

However, 2008 was not a perfect time to be popping champagne in the financial industry. Hayes's first day on the equity deriva- tives trading desk as a new graduate was the Monday that Lehman Brothers filed for bankruptcy. He recalls sitting quietly as chaos unfolded around him, thinking: 'What the fuck is going on?'

'The head of trading is running around the floor talking about which bank's credit line is cut, who you could trade with, who you can't trade with . . . I'm just sitting there. I have no Bloomberg access. I don't know what the fuck you guys do. So I'm just gonna sit here and be quiet.'

Hayes watched as poorly understood risk-taking in the bowels of the financial system blew up the global economy. He felt increasingly disillusioned. But his chief complaint was not so much the harm that banks had done to the economy and the lives they had ruined, but that traditional markets were ossifying, becoming too cautious and constrained. 'I have experienced a secular decline in finance since the day I started, and for people in my age cohort that's pretty much been the story,' he said in a later interview. 'You're not making the money you thought you were going to make, automation is coming to financial markets, you see fees getting sliced every year in different business lines, and you have this impression: how long is my job going to exist in its current form?' It was as if he had come out to Asia ready to join the party, only to find that it was over.

He returned to the theme when we spoke. 'The environment went from, like, "I get paid so much money I don't know how to spend it" to, like, "you'd better fucking pass this accounting test or you don't have a job any more".'

In 2013, having moved from Deutsche to Citigroup, he lost his job in a sweep of lay-offs. With time on his hands, and the sudden need for income, his interest in crypto grew. Like SBF years later, Hayes's first foray into Bitcoin was through arbitrage, exploiting the gap between crypto prices in mainland China and the rest of the market by buying where crypto was cheaper and selling where it was more expensive. He would cross the border from Hong Kong carrying a USB stick loaded with Bitcoin. The story about how this early exposure became the idea for BitMEX echoes the narratives attached to so many startup founders, who couldn't find what they wanted to buy so they decided to sell it themselves. 'The whole impetus was: build a platform that I want to trade on, so that people like me can trade lots of volume and make money,' he said. The product that BitMEX was set up to sell is the same product Hayes had learned to trade in his time at the big banks: derivatives.

*

Derivatives are the hard drugs of the financial markets. And like drugs they have very sensible origins: as a painkiller. The pain in this case is the pain of not knowing what prices will be in the future. As it happens, I am writing this passage in farm country, surrounded by fields of ripening corn and wheat. For farmers, on top of worrying about the weather and getting the hay in while it's dry, there's long been a concern about prices. What if you plant all your crops assuming you can sell them for X, but by the end of the season the price has dropped to somewhere less than X? You might not make any money at all. So what if, instead, you could sell your crops before they are even grown? You strike a deal to sell X tons of wheat on a certain date for a certain price. As the farmer, you eliminate the risk that prices will move against you. As the buyer, you have assured your supply, also at a locked-in price. The pain of price risk is removed. Everybody wins. Right?

This arrangement is a type of derivative, which takes its name because the value of the contract to deliver the wheat *derives* from the value of the actual crop. It is a layer of financial dealing added on top of the fundamental trade in stuff. Scholars find evidence of this kind of deal going back to trade around the Mediterranean in the ancient world. Aristotle is sometimes credited with giving the first description of what is effectively a derivatives contract, relating to olives. Their agricultural origins mean that the more recent history of derivatives markets are full of delightfully named institutions like the Butter and Cheese Exchange of New York, and hilarious capers such as the Great Salad Oil Swindle, which involved faking stockpiles of soybean oil by filling the tanks with water and pouring a thin layer of oil on the top. The CFTC, the US regulator that has played a big role in the recent story of crypto, descends from a predecessor agency, the Grain Futures Commission. The US Congress's agriculture committees still oversee the CFTC, which is why many important crypto bills and hearings come through the same committee that looks after farm subsidies.

Derivatives markets have evolved far beyond their pastoral origins. Contracts come in all sorts of structures, giving traders the option or the obligation to buy or sell something in the future, or to bet on its future price. That 'something' can really be anything. Derivatives today are based on everything from barrels of oil to interest rates. You can even buy derivatives on the weather, used as a sort of insurance policy for financial losses caused by the climate. These contracts often serve to transfer risk from someone who doesn't want to take a chance to someone who does. There are plenty of traders who want risk because, by definition, it comes with higher potential rewards. A textbook definition of derivatives will most often say that the contracts are used for 'hedging and speculation'. Those objectives are two sides of a coin. One party wants to get rid of the risk that oil prices will fall, that the weather will turn, that interest rates will rise. The other party is happy to take that risk because, if their bet pays off, the profits will be higher.

Adding to the speculation side of the equation is the other key ingredient in derivatives markets: leverage. Leverage is a word that flies around a lot in finance. In the broadest sense, it means doing something with money that isn't yours. Buying a house with a mortgage? Leverage. Taking a loan to start a small business? Leverage. Arguably even buying the bottle of 'Dom P' at a Tokyo club, on the assumption that your friends will get you back, is extending to your drinking buddies a certain form of leverage. Derivatives contracts frequently involve leverage, and traders often borrow money to amplify their positions. So when people talk about the derivatives market they most often are talking about two things. One, the market in contracts attached to the future buying, selling and pricing of stuff. Two, a market where you can trade, in part, with other people's money.

In the US, the centre of the derivatives trade is Chicago, close to the agricultural heartland. The best-known venue is the Chicago Mercantile Exchange, the CME. Hayes and his co-founders chose a name for their new company that nods to this history. 'BitMEX' is short for Bitcoin Mercantile Exchange. The choice points to their early vision for the company. Hayes had been a derivatives trader in stocks, placing him in the elite ranks of Wall Street money makers. By the time he turned his attention to crypto in 2013, derivatives on crypto assets had existed for a couple of years. Hayes found the exchanges where these crypto contracts traded, although popular with ex-Wall Street traders at the time, were primitive. They didn't have the capacity to let Hayes trade as much as he wanted to. The idea for BitMEX was to create a trading platform that would work for professional traders – for people like him. Hayes later said that they had 'started building BitMEX with the premise that Wall Street was going to flood into Bitcoin and they are going to want to trade the same types of products that I was trading at the bank.'

The exchange launched in November 2014. Hayes described the reception. 'No one came for the first six months,' he said. 'So we are sitting there with an exchange that makes no money. We make no money. And so we said we need to re-evaluate what we are doing here.' They had created an exchange to cater to Wall Street-style big-time traders in crypto. But those traders were not there. Looking around at the competitors, the BitMEX founders realised there was only really one other customer base they could target. The dominant crypto exchanges at that time were focused on China, serving its armies of amateur traders, and speculators around the world.

The candid account Hayes gives of BitMEX's false start, and its strategic pivot, comes from a recording of a private presentation he gave in 2016 that later leaked. He said BitMEX noticed that its competitors were offering similar derivatives products but were 'focusing on degenerate gamblers, aka retail traders in Bitcoin'. ('Retail' is the word finance people use to talk about do-it-your-self traders, as if people were buying shoes or washing machines.) The new strategy for targeting individual traders was to copy the competition, but to do it better. 'So we said, OK, we are going to create the world's highest leverage Bitcoin/US dollar product and we want to enable anyone who has Bitcoin to trade financial derivatives. And so that is where BitMEX came from,' Hayes concluded.

The new plan for BitMEX had two key ingredients. First, as Hayes had explained, was to offer the highest leverage. The company increased its leverage limit to 100 times, meaning that with a $10 deposit (also called 'margin') a trader could open a position worth $1,000. Adding borrowed money raises the stakes. For BitMEX, the extra risk was a selling point. 'Bitcoin is fun, but it's a hell of a lot more fun at 100 times leverage,' Hayes said in 2019. 'That's what people want to see in crypto, they want that high volatility . . . At the end of the day, we're all in the entertainment business of traders.'

Being in the entertainment business meant playing the part. BitMEX once parked three rented Lamborghinis outside a New York crypto conference. Here was the wealth you could achieve by trading crypto. In Hong Kong, the company rented a 45th-floor office, one of the most expensive in the city. Inside, they installed a giant aquarium stocked with three live sharks. A friend recalled taking a tour of the office with Hayes. 'We were in tears of laughter together at how ridiculous some of it was,' he said. 'Behind the bravado and the character he played at the height of the BitMEX boom was a genuine, caring young man.'

To make it fun, BitMEX also made trading simple. Normally, derivatives contracts expire at a fixed date. In the old world of agricultural dealing, that would be the date when the harvest would be in and the grain ready to deliver. The expiry date links the contract to the value of the underlying commodity. But they also make the markets trickier to navigate. If you want to keep your trading going, and don't want to end up with 100 tonnes of wheat on your door-step, you have to watch those expiry dates pretty carefully and move your position to new contracts with dates further in the future. The complexity of the market was a problem for BitMEX.

'Me and my co-founders, the three of us, we answered every single support ticket ourselves. And it gets really annoying after a while when your customer keeps emailing you saying, "Hey, this futures contract, it expired. I don't know where it went. Are you guys like scamming us?"' Hayes told me. 'We had all these custom-ers who didn't understand our product.'

To cut out the complexity, BitMEX's new flagship product, the perpetual contract, took derivatives and added another layer of abstraction. The contract just never expired. The design to achieve this was complicated – and much admired – but the result for the customer looked easy. 'We are trying to abstract all that complexity, take out all the jargon and make it appealing for somebody who is never going to set foot on a trading floor,' Hayes said in 2019. The perpetual product, he said, 'is extremely complicated below the surface, but to the customer it's: I can go long or short with 100 times leverage, there's an interest rate I pay every eight hours, and I can hold my position open indefinitely as long as I can afford my margin. That's very attractive.'

In 2017, the first year after the perpetual launched, Hayes said, the company's trading volumes went up 8,500 per cent as crypto trading took off. BitMEX's success in popularising crypto derivatives transformed digital asset markets. Today, around $300 billion a month trades in the straightforward buy-or-sell market, known as 'spot'. In crypto derivatives, the monthly volume is more than $1 trillion. For exchanges, derivatives are not only more popular, they are also a cash cow. At the peak of trading volumes in May 2021, Binance, by then the largest derivatives exchange, is thought to have made more than $1 billion in a month from derivatives trading alone.

Established exchanges have also joined the party. The CME, and another major venue called CBOE, both launched crypto derivatives in 2017. These regulated exchanges have provided a route for more conventional money managers to dabble in crypto, and their products lie behind many of the exchange-traded funds that were later sold to the public. However, these mainstream exchanges have stuck with the traditional design of contracts, with expiry dates, all while perpetuals have streaked ahead. 'The volume of perpetuals is infinitely more,' said Jon de Wet, chief investment officer of the crypto trading firm Zerocap. 'Dated futures are a hedging tool, whereas perps are pushing the gas . . . It is still a market dominated by excess.'

Hayes credited the rise of BitMEX, and subsequent revolution in crypto trading, to the success of the 'perp'. 'BitMEX's rise to prominence stems almost entirely from this financial invention,' he wrote in 2022. 'By 2020 all major derivatives exchanges copied this product design and achieved great success. With trillions of dollars in cumulative trading volumes to date, it has become the most traded crypto instrument ever. Mic drop, bitches!'

Why have derivatives come to dominate the crypto market? For one thing, as Hayes realised, they are easier. At no point in the process do you have to learn how to set up a crypto wallet or hold any crypto yourself. Exchanges compete to have the easiest websites for users to sign up and trade. Plenty of traders do still keep the bulk of their crypto wealth in their own wallet and only move their assets on to the exchange for trading. But many like the convenience of not having to worry about it. 'While bitcoin is supposed to be this libertarian, be-your-own-bank kind of thing, most people are pretty lazy, and are perfectly fine with buying some crypto and holding it on the exchange as if the exchange was a bank,' Hayes once commented.

For some professional money managers, the desire not to touch the actual crypto assets is not just a preference but a requirement. You might have to rewrite the terms on which you set up your fund before you can touch crypto. Certainly, you will have a lot of stress about how to store your crypto without it getting lost or nicked. And there's a good chance you'll get a bollocking from the local regulator for your trouble. Trading derivatives is often much easier, and much more familiar. They are also a more sophisticated instrument than just buying an asset and hoping it will go up. You can fine-tune your bets on future prices, calibrate the amount of risk you want to take and also bet on markets to go down. More cautious players can choose to trade on the regulated exchanges like CME. Either way, the ability to gain exposure to crypto assets without touching them directly mirrors a selling point derivatives have always had for traders. The number of people who want to trade oil certainly exceeds the number of people who have the capacity and willingness to store 100 barrels of crude. (Indeed, some contracts aren't even physically settled any more. So no one delivers any oil, or crypto, anywhere. They just settle up in cash for the value of the trade. This also works for more obscure types of derivatives. Despite the market's best efforts, you can't own the weather.)

The other huge pull factor in shifting trading towards derivatives is the magnifying effect of leverage. In the old-fashioned spot market, if you liked the chances of token X and had $100 to play with, you could buy $100 worth of token X. If the price then goes up 20 per cent, you can sell and make $20 profit. But on a derivatives exchange with 100 times leverage, your $100 deposit can buy you a position in token X worth $10,000. If the token goes up the same 20 per cent, your profit is $2,000! BitMEX nodded to the key role of leverage in its strategy when it named one of its holding companies '100x Holdings Limited'.

Nishad Singh, of FTX, which followed BitMEX in offering super-high leverage, put quite an idealistic spin on the purpose of this 100 times supercharging in a 2020 interview. 'This is sort of like the fundamental motivation behind margin and leverage. It lets users express their beliefs more strongly than their capital base would otherwise allow, but at the risk of liquidation.' There is a strain of rhetoric around these products that treats bets in the market like a form of freedom of expression. The exchanges that let their clients take leveraged bets are just lending them a megaphone to express their freedom even louder. The tail of Singh's quote notes the obvious downside . . . 'at risk of liquidation'.

What happens if instead of rising 20 per cent, X token falls by the same amount? When you open your position, the exchange will tell you a liquidation price for your trade. If X token falls below that price, you can either add more money to top up your deposit or else the exchange will close your trade, take your deposit and liquidate it. They need to do this to make sure the deposit is still big enough to cover the loss you've incurred and close out the position to zero.

Casino

The more leverage you take on your position, the smaller the margin of error will be between the price point where you enter your trade and the price point where you lose everything.

The UK allows a small but lively market in trading a different set of leveraged trading products called 'spread bets' and 'contracts for difference', attached to traditional assets. Spread betting and CFDs have something of a bad reputation. The rest of the investing world tends to look down on them as somewhere between a skeezy online casino dressed up as investment and downright larceny. Websites offering these trades are required to carry a health warning, not unlike cigarettes, right across the top of the page, that reads something like 'CFDs are complex instruments and come with a high risk of losing money rapidly due to leverage. Seventy per cent of retail investor accounts lose money when trading spread bets and CFDs with this provider. You should consider whether you understand how spread bets and CFDs work, and whether you can afford to take the high risk of losing your money.' The highest leverage allowed on these products in the UK is 30 times. BitMEX offered more than three times more. So too, for a time, did Binance and FTX.

The UK's FCA announced an outright ban of derivatives on cryptocurrencies in 2020. Sheldon Mills, a senior official at the regulator, justified the move saying: 'This ban reflects how seriously we view the potential harm to retail consumers in these products ... Significant price volatility, combined with the inherent difficulties of valuing crypto assets reliably, places retail consumers at a high risk of suffering losses from trading crypto-derivatives. We have evidence of this happening on a significant scale.' Offering these super-leveraged products in spite of the rules that limit their sale in many countries has become one of the key points of friction between the offshore crypto industry and financial watchdogs worldwide. Several major exchanges, including FTX and Binance, reduced their leverage levels after pressure from regulators and pulled these products in some regions. Still, the market in these risky trades remains huge.

What worries people about this kind of trading is the complicated structures and the speed at which they can move against the everyday trader. Traditional markets typically give traders 24 hours' notice if they are near to being wiped out, and they stop trading overnight. Many crypto exchanges trade 24/7. People will wake up to find that they lost everything while they were asleep. Cryptocurrencies also swing more quickly than almost any other market. Everything that makes crypto fun for diehards and pro traders increases the chance that it will all end in tears.

'There are no margin calls, and since these investors don't run trading bots, when markets get volatile they have to stay up all night in order to top up their collateral quickly if the price moves against their positions. This can be exhausting,' said Carol Alexander, a professor of finance at the University of Sussex, who is an expert in crypto and financial markets.

She said the playing field is tilted against DIY traders. 'Binance is like a football pitch for professional players to – they hope – play against less-informed traders. But they don't want to trade against each other – when there is only a 50-50 chance of winning. They call that "toxic flow". Because Binance is unregulated, manipulation is rife. Anything can happen, because there's no referee.

Casino

'Large professional trading firms . . . run algorithmic trading bots which are able to spoof ordinary crypto traders. The highly leveraged trades they make are far too big for the market. That size of trade would not be allowed in regulated markets.'

When you speak to people who have been on the losing end of these markets, the overwhelming feeling they express is that they have been conned. From students in their early twenties trading in their bedrooms to a 59-year-old who couldn't work after being paralysed, people believed that trading crypto could be their ticket to wealth, to paying off debt, or to retirement. They were left with a profound feeling of betrayal. 'It's like you are set up to fail,' said one trader, who estimated that they lost $500,000 during a vicious crash in crypto prices in May 2021 after China signalled a crackdown on digital assets. Their losses illustrate a particular danger. When the markets start moving against them, traders are hugely tempted to pile more and more money into their trade to try to stay afloat. In theory, the maximum you should lose on a crypto derivatives trade is the value of your deposit. That can be a lot, but it is limited. Yet around half this person's losses were cash they transferred from their bank on the day of the crash as they tried to keep their position from being liquidated. It was a painful sunk cost. 'I was so distraught that I couldn't talk to anyone about it for two or three weeks,' they said. 'You feel like you are the victim of some organised crime.' On that single day, traders saw $8.6 billion worth of positions liquidated.

It may of course seem patronising to be banning certain types of trading because we think people are such numpties that they don't know what's good for them. It comes down to your views about how far the government should go in restricting people from doing things that are probably bad for them – be it smoking or trading risky crypto products. Equally, there's a question of who has the power to make these decisions, and whether crypto players can use their international rootless status to dance around the rules that societies choose to impose. The UK's ban has enormous holes in it, since most of the trading it was trying to clamp down on happens on international exchanges, who make billions from this business and can beam their services into the UK and other countries from offshore. Crypto exchanges also spend billions encouraging more people to trade.

*

This rise to dominance of crypto derivatives is one of the most important shifts in the transition from the early days of focus on using crypto for payments and as a store of wealth to the markets we have today, which are dominated by speculation. The shift has transformed the role of the crypto exchange. The very early exchanges were somewhere between a stock exchange and the foreign currency stands at the airport. The crux of the service was swapping dollars for crypto or crypto for something else. In that quaint old world of buy-and-hold investing, it was possible for everyone to benefit if prices rose. But that market is now dwarfed by the ruthless, fast-moving derivatives trade, in which there are two sides to every contract. If I win, someone else has to lose.

'There are huge amounts of inefficiency created and they can create arbitrage. Within that, there are businesses to be created,' said Jon de Wet, the experienced crypto investor. 'Behind the scenes, in the end, it was one giant machine to encourage retail traders to lose money.'

For the pro traders and big money who do venture into crypto, the volatility and messiness is a big part of the appeal. 'The type of counterparties that we are dealing with are people who are believers or haters,' Hayes explained in one interview. 'They are coming to this marketplace and trading very emotionally, which is evident in the volatility. That's amazing for very cool-headed statistical arbitrage-type shops.' These highly sophisticated, computerised strategies do best when the market is very volatile, even irrational. Crypto, he said, is 'opaque, inefficient, fragmented. And that's just the market you want to be in in financial services because that's when you make the real money, not when everything is hyper-efficient and virtuous, scalping you for a fraction of a penny.'

Hayes is in the camp who thinks that, even if it's hard for amateur traders to make money against the pros, they should be free to try. If you think the professionals will always win, he said, 'You shouldn't trade stocks. You shouldn't trade anything in tradfi system . . . You should just buy and hold. If that's how you view the market then don't trade this stuff . . . But if you want to trade on leverage, you want to have a short-time horizon, then recognise that there are people whose whole job is to make computer programs to beat you. And do you have the skills to beat the computer program? Ask yourself that question before you start trading. And that doesn't matter if it's crypto.'

Hayes was in the vanguard of the takeover of crypto by arrivals from Wall Street. Crypto's libertarian streak clearly appealed to him. He seized on the unregulated crypto markets as a place where he could create the kind of no-rules, winner-takes-all trading environment he had dreamed about as a student in Pennsylvania. Hayes said he sees no contradiction with crypto's original vision of cutting out financial middlemen. 'Speculation is the best form of advertising for the technology. As people experience true free markets, they will ultimately learn about the technology and the ethos,' he said. 'In this way we can spread the good word of Lord Satoshi.'

One Wall Street trader who followed in his footsteps was SBF. FTX stands for 'Futures Exchange'. It was a derivatives business. The complex borrowing arrangements involved in the derivatives trade were a crucial part of how Alameda maintained, and obscured, its links to FTX. The first time I sat down to interview the FTX founder, I was preoccupied by the question of whether it is really OK to encourage inexperienced, amateur traders to plunge into these risky and unregulated markets. By then, FTX had become one of the biggest players in crypto derivatives. The ethical worldview SBF preached to the public meant constantly calculating the good and the harm you cause, and trying to come up with the biggest net positive position. I found it hard to reconcile this philosophy with running FTX, exploiting its position in the Bahamas to offer people the chance to risk their financial future on wild crypto bets that are banned in many countries.

Even if SBF promised to donate the profits to charity, wasn't his underlying business doing harm – especially since he was spending millions encouraging people to take a punt on crypto? Could philanthropy outweigh the reality of encouraging people to gamble their savings in crypto?

Casino

I have asked SBF a lot of unpleasant questions over the years. 'Did you steal $8 billion from your customers?' is one. I have never seen him more tangibly uncomfortable than when I probed the moral justification for crypto derivatives. Always fidgety, he ended up almost cowering away from the subject, sitting hunched up in his chair with his arms and legs crossed. 'You don't want it to be a way to transfer wealth from the poor to the rich,' he told me. 'There are obviously examples where that has happened. But I think there have been way more examples where there have been people who had very little, who ended up making a lot from crypto and for whom it changed their life.'

Evidence suggests otherwise. One study followed 20,000 DIY futures traders in Brazil. Most lost money. The longer they traded, the less likely they were to beat the odds. For those who kept at it for around a year, or longer, 97 per cent lost money and only one in a hundred made more than the Brazilian minimum wage at the time. A separate study in Taiwan reached similar conclusions. Less than 1 per cent of day traders consistently made any money at all. These studies come from traditional markets. When you extrapolate what they might mean for crypto, it's hard to imagine that traders fare much better in a crypto market that is more leveraged, more volatile and less predictable. Research in crypto also shows that people tend to pile into the markets when they are going up and chase rising prices, meaning they are more likely to buy high and bet on prices going even higher.

A different crypto entrepreneur I spoke to took the opposite view to SBF. Ninety-five per cent of the market, they said, is 'just a big global decentralised casino. It was all just people speculating on different tickers. It could have been a Vegas casino.' Another way of describing a casino is a transfer of money from the poor to the rich. The house always wins.

*

The one place where the casino does not operate is, in fact, the home country of Las Vegas. The US requires that companies dealing in derivatives register with the CFTC and follow its extensive rule book. Plenty of other countries have similar rules. But what they lack is America's world-policing attitude towards how and where its laws apply, and the clout to make them stick.

Crypto exchanges like Binance and FTX were sensitive to their US footprint in large part because of American derivatives rules. The US is a very lucrative market with an active amateur trading culture and plenty of money to go around. But if you serve the US, you cannot offer derivatives without going through the rigmarole of becoming regulated. And derivatives are these exchanges' main money-spinners. Binance, in its Tai Chi plan, developed a strategy, later effectively copied by FTX, that for a time let the international unit play the derivatives game, without losing its position in the US. The main US exchanges, like Coinbase, have mostly stuck with spot trading – although Coinbase in 2022 bought a CFTC-regulated derivatives exchange with plans to use it to offer some contracts in the US. FTX US also tried the strategy of buying its way into regulated status, and one of the main objectives of its vast lobbying efforts in Washington DC was to rewrite the rules to make it easier to offer more derivatives trading to US customers.

Casino

All of this careful tiptoeing around the American market reflects a real anxiety about waking the sleeping giant of US enforcement. It is the one country that seems to really scare even the most dedicated crypto pirates. Arthur Hayes's case is the ultimate example of why. Sixteen days after Hayes likened the US regulators to prison rapists in the Taipei debate, Bloomberg reported that the CFTC was investigating BitMEX. Just over a year later, in October 2020, the agency charged Hayes and his co-founders in a civil enforcement action. The same day, US federal prosecutors unveiled a criminal indictment against him and other company executives. Hayes went from being arguably the world's top crypto chief executive to a professional defendant. The infamous line from Taipei, about bribing the authorities in BitMEX's Seychelles home base with a coconut, appeared in the indictment.

The crux of the case against Hayes was that he knew full well the rules governing business with US customers, and that BitMEX made only the flimsiest pretence of stopping Americans from trading. BitMEX initially advertised the fact that you could trade without even giving them your name. 'No real name or other advanced verification is required on BitMEX,' the company's early website read. Prosecutors claimed that Hayes had consistently tried to do as little identity or compliance checking as possible. Shortly before BitMEX launched, he wrote to another executive that they should 'basically just [ask for a] valid email address until we feel significant pressure to do otherwise'. That pressure increased after 2015 when the CFTC brought its first major crypto case. Its charges against a San Francisco-based crypto company made it clear in black and white that the regulator thought Bitcoin and other cryptocurrencies were, for legal purposes, just as much a 'commodity' as wheat or oil. The rules of trading derivatives on commodities applied. 'While there is a lot of excitement surrounding Bitcoin and other virtual currencies, innovation does not excuse those acting in this space from following the same rules applicable to all participants in the commodity derivatives markets,' Aitan Goelman, the CFTC's director of enforcement, said at the time.

Some of Hayes's defenders have made the case that he's a victim of 'regulatory uncertainty'. The complaint is roughly that the government sees you doing something, then decides what rules apply to that thing, then decides that you've broken the rules that they just made up, and then charges you with a federal crime and tries to send you to jail.

US authorities went out of their way to point out that it's difficult to apply that line of defence to the facts of this case. After the early CFTC actions, BitMEX formally banned US customers, which certainly suggested that they knew – or were at least worried – that they shouldn't be letting them trade. Prosecutors argued that the ban was a 'sham'. The company had offices in the US, with customer service and marketing staff. BitMEX only checked their customers' IP address once, when they created their account. They didn't stop people using VPNs to hide the fact that they were in the US. And once you cleared the first check, you could log in from the US with no problem. Two years after officially blocking Americans, BitMEX monthly internal revenue reports still showed what share of business was coming from the US. In July 2017, an executive wrote to Hayes that '[the] United States remains the most popular country by visits and average number of active users per day.' The authorities calculated that BitMEX accepted more than $11 billion worth of Bitcoin deposits from 85,000 American users.

Not only had he broken the letter of the law, authorities charged, but the decision to do hardly any identity checks on the people moving money through BitMEX meant $200 million, and very possibly more, of dark web and suspicious transactions had gone through the platform without being reported. They also charged that BitMEX had served clients in US-sanctioned countries, and that Hayes himself had actually communicated with customers in Iran.

Hayes's sterling background, his education and experience in big name banks, could cut both ways. In one view, he was a model citizen and innovator being unfairly targeted. In another, he was a sophisticated operator who knew exactly what he was doing, and chose not to follow the law. Adding to the government's case, the US could cite examples that seemed to show what it called Hayes's 'dismissive attitude' to the rules. He had written that governments used rules requiring identity checks on customers to 'harass companies', and warned people not to buy their 'mood-altering substance(s) of choice' using Facebook's now-defunct Libra cryptocurrency because they would be tracked. It was a hard case to answer.

One major crypto executive told me that Hayes and the BitMEX leadership 'never thought of it as anything other than a casino, and they never portrayed it as anything other than that. But . . . it was just so egregious on procedural things. They got so much fucking warning and they kept refusing to comply.'

In April 2021, Hayes flew to Hawaii and gave himself up to US law enforcement. The following February he entered his plea. He paid a $10 million fine. Prosecutors sought a prison term, arguing it would be a deterrent. The judge sentenced him to six months of house arrest, which he spent in Florida. Having served the time, Hayes is out now, travelling around the world, doing lots of skiing. He launched a venture capital investment firm, and writes on his blog. He still sits on the board at BitMEX and is a shareholder, but he isn't running the company.

Hayes was in the vanguard of crypto's financial revolution. He did more than probably anyone else to create the phenomenon of crypto trading, and the financial products that facilitated it, both of which were taken to the extreme in 2021. His fall left the market that BitMEX pioneered up for grabs. Both CZ and SBF were determined to capture it.

Very Ponzi-Like

On 10 June 2022, at 1:00pm sharp, Alex Mashinsky, chief executive of the crypto lending company Celsius Network, came online as usual for his weekly YouTube livestream watched by tens of thousands of his customers, who Mashinsky called 'the community'. The video began, as always, with a slick high-speed countdown, backwards from five, followed by the title card 'Ask Mashinsky Anything' – a play on the internet format Ask Me Anything.

'Coming to you from New York live, live, live,' Mashinsky began, with a cough and an apology. 'I'm losing my voice. Sorry about that.' It was the last time he struck anything close to an apologetic tone in the hour-long broadcast. Even for the pugnacious business-man who had built Celsius into a multi-billion-dollar lender, the livestream was a remarkable performance. Mashinsky's job was to project confidence, and it was something he excelled at. He was never more animated than when hitting back at crypto sceptics or blasting the self-seeking behaviour of mainstream banks, bidding customers to HODL in the face of FUD. In the five years since he had founded Celsius, Mashinsky had crafted his persona as a straight-talking champion of the little guy – Robin Hood from New York. In his mid-fifties, jowly and grizzled, he spoke to a clientele of crypto enthusiasts, many of them a generation younger, with a tone of world-weary experience.

The hour-long Friday YouTube show was a key component of Mashinsky's marketing engine. (The Celsius founder nicknamed himself 'the machine'.) Sometimes he seemed almost bored as he fielded endless questions from clients, provided updates on the business and introduced employees for short interviews about their role within 'the community'. New recruits in particular were often singled out for two minutes in the sun with the company founder. The laid-back delivery added to his air of authenticity. He did not have the manner of a salesman. Mashinsky made it seem like he was doing customers a favour. He took time to share mantras and deliver lessons from his decades-long business career. The whole performance spoke to Celsius's dual character as a cross between a financial institution and a self-help movement, which promised customers that crypto was their way out of an American financial system that had been rigged against them.

What made the 10 June broadcast different was that Mashinsky's 'community' was suffering a crisis of faith. The crypto sector was in meltdown in the late spring of 2022, with token prices falling sharply and corners of the market seizing up. Celsius was said to be hiding massive losses – the result of a number of obscure and risky trades that had gone badly wrong as the market tanked. Jittery customers had pulled $1.8 billion from the platform in May. But the scale of the withdrawals wasn't yet widely known. In a blog post a few days earlier, Mashinsky thundered back against the critics, quoting the line attributed to US Civil War admiral David Glasgow Farragut: 'Damn the torpedoes – full speed ahead'. Still, Celsius's detractors on Twitter and in the media had kept on firing torpedoes thick and fast. In his Friday livestream, Mashinsky took another opportunity to shoot back. 'All these naysayers and haters haven't built anything,' he said. And he promised that any client who wanted their money back could have it, right away: 'Celsius has billions in liquidity, and we provide immediate access to anyone who needs access to the liquidity.'

Mashinsky also called up a pre-recorded message from Celsius's chief financial officer, Rod Bolger, to underscore his confidence in the company's financial strength. Bolger had joined Celsius just five months before, after a decade at the Royal Bank, Canada's largest lender, including five years as CFO. As I watched the video, it struck me as odd that his contribution was taped, rather than him appearing live. When he came on screen, Bolger did not look happy. He looked more like Mashinsky had him locked in the basement and was holding his dog hostage for good behaviour. Bolger's statement was less than a minute, and could not have seemed more detached from the reality of the crisis which Celsius was trying to stare down. Under the caption 'Why is Celsius so active in being transparent?', the CFO rambled about the importance of good regulation, alluded to the Basel committee on banking standards and how Celsius aimed to become a public company, and concluded that transparency was important to 'build the level of trust in the community'.

Bolger's appearance was indeed calculated to boost trust in the company. A Celsius executive had suggested the segment as a 'high priority', writing in an internal email that hearing from the CFO would 'help soothe our community and reduce the FUD and noise currently out there in the market'. The messaging obscured the reality inside Celsius. Bolger had clashed with Mashinsky in the days before about how to handle the financial crunch, customers' fears and the mounting withdrawals. The same day as the broadcast, Bolger wrote an email pushing back against Mashinsky's demands that Celsius offer 40 new crypto tokens on its platform as a way to generate enthusiasm from clients, and hopefully bring in new money. 'I haven't seen a business case for any of this,' Bolger wrote. Perhaps Mashinsky didn't want his CFO to have the chance to speak live on air.

The video, and Mashinsky's other public statements, also dramatically misrepresented Celsius's real financial position. The company had patchy internal records. In response to staff worries about its bookkeeping, Celsius had started to produce what it called the 'Waterfall report', a real-time statement of its liquidity: the amount of money it had on hand in cash or assets that could easily be converted into cash. Some employees still thought the Waterfall report was inaccurate, and tended to make the company's financial position look stronger than it really was. Still, the reports generated in the lead-up to 10 June showed that Celsius was on the brink of disaster. Too many people wanted their money back, and there was not enough money to pay them. Mashinsky's confident salvo in his Friday video was not enough to reverse the trend. Between Friday and Sunday, customers demanded the return of another $428 million. Over the weekend, clients received some funds back but began to notice that the company's systems were bogging down, throwing up unfamiliar errors and taking longer to process requests.

Even as he had been promising customers that their money was safe, and that they could have it back any time, Mashinsky had been pulling $8 million of his own money out of his Celsius accounts since mid-May. By the time of his broadcast, US prosecutors now allege, he had removed most of his own crypto from Celsius. Late on Sunday night, Celsius announced it had frozen withdrawals. That is the other thing that makes Mashinsky's 10 June livestream remarkable. It was the last one he ever gave. A month later the company filed for bankruptcy.

Celsius was the last act in Mashinsky's remarkable and dubious career. Starting the company in 2017, he was one of the pioneers of the large-scale crypto lending market that began during the first crypto bubble, before expanding rapidly during the 2021 boom and then playing a critical role in the 2022 collapse. I interviewed Mashinsky several times while he was running Celsius in 2021 and 2022. My first impression was a lasting one. I would not have bought a used car from the man, let alone given him my money.

In one interview he tried to persuade me how crazy it would be for him to do anything illegal under US law, since he lived in a Manhattan penthouse where American authorities could easily get at him. Why would a man like himself, with a wife and six children, risk losing everything? The bravado now looks ironic, even tragic. Mashinsky has been sued for fraud by New York's Attorney General, the Federal Trade Commission, the CFTC and the SEC. A year to the day after Celsius went bankrupt, he was arrested and charged with fraud and market manipulation. Celsius's former chief revenue officer pleaded guilty. Mashinsky denies wrongdoing and has pleaded not guilty. His trial is scheduled for September 2024. In legal filings, his lawyers said Celsius failed because of a 'series of calamitous, external events'.

The huge expansion of risky lending before the crash set the crypto market up for disaster. Mashinsky was a central figure in the lending market, and played an outsized role in convincing hundreds of thousands of people to plough their savings into crypto loans – linking their financial fortunes to the games being played by the crypto elite. He is someone who had no deep roots in digital assets or an obvious ideological connection to the idealism of 'first wave' crypto. He used the promise of a fairer financial system and the shadow of big banks' wrongdoing in 2008 as a marketing tool to attract money from disillusioned Americans, many of whom were relatively unsophisticated and financially vulnerable. His favourite T-shirt, which he often wore when promoting Celsius, read: 'Banks are not your friend'. As it turned out, neither was Mashinsky. For him, crypto's appeal to people struggling in today's financial system was a golden opportunity. He capitalised on the latest hot technology to rip them off.

*

The Celsius founder liked to say he was born under communism, raised under socialism and thrived under capitalism. The child of Jewish refugees from the former Soviet Union, he was raised in

Israel and then moved to the United States. He used his backstory and apparent success in business to full effect in promoting Celsius. On his personal website, Mashinsky described himself as a 'maverick investor and entrepreneur'. Even months after Celsius filed for bankruptcy, facing fraud accusations, his LinkedIn still proudly described him as a '4X Unicorn Founder', touting his record at four startups valued at more than $1 billion. Like many of Mashinsky's claims, there are good reasons to doubt parts of his self-promotion. What is true is that Mashinsky's career followed the latest high-tech booms since the early days of the internet in the 1990s. His chief claim to fame is that he was one of the inventors of VoIP – Voice over Internet Protocol – which enabled online phone calls and paved the way for the likes of Skype, FaceTime and WhatsApp calls. Other technologists who were involved in VoIP's inception have said publicly that Mashinsky's claims about his role in the invention are exaggerated. But that never stopped him from using the achievement to craft a compelling narrative to promote Celsius, which he founded during the first crypto bubble in 2017.

Mashinsky played up one of the well-trodden metaphors between the development of crypto and the early days of the internet. He cast the big banks as the equivalent of the old-school phone and telecoms companies, a small group of monopolistic players who kept prices high to screw money out of customers and who used their clout in Washington to protect their entrenched position. Crypto was like the early internet entrepreneurs, whose disruptive innovation cracked the communications monopoly and gave consumers benefits like free long-distance calls and easier access to information. The legend Mashinsky spun cast him as the leader of the plucky financial rebels, using lessons from the fight against the telecoms monopoly in his quest to smash up the banks. 'When I built Voice over IP, we didn't have to get permission from AT&T,' he once told me. 'The same thing is happening right now in finance.'

There are lots of flaws in the internet-to-crypto analogy. But when it comes to Mashinsky, the biggest hole in the story is that he was much more of a financial opportunist than a crypto innovator. Someone who was closely involved in discussions with Mashinsky and the company's other founders around its launch told me: 'Mashinsky loves to argue . . . We would have long dinners where we would argue about everything from the philosophy of crypto to their strategy . . . They were outsiders coming in after the first bubble . . . I think he knew very little about blockchain or crypto coming into things.' In an interview with a bankruptcy investigator, Mashinsky said that crypto was a 'totally new field' for him when he drew up plans for Celsius in the summer of 2017.

Mashinsky was not the only entrepreneur who sniffed out a business opportunity in lending and borrowing crypto around that time. Rival lenders BlockFi and Voyager, both of which also came to grief in 2022, were founded in 2017 and 2018. As crypto grew, adding lending into the digital financial system made good sense – even if it later became a ludicrous tangle of financial engineering. Max Boonen, the former Goldman Sachs trader and well-known crypto entrepreneur, believes he executed the first significant loan, borrowing from a billionaire Bitcoin enthusiast to get the capital he needed to run his own crypto trading business. The logic of this deal was clear. Boonen's firm needed an inventory of Bitcoin to run its operation, but it didn't want to take the risk of owning the coin and enduring its wild price swings. The billionaire lender was a Bitcoin believer, and he wanted to hold on to his coins in the faith that they were going up. In the meantime, he was happy to be paid some interest.

As crypto prices surged in 2017, more and more Bitcoin owners were sitting on huge profits. Many thought Bitcoin would rise further, and didn't want to sell. But they did want to get some income from their crypto winnings. You couldn't buy your Lamborghini with Bitcoin, let alone pay your rent. So how could crypto enthusiasts use their new-found wealth? Selling Bitcoin or tokens to get dollars was not an attractive option. The process was clunky and involved high fees and tricky tax obligations. Lenders offered a better solution. Crypto holders could hand over their digital tokens as security, and take a loan in hard currency like US dollars, which they could use for real-world expenses. Since they never sold their crypto, the clients didn't have to pay tax on their 'investment' gains, and they also kept their feet in the crypto market, so they would benefit if crypto prices continued to rise. As crypto businesses go, this type of lending was pretty sensible. But it was a small niche and the interest rates lenders could charge, while hefty by normal standards, were not going to make the enterprise wildly profitable.

Mashinsky was one of the entrepreneurs who pushed crypto lending into a new area. 'His big hypothesis was that to make a crypto business succeed you would need to offer yield,' said the person involved in his early plans. The focus on 'yield' came to be a dominant force in the crypto industry. It simply means the interest rate you can earn by pledging a crypto asset to a particular company or project, the same way you might earn an interest rate by depositing money at a bank or get a return by investing your money in a stock. The tricky thing about the use of the word 'yield' in crypto is that it blurs the line between those two fundamentally different ways of putting your money to work. The cash you deposit at a bank allows the bank to make loans to other customers, such as mortgages. But you expect to have access to your cash whenever you want. So the bank has to be very conservative in how it handles your money, and the interest rate you earn is small. Banks also have a government guarantee backing their deposits, which comes with particularly intense supervision. With an investment, such as a stock or lending to a company, you accept the risk that you might not get all your money back, and therefore get a higher return.

Celsius's pitch when it launched in 2018 appeared to overcome that ever-present trade-off between risk and return. It promised that crypto deposited with the company would be just like savings in a bank. But it also offered incredibly high yields, much higher than even risky traditional investments. Mashinsky always pushed for Celsius to pay the highest yields in the market, as high as 17 per cent annual interest on some coins. Clients, attracted by those juicy rewards, did not pay enough attention to the glaring question of how Celsius could afford to pay such high interest rates. The crypto market was so new, so innovative, so buoyant and baffling, that people accepted that the rules of financial gravity – that higher returns mean higher risk – simply did not apply. By the end of the first year, 2018, Celsius had pulled in $50 million, according to Mashinsky's account, given in court documents. Despite the slowdown in crypto as the first bubble deflated, Celsius quadrupled its asset by May 2019 to $200 million. The arrival of the second crypto bubble vaulted Celsius from that modest scale to stratospheric growth. By March 2021, its assets had ballooned by 50 times to $10 billion. In total, half a million customers trusted Celsius with their money.

The bond of trust was established, partly, by playing to the anti-establishment zeitgeist. Crypto has a strong appeal to people who are already primed to distrust experts and established institutions, and to believe in 'alternative facts'. The resentment people justifiably feel for the long and painful legacy of the 2008 financial crash easily tips over into thinking that big banks and US regulators are literally conspiring to screw you over. At times, there was something Trumpian about Mashinsky's pitch. He was the man who had beaten the corrupt elite at their own game, who knew how to play the system and win, and who was ready to share his success to lift up people who had been left behind. 'Remember, we get institutions to pay us so we can pay you,' he once said. 'When in history have institutions paid the average person anything? They don't like it, believe me. They hate paying us that yield. Right. And then we take most of it and deliver it to you.'

None of that salesmanship, or the growth Celsius achieved, could answer the fundamental question of how it could earn enough money to pay interest rates as high as 17 per cent. As I write, the average interest rate paid on 'junk bonds' (yes, that is the technical term for risky corporate debt) is around 8.5 per cent. Lending your money to companies who have been assessed by credit rating agencies as officially dodgy (not a technical term) would make you around half the interest rate that Celsius promised to pay while still promising that clients' money was safe. (In fact, rates were much, much lower across the traditional market when Celsius was in its heyday.)

The company's original plan had been to operate like a bank, using client deposits to fund lending activities and keeping a cut of the interest rate on those loans. 'I think originally his plan was to make a little bit of yield by lending out the Bitcoin they took in,' said the person involved in Celsius's launch. '[Mashinsky] embarked on the business before he realised that doing it properly would be impossible.' What my contact meant by 'impossible' was that to turn a profit, Celsius had to be able to take customer deposits and earn more interest than what it was promising to pay. According to an investigator appointed by the bankruptcy court, the gap between what Celsius promised to pay customers and what it was really earning by deploying their deposits grew over time, eventually reaching a shortfall of $1.36 billion.

'When regulators asked Celsius how it set its reward rates, Celsius explained that there was no correlation between the interest rates it paid to customers and the yield it generated from investing customer assets,' the investigator, a former US federal prosecutor named Shoba Pillay, wrote in her report. 'Celsius consistently set its reward rates based on what it perceived was necessary to beat the competition and not based upon the yield it was earning from investing customer assets.'

Pillay's analysis is that because Celsius promised to pay customers more money than it could reliably earn for them, it created a financial chasm that the company became increasingly desperate to fill. When it was growing like fury in 2021, Celsius lost $800 million in the year, plus another $165 million in the first quarter of 2022, according to the SEC. How did Celsius keep afloat for so long? The answer lies partly in a special ingredient that it brought to the crypto lending market. That ingredient was CEL, a crypto token created and controlled by Celsius. The company portrayed CEL as a sort of supercharged version of loyalty points offered by normal businesses. The highest yields were paid to customers who would accept part of the payment in CEL. That meant Celsius didn't have to come up with cash, or even valuable crypto assets, to meet its entire weekly bill of interest payments to customers. Instead, it kept the ship afloat through an ingenious, circular financial operation that even one of its own employees described in an April 2022 Slack message as 'very Ponzi-like'.

The first step in the scheme, according to the bankruptcy court investigation, was drawing in new customer money, using the promise of high interest rates and Mashinsky's marketing machine. New inflows of cash or valuable crypto assets like Bitcoin or Ether would be used to buy CEL tokens on the open market. Those purchases kept the price of CEL high, making the coins that Celsius then paid out in rewards to depositors more valuable. US prosecutors say the company also bought extra CEL tactically to boost the price when there was bad news around, understanding that its customers saw the price of CEL as a proxy for the company's strength. Mashinsky always denied this. In March 2021 he told his YouTube audience: 'We obviously want [the] CEL token to go higher in price, but we don't control it. It's not like we are the invisible hand that controls the pricing here or anything like that.'

In the classic Ponzi scheme, money brought in from new clients is used to pay the fictional investment returns to existing clients.

The crux of the allegation that Celsius was essentially a Ponzi scheme is that it bought CEL tokens with customer money, rather than earnings from the business. This added a modern crypto twist to the Ponzi structure, mediating the payments through CEL. Pillay, the investigator, concluded: 'In total, Celsius spent at least $558 million buying its own token on the market . . . In effect, Celsius bought every CEL token in the market at least one time and in some instances, twice.' The other important consequence of using new clients' money to inflate the price of CEL was that it benefited Mashinsky, his wife and other company insiders. Although he fiercely maintained in public that he was holding on to his own CEL, in reality Mashinsky made at least $42 million by selling the tokens in secret deals, prosecutors charged.

*

In the summer of 2022, in the aftermath of Celsius's collapse, the *FT* was the first to report on these insider sales in a piece I wrote with my colleague Kadhim Shubber, a brilliant reporter on the investigations team. Kadhim had got hold of internal company spreadsheets detailing some of the trades. We reported both on the sales and the shockingly poor management of customer money. The first clue to the importance of CEL came a year earlier, when I was trawling through LinkedIn in search of leads. I got in touch with a former junior Celsius employee who had been close to the CEL trading operation. Just a few years out of college, this staffer had spent just months at Celsius before moving on. With scarcely any training, the crypto firm gave him substantial responsibilities on its trading desk, demanding he work around the clock. He did not have a clear picture of the alleged CEL manipulation that would later come to light, but he shared with me the strong impression that the token was central to the operation. 'I think the whole company rests on how the CEL token performs,' he said. 'If that was to fail, I don't know how they would cope.'

My young source got cold feet after the first call and wouldn't speak to me again. It took the company collapsing under its own weight to unlock the story. Later investigations show that multiple Celsius employees were aghast at what Mashinsky said in public. They compiled lists of his public misstatements. Sometimes, staff edited the recordings of his live broadcasts to remove damaging and misleading claims, and conferred in private about how much trouble they would be in if any of this got out. 'If anyone ever found out our position and how much our founders took in USD, it could be a very very bad look,' one employee wrote. Staff also warned Mashinsky to stop lying to customers. Commenting on the CEO's claim about their lending practices in a draft article, one executive emailed: 'That is not true and we cannot say that.' The warning was ignored.

Meanwhile, Celsius tried out all sorts of different schemes in its search for income to meet its exaggerated promises to customers. It invested a small fortune into an ultimately unsuccessful foray into cryptocurrency mining. And it tried out lots of different strategies trading in the cryptocurrency markets. One of these, a trade involving an investment vehicle called the Grayscale Bitcoin Trust, was for a while the most popular money-maker in crypto. Other lenders, including BlockFi, joined in.

Hype Machine

The so-called 'Grayscale trade' was not a work of financial genius. The Grayscale trust had been set up as an investment product to give people access to Bitcoin, much like funds and trusts that let people easily invest in gold or stocks. Investors could buy shares in the trust, which in turn would hold the Bitcoin. It was a simple and popular way to get a little slice of crypto through a familiar financial structure. So popular, in fact, that demand for the shares was high enough that for many years the shares were valued at more than the corresponding amount of Bitcoin. The structure of the trust meant that small-ticket individual investors could only buy shares on the open market and would have to pay a premium over the amount of Bitcoin the shares were worth. Big-ticket investors, however, could give Bitcoin directly to Grayscale and receive an equivalent number of shares in return.

The route to profit was simple. Big investors bought Grayscale shares directly. They waited six months (which was required by the trust's rules). And then they could sell those shares on the open market at a higher price than they had paid. The only reason institutions could make money on this trade was that they had privileged access to buy shares at their true value, and that small investors who wanted shares had little choice but to overpay. There was no way this could last forever. In February 2021, Canada allowed the first North American Bitcoin ETF. Exchange-traded funds are a popular way for people to get into all sorts of assets, and the launch of a Bitcoin fund had been the 'holy grail' for crypto investors, one strategist told me at the time. Small investors flocked to the new funds. Almost immediately, the lack of demand for Grayscale shares meant that their price on the open market swung from being more than their Bitcoin value to much less. Big traders who had been creaming money off the Grayscale premium now faced a loss on all the shares they were waiting to sell. A lot of companies got burned.

The undoing of the Grayscale trade now looks like an early warning of what would happen to seemingly foolproof crypto trades when prices stopped going up. At the time, Mashinsky and others were just focused on finding a replacement money maker. The Celsius founder was a domineering and erratic figure. He interfered in trading strategies, overruling the professionals he had hired, constantly pressed for faster growth, and basked in his dual role as CEO and cult leader. His employees agonised about how to rein him in. When he personally took control of Celsius's trading in January 2022, one employee WhatsApped a colleague: 'Seems like Alex is unilaterally trading large positions of our book? . . . So at what point do we seek outside intervention to get the thing under control?' At a party in the wings of a Lisbon crypto conference, a former staffer recalls, Mashinsky stood up on a table in front of employees and clients and gave an 'extraordinary . . . impromptu speech that went on much, much, much too long'. The former employee found the image Mashinsky tried to foster 'bizarre'. No one would turn out to an event hosted by their bank. Yet Celsius wanted its clients to hero-worship its chief executive. 'I don't know anyone who was signed on to the cult. But that seemed like certainly it was [Mashinsky's] expectation. I mostly found it very cringeworthy,' they said.

*

If employees had doubts about their CEO, Mashinsky had managed to make a good impression on some big name investors. In late

2021, Celsius announced that it had raised $400 million from two heavyweight investors: WestCap, a well-known investment fund, and Caisse de dépôt et placement du Québec (CDPQ), Canada's second largest pension fund, which manages the retirement money of public sector workers. The funding round was later expanded to $750 million. Mashinsky was triumphant. 'It's not the $400 million. It's the credibility that comes with the people who wrote those cheques,' he told the *FT* at the time. Investors valued the company at more than $3 billion.

The investment, and the vote of confidence it brought, was surprising. By this time, it was public knowledge that several US regulators had concerns about Celsius. Another public red flag came from crypto custodian Prime Trust, which dropped Celsius as a client earlier in the year. It was widely reported in the press that Prime Trust was worried about how Celsius handled its assets.

During the peak of crypto enthusiasm, from spring to autumn 2021, WestCap and CDPQ spent months digging into Celsius. They employed more than a dozen consultants to interview Celsius staff and pore over its records as well as lawyers to study its regulatory risks. One person involved in the process estimated the cost of the diligence was more than $4 million. The company appeared to have robust earnings and even better prospects. Background checks portrayed Mashinsky as a 'driven, sharp-elbowed executive', the person said, which is the kind of guy you probably want running a company you're going to invest in. He looked like the charismatic founder of a fast-growing company that was perfectly positioned to bring crypto to the masses.

A document prepared by WestCap as part of the investment process, in September 2021, did identify the weakness of Celsius's bookkeeping, which they called 'underdeveloped financial reporting muscle'. It structured its investment to include a 'review period' that would allow 'WestCap, along with CDPQ, to get intimately involved and familiar with the Company's accounting practices' before making the full financial commitment.

Chaotic record-keeping is not unusual at a young, fast-growing company. Perhaps it should have been more of a concern when the company was looking after billions of other people's money in the Wild West of crypto. The investors helped bring in more professionals, and pushed for Celsius to clean up its act. They thought the company could settle with US regulators over past issues, and find a new way to operate within the law.

The investors misjudged the risk of getting into bed with Celsius. Although they modelled what would happen when crypto prices fell, they did not anticipate the scale of the crash that was just around the corner. They did not spot the alleged manipulation of the CEL token behind the scenes. And they didn't fully grasp Mashinsky's character. 'The wild card in this is Mashinsky's behaviour,' the person involved in the investment said. 'He is almost impossible to control.'

WestCap lost $250 million on Celsius. CDPQ lost $150 million. CDPQ's chief executive, Charles Emond, later said it was 'disappointed with the outcome and not happy', and has 'a lot of empathy' for customers who lost money. He said the due diligence on Celsius was 'quite extensive' but that 'due diligence is not a guarantee of success'. It was not the last pension fund that would lose people's retirement savings in cryptoland.

*

What finally pushed Celsius over the edge was its entanglements in the increasingly complex world of crypto lending as the second bubble expanded in 2021 and early 2022. Seeking new ways to make the types of returns it was promising to pay clients, Celsius committed itself more and more heavily to decentralised finance, so-called 'Defi', where crypto lending had mutated from straight-forward transactions to a wild level of complexity.

The basic idea of Defi is that you can remove the middleman from the normal functions of the financial system. Just like decen-tralised exchanges that try to replace companies like Binance by automatically facilitating trades, Defi entrepreneurs had come up with computerised lending systems. Instead of applying to a bank or another lender for a loan, a crypto project that needed financing could open up a 'pool' that would accept money and return interest payments according to pre-programmed rules. These pools were often highly lucrative for the lenders, but were also incredibly risky. Crypto projects frequently fail. The smart contracts and code that governed the transactions were liable to hacking. And the payment was often made in obscure crypto tokens that might be temporarily valuable but whose worth was unreliable.

Still, Defi appeared to offer the sort of yields that would help Celsius earn the income it needed, interest rates higher than 20 per cent and sometimes briefly reaching 100 or even 1,000 per cent. The company hired and contracted with Defi traders and threw ever larger sums of money into the frothy market. Its record was disas-trous. Celsius put several hundred million into a company called KeyFi, run by a trader named Jason Stone, who was supposed to deploy the funds into the best Defi opportunities. Mashinsky had previously invested in another of Stone's companies and insisted he could be trusted. The relationship between KeyFi and Celsius quickly descended into squabbling over issues like what Stone could invest in and how he would report back to Celsius. Within months, Celsius demanded its money back. Stone refused, blaming the company for sabotaging the arrangement. Their dispute is being litigated in Celsius's bankruptcy. In another case, Celsius gave funds to a Defi company called StakeHound, which within five months lost the cryptographic keys to the tokens, rendering them permanently unrecoverable and costing Celsius $105 million.

On the surface, Defi has grown spectacularly. The amount of money circulating in the 'ecosystem' reached nearly $230 billion by late 2021. And people were briefly able to make substantial profits. One trader I met at a London crypto party had given up entirely on speculating whether token prices would rise or fall, and instead hopped between the most lucrative Defi 'pools', made enough money to live in a posh West London mews house and smoked an astonishing amount of weed. But Defi's growth was illusory and the easy profits were fleeting.

The lack of lending standards, or really any rules, in crypto allowed traders to recycle their assets to obtain multiple loans. The basic outline of this scheme was to lend money in one pool and then use whatever tokens you got back as a deposit to borrow tokens in a different pool. They would then use the money from the second loan to lend even more back into the first pool. And repeat. This strategy, dubbed 'recursive lending', was commonplace in Defi circles. If you weren't recursive lending, you really weren't one of the cool kids.

It should not be hard to imagine how this would go wrong. Each addition to the debt stack increased the risk that the whole pile would collapse. But in the buoyant crypto markets of 2021, people were too concerned about not missing out on the next hot Defi pool to worry about what might happen if prices ever went down.

Inside Celsius, one former employee compared the atmosphere to the film *Bugsy Malone*, a 1976 riff on the classic gangster movie genre where the thugs and criminals are all played by children – and the machine guns fire whipped cream. Mashinsky's crew at Celsius were wannabe financial sharks. With no boring grown-ups to spoil their fun, they were seeking to play a very aggressive and sometimes dishonest game with their customers' money. What made all this possible was the inevitable gap between new technology emerging and the forces of law and order catching up. As far as many of its customers were concerned, Celsius was just as good as a bank – or better. Its marketing portrayed it as an alternative to banks. It described its product in terms of deposits and interest rates. And it promised customers that their funds were safe, and available to be withdrawn at any time. But in the background, Celsius wasn't subject to any of the same rules and oversight, or backed by the government guarantees, that make banks reliable. Should customers have been more sceptical? Well, clearly yes.

*

Celsius's brushes with financial regulators are revealing of how the crypto bubble was allowed to become quite so damaging. Unlike BitMEX and Binance, it did not operate from an offshore base.

Very Ponzi-Like

It pitched itself not as an adventurous trading venue, but as a reliable alternative to banks. Being based in the Cayman Islands or Seychelles would surely clash with that image. Originally operating from London, Celsius even applied for registration with the Financial Conduct Authority. At the FCA, early optimism about the potential for crypto to revolutionise financial services had turned into deep scepticism. 'There was a lot of unease about crypto,' said a former FCA official who worked on digital assets. Regulators had watched the 2017 ICO boom thinking: 'This is absolutely ludicrous. Everyone is investing in this. It behaves like a financial instrument. People are going to lose a lot of money.'

The FCA worried that regulating crypto would be seen as an endorsement. But it had to implement regulations to combat money laundering, so it did set up a registration system for crypto companies. Although the scheme was focused on controls to block dirty money, the FCA took a pretty detailed look at the overall character of the companies before handing out its seal of approval. Exactly what the FCA thought when Celsius applied for registration we cannot say. We do know that the regulator was not prepared to grant it registration in a month of Sundays. But that rejection was private. The FCA will inform firms that it isn't going to register them, and let them gracefully withdraw their applications and go elsewhere. It saves the FCA time and grief. It also means that whatever red flags the FCA finds, it does not always share with the public – who, after all, the regulator is supposed to protect.

Celsius could spin the situation to its advantage. The company put out a press release saying it had decided to move from the UK to the US, blaming 'regulatory uncertainty' in Britain and saying that it had 'chosen to withdraw our application from the UK Financial Conduct Authority'. Here again, 'regulatory uncertainty' is what crypto companies say when they hit upon regulations that they don't like. In this situation, the message from the FCA was pretty clearly 'bugger off'. Celsius's statement might be technically accurate but it is also hopelessly misleading. A more honest version would be: 'The FCA said they won't touch us with a ten-foot pole, so we're going to try our luck in America.'

Celsius's luck in America was not much better. To give them credit, US regulators, including state-level authorities and the SEC, caught on to the problem of crypto 'deposit accounts' pretty quickly. They first went after Celsius's rival BlockFi. Celsius was targeted by several states within months of arriving on US shores. Still, the process for getting these claims to court is itself months long. And Mashinsky spun the intervention as regulators seeking to protect the monopoly of their buddies at the big banks, a narrative that many of his clients bought. In an interview, he told me that SEC chairman Gary Gensler was up to no good. 'The fight is over all the money in the world. Gensler is trying to slow everybody down to let the old guard catch up by putting in roadblocks,' he said. Ultimately, the regulator's action forced Celsius to stop accepting new clients for its yield-bearing accounts in the UK and later in the US, just two months before it collapsed. This stopped more people losing money, but it did not save existing customers.

The FCA has never been called to account for letting Celsius slip away. Frauds and failures within the UK's regulated financial sector normally mean months of ritual humiliation for FCA leadership in front of Parliamentary committees and in the press,

Very Ponzi-Like

blighting the résumés of the people in charge. By pushing Celsius out of the country, the FCA avoided association or responsibility for its collapse. Documents from the autumn of 2021 show that 6 per cent of Celsius's deposits came from people in the UK. Yet, there have been no *Daily Mail* editorials or speeches from legislators blaming the FCA for the hundreds of millions that British customers lost. In fairness to the FCA, there are legal constraints on what they can do and the scope of their jurisdiction over crypto is limited. Equally, the FCA has been reluctant to get its arms around digital assets. 'The FCA hated the idea of being responsible for crypto asset providers. There was a lot of discussion around massive risks that weren't really known to them. So no one wanted to take responsibility for these firms. And no one wanted to give these firms legitimacy by having an FCA registration,' said the former official at the watchdog. 'There is a perceived huge reputation risk for the FCA.' A senior UK crypto executive said: 'Their focus is making sure there isn't a problem on their watch, not on whether the consumer loses money. I don't think that's right.' It's troubling to think that anyone inside the regulator might be preoccupied with protecting their own reputation over protecting the public from fraud.

The absence of a cop on the beat is what let Mashinsky and his Celsius followers run around like child gangsters, screwing money out of unsuspecting customers. The thing that finally stopped them was not enforcement action but the downturn in the crypto market. Then, people realised the one thing that made Celsius quite different from *Bugsy Malone*. While crypto was rising, all money seemed like play money. It was all a game that you couldn't lose. But in reality the machine guns did not fire whipped cream. They were firing bullets. It was real money, belonging to real people, and it was gone.

*

Celsius was the most outrageous crypto lender killed off by the 2022 crash. But it was not the only one. BlockFi and Voyager, two other crypto lenders, have both filed for bankruptcy. Genesis, another large crypto firm, has put its lending unit into restructuring. Numerous smaller operators have failed too. Genesis, its parent company DCG and its partner exchange Gemini, as well as Voyager's former CEO, have each been sued by US authorities alleging fraud – accusations they contest. There are important differences between all these companies, particularly around the severity of the alleged wrongdoing. What the lending industry has in common is that all these companies got carried away during the crypto bubble and ran big risks.

Publicly, many crypto lenders talked a lot about 'overcollateralised' loans. Collateral is an asset that the borrower offers up to the lender to make them comfortable with extending the loan. The most commonplace example is a residential mortgage, where the house is the 'collateral'. If you stop paying, the bank can take the house and sell it, which means the loan is much less risky for the bank. Mortgages are almost always 'overcollateralised' because the house is worth more than the value of the mortgage. The rule of thumb in the UK is that banks will lend you 85 per cent of the value of the house you want to buy. The remaining 15 per cent you have to pay yourself, as the deposit. Some banks will go further, say to 95 per cent, reducing their own margin of safety to just 5 per cent. Collateral provides that margin of safety.

Still, even in an 'overcollateralised' loan, the bank is taking a risk. If the economy really tanks, people lose their job and the housing market falls, the bank might find that borrowers can't make their monthly mortgage payments and at the same time the value of the house has dropped to less than the amount of the mortgage.

Crypto lending is not fundamentally different. If someone wants a loan of $100 million, they might be asked to put up $115 million worth of Bitcoin as the collateral. Crypto lenders made a song and dance of being 'overcollateralised' to try to say that they were playing it safe. The price of Bitcoin moves around sharply. The loan could be overcollateralised when it's made on Monday, but under water by Wednesday if the price of Bitcoin against the dollar falls far enough. In theory, though, price movements are all manageable. If the loan starts to get too close to the danger zone, the lender will ask for more collateral to top up their margin of safety (this is called a margin call, which people in finance love to say because it was the title of a 2011 film starring Jeremy Irons). If the borrower can't stump up any more collateral, the lender can still cancel the loan before it dips into negative collateral territory, and sell the collateral to pay itself back. So far, so idiot proof.

'Idiot proof' is a concept that people in crypto love to test. Crypto lenders did two things that broke the theoretically 'unfuck-upable' lending model. First, they accepted collateral in the form of assets that were way, way more prone to changes in value even than Bitcoin. Second, they also made plenty of loans that were never overcollateralised in the first place. By 2022, Celsius had more than

$1.3 billion of loans on its books with no collateral at all, more than a third of its lending, according to the SEC. One of the biggest clients for these loans, across the crypto industry, was SBF.

These loans were riskier, so Celsius could charge higher interest rates – which the ever yield-hungry company was keen to do. In January 2022, Mashinsky flew to the Bahamas and met SBF and Caroline Ellison. After the meeting, he wrote to an executive: 'Alameda wants to borrow [US dollar tokens] on 6-12 month terms up to $2B so work with Risk to see how far we can go. I met their CEO Caroline yesterday in Bahamas.'

'Risk', that is Celsius's risk team, along with other executives, pushed back and tried to limit the scale of the relationship. Celsius was just one of the lenders that SBF and Ellison targeted. BlockFi and Voyager also made large loans. Genesis lent Alameda $6.5 billion at one point, with only 50 per cent collateral, according to reporting by the *Wall Street Journal*. The easy access to debt allowed SBF to get in over his head.

*

Why did the crypto lenders take the risk of lending large sums, with shaky or non-existent collateral, not just to Alameda but to many other borrowers? A big part of the answer is the intense pressure they were under to grow. The more they could lend, the bigger their business, the more money they could make. One early investor in a major crypto lender, who sold their shares before the crash, explained the dynamic. '[The lenders'] business model doesn't necessarily mean you're gonna go bankrupt. But these guys are just all bad at it. Really bad at it. It's a really simple game,' the investor said. 'They were pushed . . . they needed to show numbers.'

Who pushed the lenders to make riskier loans? The investor blamed venture capital backers, like himself. The lenders were trying to appeal to investors and achieve higher valuations for their businesses. 'The market says: "I value you on your loan book. How big is your loan book? What's your net interest margin?"' If the lenders said, 'There's only, like, one credible person to lend to in Bitcoin, who could actually pay me back at a reasonable rate,' the response from the market was, 'Wrong answer. Your company's worth fuck all.'

'On the other hand,' the investor went on, lenders could take risks on uncollateralised lending, but 'show a massive loan book and a massive net interest margin'. The investor response? 'Oh, great, you're the next deca-unicorn company. You're gonna go public. You're rich now.'

'And then it all ended how we thought it was gonna end,' the investor concluded. 'But it's the incentives scheme of a [venture capital] led company that has a bunch of dollars. You've got to spend them. So you'd better be growing that loan book. Find someone to take that money, right. And they found somebody.'

A senior executive at one of the crypto lenders agreed. 'All the big lenders are done – BlockFi, Voyager, Celsius, Genesis. Not a single person is alive. Something was wrong,' they said. The trick about lending, they said, is that there is a natural limit to the number of reliable people you can safely lend money to. And so there should be a limit to growth. With regular products, 'the quality of your product doesn't go down the more people you try to sell it to,' they said. 'Lending isn't the same as selling software.

'Competitive pressure in lending markets can be unhealthy,' they concluded. 'If you look at the crypto lending industry, it was definitely too much too fast.'

For lenders across the crypto industry, a lot of the money that went into these risky loans came from small investors and depositors. The spate of bankruptcies has stacked up tens of billions in losses. In the Celsius bankruptcy proceedings, its customers have written letters to the judge describing the consequences for their lives. Researcher Molly White has done admirable work sifting through these letters and highlighting the human cost of Celsius's deception.

'The devastation to my life situation is irreparable, its despair, hopelessness, its failure, a slow death, that eats at you every minute of every day. It takes your heart, mind, soul and body. I have become a shell of a person and obsess on how to fix it,' wrote one client.

Another customer was left wondering why authorities didn't stop Celsius earlier. 'Your Honor, I have worked hard all my life and it has taken me years to save this money. I don't understand how this can be allowed to happen. Celsius Network was operating in New York and New Jersey which are under SEC rulings. The SEC has been so stringent regarding cryptocurrency regulations yet this was allowed to happen.' A third, who deposited his baby daughter's education fund at Celsius, said that WestCap and CDPQ's investment gave him confidence. 'Seeing that companies of this magnitude invested with Celsius gave me the indication that Celsius is a good safe investment.'

Very Ponzi-Like

In retrospect, it's easy to dismiss the risk that people took as foolish. But in crypto's boom times, the desire to lend was matched only by the insatiable hunger for borrowing. Reasonable people might wonder why SBF and Alameda went around hoovering up as much money in loans as they possibly could on the most aggressive terms possible. FTX was already a highly profitable business, sufficient by itself to make SBF as rich as anyone could wish. Why take the risk of getting in hock to all these lenders?

This is not a question that would make much sense to people steeped in the culture of high finance, especially the supercharged version of that culture that prevailed in crypto at the height of the boom. The more money you can borrow, the more money you can make. If you have $100 million and invest it to make $1 million a year, that sounds pretty good. But if you can take that $100 million and pledge it to get a loan worth $200 million, you can invest that and double your return. In the risk-taking mindset that prevailed within crypto, and certainly at the court of SBF, failing to maximise your borrowing meant you were effectively losing money. You were leaving profit on the table, and were therefore an idiot. What they forgot was the other side of the coin. The more money you can borrow, the more money you can lose. If you invest your own money and fail, you might be wiped out to zero. If you invest borrowed money, you can end up somewhere worse. In the spring and summer of 2022, this is exactly what happened to SBF.

Legendary

Bitcoin 2021 was billed as the largest crypto event in history. A crowd of 12,000 people descended on Miami at a time when many places were still in some degree of lockdown. Sam Bankman-Fried didn't make top billing on the list of speakers. The FTX founder appeared on the agenda behind the libertarian former presidential candidate Ron Paul, Twitter founder Jack Dorsey and 'skateboarding legend' Tony Hawk. But SBF arrived in Miami ready to make a splash.

Months early, FTX had clinched the $135 million deal to rename Miami's 19,000-seater stadium. For more than two decades, the venue had been called the American Airlines Arena – the 'triple A'. It was home to the three-time NBA championship-winning Miami Heat, and hosted performances by every A-list musician you could name, from Kanye West to Celine Dion. The name of the stadium was repeated, game after game, show after show, to millions of fans across the country. Now, the Covid cash-strapped airline was ceding its place to the rising star of the crypto world. On NBC News, the reporter announced: 'A name that we have all come to know, American Airlines Arena, is now a thing of the past. It is official, the new name of the arena, FTX Arena, named after the cryptocurrency trading platform.' Alongside the Bitcoin event, SBF led the renaming ceremony, complete with smoke machines and confetti. Outside, TV cameras filmed crews in high-visibility jackets working with cranes to change the signs over the stadium doors.

Back at the Bitcoin conference, on stage in his signature shorts and scruffy FTX T-shirt, he modestly introduced his company to the crowd. 'FTX is a global crypto exchange,' he began, interrupted by a whoop and a round of applause from the audience. Clearly, FTX needed no introduction. SBF grinned bashfully, shuffling his feet and staring down at the floor. 'We're one of the bigger ones,' he continues, smiling to acknowledge the audience reaction. 'Not the biggest yet.'

SBF's star was on the rise, and his next ambitious move was taking shape. But first, he had to endure the return journey from Miami to FTX's base in Hong Kong, serving the city's strict quarantine. It was fortunate that Hong Kong was so stringent. Bitcoin 2021, with thousands of maskless crypto fans jammed into the audience, became infamous as a Covid superspreader event. SBF dodged infection and cleared quarantine in time to execute the next crucial play in his strategy to make FTX the biggest name in crypto.

The company had been working for months pulling together a major round of investment from outside funders. SBF had been invited to present to Sequoia Capital, who were looking at whether to join the fundraising. Sequoia is at the very top of the venture capital world, managing tens of billions of dollars with a track record of backing ultra-successful tech companies including Apple, Zoom and Airbnb. The firm can write cheques for tens of millions, but its reputation is worth even more. The deal for the naming rights to the Miami stadium put FTX's brand in front of millions of Americans, and many millions more around the world. But a signature from Sequoia would show the elite financial world that FTX was the company everyone had been searching for, the one that could finally bridge the gap from crypto into the upper echelon of Silicon Valley.

If SBF was at all anxious about facing a panel of Sequoia's partners for a quiz about his business, it didn't show as he signed on to the Zoom call. But there was nervousness on the other side of the table. Michelle Bailhe, a chipper Google and McKinsey alumni and one of Sequoia's crypto experts, was worried that some of her colleagues, either ignorant or sceptical of digital assets, would alienate SBF.

'Before we even met Sam in an official Sequoia meeting, I had sent this email to all the people on our side that were going to join [saying] "Guys, don't ask silly questions in the meeting,"' she said in a later interview. '"This is an amazing company, like, please bring your A-game."'

FTX's financials were indeed impressive. Since being founded in 2019 as an upstart rival to much more established exchanges like Binance, FTX had grown swiftly into the top ranks of crypto trading sites. The company made around $10 million of revenue in 2019 and $80 million in 2020. In 2021, FTX was on course to earn $1 billion in revenue. This electrifying growth was the stuff of investors' dreams.

Even better, FTX was already profitable. Most startups use venture capital funding to operate at a loss, often for years, as they throw money into trying to grow. Uber was more than a decade old before it finally turned a profit. Because FTX's high-tech trading systems required little investment beyond its small, super-hard-working staff, SBF was managing to grow the company and make money at the same time – even while splashing millions on marketing. The brand-new company looked set to make $300–$400 million of profit that year.

With those kinds of numbers, investors were ready to love FTX. And its founder did not disappoint. SBF was quick and fluent, with an answer for everything. The Sequoia panel was wowed. The real-time comments from partners in the Zoom chat were ecstatic, according to an account later published by Sequoia itself. 'I LOVE THIS FOUNDER.' 'I am a 10 out of 10.' 'YES!!!'

On the other side of the screen, in FTX's crowded Hong Kong office, SBF was playing a quick game of 'League of Legends'. The ability to pitch Silicon Valley kingmakers with half his brain became one of SBF's most famous power moves. Far from being infuriated by his rudeness, Sequoia apparently loved the bravado – including the detail proudly in the profile of SBF that they published. It was just the kind of antics that venture capital investors love to see.

Although they formally put their money behind companies, many venture capitalists would tell you that they really invest in people. Inspired by examples like Steve Jobs, Mark Zuckerberg, Jeff Bezos and Elon Musk, these investors see huge value in exceptional individuals as the architects who can build multi-billion-dollar companies on top of a good idea. Eccentric behaviour – in SBF's case playing

Legendary

video games in meetings or sleeping on a beanbag so that 'my mind stays in work mode, and I don't have to reload everything the next day' – easily fits into the myth of this kind of genius. An executive at an investment firm that got burned elsewhere in crypto told me: 'For this kind of thing, you almost want a maniacal leader . . . It's not normal people who do this kind of stuff.'

I have never felt that SBF's weird behaviour was particularly calculated. He is authentically unusual. But he certainly knew the game he was playing, often quite literally. He told me that he played games on his computer during most of his investor meetings. It kept him from getting bored and combative on long calls that he said were 'excruciating for me . . . They are so dull and slow.' And it didn't hurt his pitch. 'If you do that shit and then nonetheless ace the interview, rather than feeling disrespected, [the investors'] takeaway is more that, "with half their brain, they can do well at this. What must that mean about their whole brain?"' he said.

I might once have naively thought that a startup pitching for investment and a venture capitalist doling out millions would look a lot more like *Dragons' Den* – with the entrepreneur pleading for backing, ready to give up a large share of the ownership in their company. In fact, the interaction is often much more finely balanced. For super-hot startups like FTX, as Bailhe's email attests, the venture capitalists are frequently also preoccupied by making a good impression.

In SBF, Sequoia thought it had found another visionary, who could fulfil the firm's mission of building 'legendary companies'. They were not alone. When FTX's new fundraising round was announced in late July, the list of backers included Thoma Bravo, SoftBank,

Third Point, Paul Tudor Jones's family, Izzy Englander and Alan Howard among a host of top-tier supporters. Although few are household names, it's hard to overstate how much this roster represents financial royalty. With $900 million of fresh investment, the 'Series B' round valued FTX at $18 billion. Securing their backing was probably the most important moment in FTX's rise. The credibility that came with these established investors transformed the company from being the rising power in the niche world of crypto to becoming a major player in global finance, media and politics. Over the course of the next year, SBF would cement his position, wielding financial clout, political access, splashy marketing and the press to become unquestionably the most influential figure in crypto. The Series B round increased the momentum that would see venture capital investors put a total of around $2 billion behind the company. It was a decision each of those investors no doubt wishes they could take back.

Venture capitalists are not afraid of losing money. Mostly they back companies that have little more than a good idea, an enthusiastic team and big plans for growth. Just like an athlete takes to the field knowing they might lose, making investments that don't pay off is part of the game venture capitalists play. If you end up sitting next to a venture capitalist at a dinner party, the most likely explanation you'll hear is roughly this. You back 20 young companies with a moderate amount of money. If two or three of them are moderately successful, and one or two are very successful, you can make good money. (And if even one of your picks becomes the next Facebook, you make more money than you'll need for the rest of your life.) So you don't need to lose too much sleep over the rest, the companies that plod along or fizzle out.

Legendary

FTX is the rare failure that scrambles that logic. Its collapse was so spectacular, the billions in losses for its customers so painful, and the fraud accusations so scathing that its venture capital backers don't just look like bad financiers. They look hopelessly gullible or, worse, complicit in hyping up SBF. The recriminations have focused on the 'due diligence', or lack thereof. For investors who like to be seen as some of the smartest people in finance, and whose industry thrives on its mystique and reputation, it is deeply uncomfortable to now have people asking: 'How did they get FTX so disastrously wrong?'

*

SBF showed a seemingly insatiable appetite for new capital. FTX ran three fundraising processes in 2021, condensing a series of milestones that many companies would have spread out over many years. The July Series B was followed by an add-on round, the B-1, in October for all the investors who missed the boat the first time round and still wanted in. The autumn round added $420 million of fresh cash, and took FTX's valuation to $25 billion. (It's called the 'meme' round because the $420.69 million came from 69 investors.) The pinnacle came in January 2022, when together with its US arm, the company announced a new round, the Series C, valuing SBF's empire at a combined $40 billion.

The pace of this ascent and the succession of millions and billions is dizzying. The speed with which FTX could raise money reflects the strange times in which it set out its stall. All three rounds were concluded in just over a six-month span, which will go down as one of the most remarkable periods in modern financial history.

What we are talking about is a period of very, very 'cheap' money. The first few times I heard that phrase I remember thinking it strange to talk about money having a price. Surely a dollar is worth a dollar? 'Cheap money' is the phrase the financial hive mind has come up with not for the cost of buying money, but for the cost of borrowing money. A $1,000 loan paying the bank $10 a month is a 1 per cent interest rate. That's cheap. Paying the bank $50 a month is a 5 per cent interest rate, which is getting more expensive.

From 2020 into 2021, money was as cheap as it has ever been. And the cause was not financial. It was biological. When the pandemic hit in March 2020, governments and economists were rightly worried that the sudden impact of everyone staying at home – and many people being unable to work or losing their jobs – would collapse the economy. Governments and central banks faced an impending economic disaster. Controlling the price of money is one of the key tools central banks have to fulfil their responsibility to keep the economy on an even keel. The basic mechanism is fairly straightforward. In the UK, the interest rate set by the Bank of England acts as the baseline for the rates that commercial banks will, in turn, pay on savings accounts and what they will charge on loans and mortgages. Making money cheaper is a powerful tool for juicing up the economy. With cheap loans, people can afford to buy cars, houses, washing machines and holidays. Companies use lines of credit to buy new widget machines or open new stores.

The central bank controls the dam that drives the mill. The more they increase the flow of money, the faster the wheels of the economy start to spin. Going into 2020, money had already been unusually cheap for quite a long time. Interest rates had been set at a low level to help keep the economic wheels spinning after the 2008 financial crisis. Money had been flowing through the dam in a steady stream. In response to the Covid pandemic, central bankers around the world stepped away from their carefully calibrated controls and hit the big red button for an emergency release. In the US, UK and elsewhere, rates were cut, effectively to zero.

Simply being able to borrow for next to nothing wasn't going to solve the Covid economic crisis. The problem wasn't that people needed a little push to get economic activity going. The problem was that most economic activity requires people to get together, and we were all stuck at home. So on top of cheap money from the central banks, governments added free money – literally paying people to stay at home. Probably the most remarkable example of this was in the US, where instead of subsidising the wages of people who couldn't work because of lockdown, the government simply mailed out stimulus cheques. It truly was free money for everyone.

The double act between central banks and government is formally known as monetary and fiscal policy. And the government (fiscal) could afford to scatter money like confetti to keep us all going through Covid because central banks (monetary) decided to back them up. The US Federal Reserve, the Bank of England and others doubled down on an interesting trend in monetary policy that caught on after the 2008 crash, when simply having low interest rates was judged not enough to boost the economy.

This scheme, called quantitative easing, very simply, consists of the central bank buying stuff, often government debt in the bond market, as a way of pushing even more money into the economy. The phrase 'buying government debt in the bond market' effectively means 'being a lender to the government'. In the first nine months of 2020, the UK government issued £261 billion of new debt into the bond market – up from just £34 billion in the previous nine months. In the same period the Bank of England was buying up a 'roughly equivalent quantity' of bonds in the market, according to the independent Office for Budget Responsibility. Over a longer time span, from April 2020 to July 2021, the Bank of England bought £412 billion of government debt, equivalent to 99.5 per cent of public borrowing in that period, analysis by the New Economics Foundation found.

Normally, if the government wants to up its borrowing from say £34 billion to a cool £261 billion, the bond market would, to use a technical term, freak out. (This actually happened when Liz Truss proposed huge unfunded tax cuts in her 2022 'mini-budget'.) Central banks' stupendous bond-buying programme effectively slipped the market a tranquilliser, keeping debt costs down and making it possible for the government to borrow like it was going out of style. The same thing happened in the US during Covid, where the Fed loaded up on US government debt. Where do central banks get the money for all of this? They print it. That's their superpower.

Long before I started writing about finance, I was aware that some people thought QE was a dodgy practice. One reason to have your central banks as a politically independent institution run by experts is that the ability to click your fingers and *have more money* is so powerful. Independence stops spendthrift politicians from printing money to solve short-term problems, thereby making their currencies worthless and hobbling their economies. QE sceptics think that the whole complex dance of bond issuance and bond purchases looks uncomfortably similar to the central bank recklessly printing money and handing it to the government. Some think central bankers need to show the government more tough love, for the sake of the long term. But in the face of the Covid crisis, those concerns went out of the window. All the economic power brokers were pointing in the same direction – and that direction was to get cheap money out of the door fast.

Watching the effect of cheap money transmitting through the economy is like watching the tide. You can't see the change as it is happening. But if you look away for a little while and then glance back, the effect is obvious. If you woke an economist up from a 20-year coma in the midst of the crypto craze, showed them SBF's Twitter feed and asked them to guess whether money was expensive or cheap – ten out of ten economists would say 'cheap . . . dangerously cheap'.

*

Within a year after central bankers and governments went all-in on pandemic stimulus, the first genuinely weird behaviour started to show up. It is a general rule of the internet that there is a Reddit chat forum for everything. But until January 2021 few people had probably ever heard of Wall Street Bets, outside the people who used the Reddit forum to share wild trading strategies and even more wildly profane memes. Traders caught on to the fact that short sellers were targeting the video game store GameStop. Short selling simply means betting that a stock will go down, a fairly aggressive strategy often pursued by hedge funds – a category of investor frequently cast as the bad guys of the financial world. I think it's safe to assume there's some healthy overlap between people who like to chat about trading strategies on Reddit and people who have fond memories of shopping for video games at a time when that still meant going to a store. Affection for the brand GameStop overlapped with a financial opportunity. If enough small traders could organise to buy GameStop shares, pushing up the price, they could hope to trigger a market dynamic called a 'short squeeze'. The flip side of short sellers betting a stock will fall means that if it rises, the short seller starts to lose money. The squeeze comes in when they rush to close out their trade and limit their losses, which involves buying up shares, pushing the price even higher. The result would be profits for the Reddit investors who owned GameStop shares, and losses for the hedge funds who had bet on it to fail. The name of the trading app that became popular as a place to execute this daring plan to steal from the rich could not have been better chosen: Robinhood.

At the start of 2021, about 10,000 accounts traded GameStop shares on a normal day. By the peak of the Reddit traders' insurgency on 27 January, that number had risen to 900,000 – and the shares had risen 2,700 per cent in value. The GameStop short squeeze became one of those pivotal moments that define a trend. The idea that 'dumb money' retail investors could rebel against the supposedly super-smart hedge funds was electrifying. Hopeful amateurs tried to replicate the trick or exert their influence all over the place. And suddenly everyone was talking about trading. For a new generation of traders, the stock market looked like a great game. Here was a quest for untold wealth that you could take from the comfort of your living room.

Many explanations have been advanced for the wild rise of the 'meme stock' traders. But two crucial ones are that people had time on their hands and a little bit of money in their pockets. Americans saved $1.7 trillion in 2020, because Covid meant they had less opportunity to spend money. Most normal recreation and entertainment, like sports on TV or going outside, were still on hold. And government programmes had dished out quite a lot of cash, particularly the indiscriminate US airdrop of thousands of dollars to its citizens.

These factors certainly played a role in the next trading frenzy to catch people's attention: crypto. Trading volume in crypto skyrocketed from around $2 trillion per month at the end of 2020 to more than $10 trillion in May 2021. Crypto's appeal during that spring was compounded by a worry that the scale of central bank money printing during Covid was so epic that it might destabilise the value of real currencies like the dollar and the pound. Nearly a fifth of US dollars in circulation by early 2021 were created in 2020. People still thought Bitcoin might be a hedge against inflation.

The surge of interest first into meme stock and then into crypto trading is a textbook example of what happens when money is very, very cheap. It takes time for the effects to be visible, but financial markets tend to go feral simply because there is too much money and not enough places to put it. Once all the sensible ideas are used up, people go for the wackier ones.

Even the more polished world of professional investors is not immune. Lending money, particularly low risk lending to big companies or even governments – who are very likely to pay you back – is just about the safest option for investors who have a big pile of cash and want to see it grow. When money is relatively expensive, this can be a pretty profitable enterprise. If you have $10 million today, you can easily clear half a million in annual income while taking almost no risk at all of losing your fortune. But when money is cheap, these easy ways to make income dry up. Everyone from wealthy individuals to pension funds starts to hunt around for new options. They put pressure on the professional investors who are paid to manage all this cash. Investors get nervous about earning their keep, and hungrier to make a buck. The only way to do that, really, is to be more adventurous. Higher risk, higher potential reward.

Venture capital is one of the riskier corners of the market that benefits when investors are hungry for profits, and ready to take some extra risk to get it. Venture funds raised the most money on record in 2021. The sector's reputation was cemented by the enormous successes scored by those who invested early in the Big Tech companies. Facebook's 2012 IPO made many of its investors billionaires. When Facebook in turn bought WhatsApp in 2014, Sequoia reportedly made $3 billion off its initial $60 million investment.

Enthusiasm for the fundamentally speculative business of backing unproven companies was barely dented by two stunning failures, which followed the glory days of the early tech giants. Elizabeth Holmes convinced investors to part with around $1 billion before it turned out that the blood-testing machines made by her startup Theranos didn't work. The year Theranos came unstuck, 2018, Adam Neumann convinced investors to let him burn $150 million a month. The mission of his unprofitable co-working startup, WeWork, wasn't to make money. It was to 'elevate the world's consciousness'. Holmes went to jail over Theranos's failure. Neumann never faced similar allegations. He got paid a fortune, reportedly more than $1 billion, to go away. Both founders had big ideas and even bigger ambitions. They cultivated over-the-top personas. Their undoing was not enough to make people think twice about SBF.

*

By the summer of 2021, powerful tectonic forces in the financial markets had combined to create the most fertile possible ground for SBF to raise money. Venture capital firms were flush with cash and under pressure to get it out of the door. These firms like to think that their wins in funding the rise of Silicon Valley were not just financial. These are investors who want to change the world. They are always on the lookout for the next big thing. And the flood of easy money into the financial system had created a boom in speculative trading, which vastly increased prices and activity in crypto, making it look like a very plausible candidate for an innovation whose time had come.

SBF was clear-eyed about the dynamic he took advantage of. 'Especially in 2021, every VC had to invest in at least one crypto company,' he told me. 'If you don't do it, and crypto goes up more, every single one of your investors is going to come to you and say: "My neighbour invested in this VC and got 10x returns because they invested in crypto. Did you invest in crypto?" Collectively, they had to invest at least $10 billion in crypto that year.'

His analysis reflects the fact that, in the minds of many venture investors, missing the crypto train as it pulled out of the station would be much worse than putting some money into a couple of crypto companies that ultimately went off the rails. Their model tolerates bad bets, and prioritises getting in early. As it turned out, SBF was right about the trend but wrong about the size. Venture capital invested $33 billion into crypto in 2021, more than in every previous year in the history of crypto, combined.

'To my mind, this is a VC story. They are the ones who built the industry,' said Hilary Allen, the American University professor. 'I think we are long past a reckoning with VC. They are so prone to inflating bubbles.'

The popularity of crypto also benefited the VCs themselves, who used the enthusiasm to raise vast sums of new money for their own funds. Facebook veteran Marc Andreessen's firm a16z led the charge with a $2.2 billion crypto fund raised in June 2021, one of dozens of mammoth funds opened that year. The pressure to invest all that money, combined with the relative lack of grown-up-looking crypto companies, meant that by the time SBF logged on to his Zoom call with the Sequoia partners, the balance of power had shifted heavily in favour of startups like FTX and against the investors who they were supposedly pitching to.

Still, at some point in the process, even the keenest investor should sharpen their pencils, open up a company's books and do their homework on whether it really is as good as it appears. Looking back on that due diligence must be the most uncomfortable part of the story for FTX's investors.

Legendary

'I think you can argue investors overpaid by a factor of two. If this deal happened in 2018, then arguably the valuation would have been half,' said someone closely involved in the investment process. They added: 'It doesn't seem like an egregious example of decision-making.'

It is hard to believe that anyone could defend an investment process that ended so disastrously. Certainly, it's not a position people are very comfortable taking in public. But my contact is not alone. The accusation that investors simply 'didn't do their due diligence' on FTX is not true. Some later investors did rely on the work that their peers had done, and trusted that the early, big name investors had put FTX through its paces. That is not unusual. 'Not every single investor does diligence. The way it typically works in the startup space is that you have a lead investor and other investors rely on them to do diligence,' said another person closely involved in FTX's fundraising.

FTX had been made to jump through hoops. Investors pored over data, prepared vast memos, held meetings with executives and even commissioned background checks on SBF and other top executives. Some of the big name firms spent months on the process. Crypto regulation was a major focus. Investors did not want to see FTX end up in the same kind of trouble as BitMEX.

The fact that investors did these checks makes the puzzle even more interesting. How did these enquiries fail to spot warning signs? One reason is that the diligence process relies heavily on general information about the market and specific information provided by the company itself to assess the potential of the business. It is not a forensic audit. Asked about their diligence process in

January 2022, Sequoia partner Alfred Lin said: 'In retrospect, we looked at a bunch of things but, reflecting on it, we were misled.' In other words, Lin is saying, *It's not our fault. FTX lied to us.* One of the people involved was more blunt. Catching fraud, they said, 'is not the business model of venture capital. Even if it were, it is such a hard fucking thing to do.'

The other insider echoed this. 'Diligence is not 100 per cent bulletproof or foolproof. You need to know where to point your questions,' they said. Investors 'were not thinking about Sam potentially stealing user money . . . [they] just didn't point the light bulb in that direction'. In fairness, they added, many of the investors did their checks in 2021, a year or so before the worst of FTX's misdeeds. 'It's a matter of one, the timing of the diligence. And two, it doesn't prevent the CEO and a close group of confidants from – after you have invested – stealing customer funds.'

*

SBF himself still denies that he ever knowingly lied to investors. 'I was, in general, pretty careful not to lie,' he told me. 'I don't necessarily think that I was maximally forthcoming in what I was saying . . . but I was answering the question that was asked.' He said he thought the venture capital industry was '60 to 70 per cent bullshit. There is something real going on there, but a lot of it is bullshit.'

'There is very much a great leader philosophy among VCs,' he went on. 'There are huge positive feedback cycles with investors, because they all talk to each other . . . In context, no one was looking to create red flags if they didn't have to.'

Another element that played into SBF's favour is the sheer speed at which these investment processes were sometimes taking place, particularly in ultra-hot markets like 2021. Speaking later in the year, after backing FTX, Bailhe said: 'We try to move extremely quickly . . . Especially this year, you might have to make a decision within five days or less.' By that standard, the time they spent on FTX looks generous.

The way venture investors make these tight timelines work is by doing lots of research in advance, studying the market so that they already know which companies they would like to invest in if the opportunity comes along. Bailhe recalled a conversation with Ramnik Arora, the FTX executive who ran its fundraising, talking about SBF's bravura performance in the Sequoia partners' meeting. 'Ramnik was joking later with us, being like, "Did you guys just invest because Sam is so charismatic?"' she said. '[We] were like, "No, we do our home-work. We did our homework way in advance. We knew FTX was an amazing company and we knew Sam was an amazing founder."' Her comment is revealing of the way in which doing so much research in advance, before having the chance to look at the nitty-gritty of a company's internal data and how it's run, can introduce bias.

It's worth saying, there's no evidence that Sequoia's investment process around FTX was particularly weak. If anything, the firm has a reputation for being among the most diligent venture capitalists, and other people involved in the FTX process were impressed by Sequoia's thoroughness. The firm has highlighted the relatively small scale of its FTX investment compared to the giant scale of its fund.

'If you want to look at egregious examples of investing in 2021, FTX is not at the top of that list,' one person involved in the process told me. The VC process is tilted towards trying to judge how fast a race car can go, rather than figuring out if the driver might veer off the road and crash into the stands, or if under the bonnet some of the spark plugs are made of cheese. And from 2019 until late 2022, crypto looked like the fastest car around. The crash has left many venture firms badly bruised, and some investors with what looks like a crisis of confidence.

Lin, the Sequoia partner, was grilled about his leading role in the FTX investment by a TechCrunch journalist at an event in early 2022. Formerly a key executive at Zappos, Lin has sat on the boards of major companies including DoorDash, Airbnb and the financial group Citadel. At times he seemed to defend the firm's decision-making, noting that it expects to strike out on 30 per cent of its bets. But he also alluded to how profoundly cases like FTX challenge the venture model.

'The one thing I think about . . . the venture industry, it's a trust business. And yes we need to trust and verify. And we try to verify what we can. But we start from a position of trust. Because if we don't trust the founders that we work with, why would we ever invest in them?' he said.

'The thing that gets me to reassess is, it's not that we made the investment. It is the year and a half working relationship afterwards, that I still didn't see it. And that is difficult.'

*

SBF loved to see FTX do the impossible. One of the most remarkable capers the company managed to pull off is also one of the most famous. In February 2022, somewhere around 80 million people watched as FTX achieved the ultimate prize in US marketing: a 60-second slot at the Super Bowl. For anyone who hasn't seen it, the ad is really worth watching in full for an insight into genuinely lethal advertising.

The main character is a time-travelling curmudgeon who flashes forward through the centuries, from the invention of the wheel to the US Constitutional Convention to the workshop of Thomas Edison. At every breakthrough, he is unimpressed. The wheel? 'One of the worst ideas I've ever heard.' Democracy? 'No King? Gentlemen, have you taken leave of your senses?' The light bulb? 'It stinks.'

You'll have guessed what comes next. 'It's FTX, a safe and easy way to get into crypto,' says a reasonable-looking chap in a blue checked shirt. 'Ahhhh, I don't think so. And I'm never wrong about this stuff. Never,' says the sceptic, played by, of all people, Larry David.

The comedian was perfect for the role. The co-creator of *Seinfeld* and star of *Curb Your Enthusiasm* had made his career through a sceptical brand of humour. He is a household name who has maintained enough of a cynical reputation to make him the last person you'd cast as a hype man or a corporate shill. Equally, the concept of the ad brilliantly upended the position of crypto sceptics. Reluctance to jump on the crypto bandwagon is not prudence or good sense, the ad is saying. It makes you a flat-Earther, a dolt, a stick-in-the-mud standing against the inevitable march of progress.

The addition of not just conventional 'tech' breakthroughs, like electric lights, but also political milestones, like the American

Constitution, and everyday objects we now take completely for granted, like the wheel, is particularly shrewd. Crypto isn't just tech. Maybe we all rolled our eyes at the latest new VR gadgets coming out of Silicon Valley. Crypto is bigger than that. It's a world-changing, historic invention that will make people rethink how they live their lives in a form just as profound as representative government or rolling stuff around. By the time the ad aired, cryptomania was at such a peak that refusing to follow the herd chasing digital assets could actually start to look like the smart thing to do. The ad combated that logic with a rebuttal that was based on an obvious truth: there have been sceptics who pooh-poohed every great breakthrough in history. In retrospect, they look really dumb. Suddenly, the slogan that flashes on the screen at the end of the commercial – 'Don't miss out' – isn't a dangerous incitement to 'FOMO'. FTX is giving the viewer the opportunity not to be stupid.

SBF watched the game in a box, taking pictures with Katy Perry, Orlando Bloom and Kate Hudson. The ad was viewed by the massive Super Bowl TV audience, shared far and wide on social media and viewed tens of millions more times on YouTube. And it bought FTX reams of free promotion in the world's media. The multi-million-dollar price tag looked cheap at twice the price. And it also almost didn't happen.

The origins of the ad went back over a year, to just before the previous year's Super Bowl, when FTX executives were brainstorming about 'what is the biggest impact we can have in the shortest amount of time' to raise the company's profile, according to Nathaniel Whittemore, who had led FTX's marketing since late 2020.

Legendary

'My memory is that Sam said, "Well, have we thought about doing a Super Bowl ad?" We are talking about literally three weeks before the Super Bowl or something,' said Whittemore in a later interview. While it was too late to secure a slot for the 2021 event, the idea of shooting for this ultimate target stuck around. FTX called for ideas from ad agencies. It was Dentsu Creative – an agency that has worked with brands from Oreo to Volkswagen – that won the pitch with the idea of a sceptical time traveller. From the start, FTX had its heart set on Larry David: 'The image that was used to first pitch it was Larry David. That was immediately the only person who we were interested in having do it,' Whittemore recalled.

One problem. David had never done a commercial for any brand. Ever. Why would he start with a risky foray into crypto? Luckily for FTX, David was already within reach of its growing network of stars. The comedian's agency, WME, is part of the powerhouse talent group Endeavor, run by Hollywood's most famous agent, Ari Emanuel. Emanuel invited David to officiate his wedding later that year. Another spoke of the Endeavor network is IMG, an agency that represented supermodel Gisele Bündchen. Both she and her husband at the time, NFL superstar Tom Brady, were shareholders in FTX, alongside their own endorsement deals. The agency IMG had also invested in the company.

Sina Nader, a former Morgan Stanley and Credit Suisse banker, who had ditched finance for crypto and became pivotal to building FTX's celebrity network, explained that connections were key to clinching the deals. 'It still required some convincing. Because crypto is a new thing for many people. Larry had never done anything like this. And he didn't know who the hell we are. So he had to get some validation, and he was able to get that validation from another one of our partners that he had worked with,' he said in a summer 2022 interview. It certainly can't have hurt that FTX agreed to pay David $10 million for a one-year contract, according to the company's records.

Early on, convincing celebrities to stake their reputation on an unknown crypto company had been an uphill struggle. Nader used a former college football teammate who had gone on to play on Brady's winning Super Bowl teams to open the door to the legendary quarterback. One celebrity connection led to another. 'The interesting thing there was that once you sort of get the ball rolling and once there's a few partners that have validated you . . . that word validation I think is very accurate, then it becomes easier for others to be open to validating you,' he said.

That word, 'validation', is borrowed from the language of crypto tech. Different nodes in a network validate a transaction to establish trust. It is indeed a perfect description of how FTX made itself an accepted player in US media, politics and celebrity culture. Its entrance into the mainstream was supported by a sort of quadruple helix of blue chip investment, celebrity endorsement, promised philanthropy and political clout. The four strands supported each other in a spiral of increasing confidence. Splashy marketing raised SBF's profile and made FTX look hot to investors. Prominent early investors convinced people outside finance that FTX's business must be legit. Financial success gave credibility to SBF's extraordinary plans to give away his fortune, which appealed to celebrity backers (alongside plenty of cash). High profile endorsements brought more customers, and raised SBF's profile to the point where he came on the radar in Washington DC. Having the ear of the powerful, from Capitol Hill to Hollywood Boulevard, made FTX even more the hot deal that yet more investors wanted to back. And so the cycle escalated. Documents sent to investors in 2022 read: 'FTX has an industry-leading brand, endorsed by some of the most trustworthy public figures, including Tom Brady, MLB, Gisele Bündchen, Steph Curry, and the Miami Heat, and backed by an industry-leading set of investors. FTX has the cleanest brand in crypto.' Everyone was validating, but no one was checking. Surely someone else had already made sure that this guy was for real?

FTX's approach to celebrity marketing was unique. In interviews, FTX executives liked to talk as if they were slightly too smart for the marketing world and above its tedious conventions. The idea of 'performance marketing', where companies try to carefully measure the impact of publicity and tabulate the value for money, was too pedestrian. FTX didn't buy that all these metrics were reliable. In this, they may have had a point. But the bean-counting approach also didn't fit with the company's hyperspeed culture. Instead, FTX threw itself into a steroidal version of 'brand marketing', which is all about simply getting your name out there and not worrying too much about whether the cost is worth the pay-off.

'We didn't use the term brand advertising versus performance advertising versus endorsement. We used some of those words but they didn't mean what other people would have thought that they meant,' said Whittemore. 'Really it was the "Cambrian explosion" of short-cutting and supercharging and super-speeding how fast people get to know who we are.

'The end goal is not a specific set of numbers that get spun out of that Rube Goldberg machine to help us know how it performed from a user acquisition standpoint. It is when I walk down the street, when we were just meeting our neighbours for the first time, and he said, "Oh, you're the Tom Brady exchange." That's kind of the goal . . . A lot of brand recognition is just repetition, repetition, repetition.'

What FTX understood about how marketing and celebrity works is that it's almost impossible to compare the value of a celebrity deal with Tom Brady or a Formula One team with normal advertising. FTX thought the endorsements, even if they cost tens of millions, were worth an infinite amount of carefully targeted Facebook ads. Their spending was jaw-dropping. Some deals included payment in FTX stock, not pure cash. Others were long-term commitments, like the decades-long Miami stadium agreement. Still, company records show FTX paid nearly $150 million for its celebrity and sports sponsorships in 2021. In 2022, they were on track to spend almost $200 million. Overall, the company had committed to deals that could cost $1.13 billion.

SBF would also pay handsomely for access to valuable connections. He committed millions to an investment deal with a former aide to Hillary Clinton, turned celebrity agent and investor, named Michael Kives. Kives impressed SBF as 'probably, the most connected person I've ever met'. SBF attended a dinner at Kives's house with Clinton, Kamala Harris's husband Doug Emhoff and a laundry list of celebrities including Katy Perry, Orlando Bloom, Kate Hudson, Leonardo DiCaprio and Jeff Bezos. In a memo shortly after, SBF praised Kives's 'essentially infinite connections' and the possibility of working together on 'potential unpaid partnerships with celebrities . . . political relationships . . . [and] electoral politics'. Kives lawyers have said that he was 'as surprised and dismayed as everyone else' to learn about SBF's fraud.

SBF told me that the reputation building was targeted, mainly, at elite circles where he needed to have influence. 'Branding stuff just helped us with everything,' he said. 'You get major implicit regulatory points for having an NBA stadium named after you. Even if no one explicitly makes that argument . . . Regulators, banks, policy makers, large potential institutional clients, media, politicians, investors; those are all categories of people who mattered to us and would hear about FTX Arena.'

He said he thought the marketing blitz made a '2x' difference to FTX's valuation. In other words, having Tom Brady onside and a stadium named after them led investors to think the company was worth double the value they would otherwise have attached to it. That makes $135 million look cheap. It was also remarkably circular, since you could spend investors' money on branding moves that would make more investors give you more money. 'Empirically, it did seem to have impact. They all brought it up,' SBF said. 'I did feel like it revolutionised our reputation in institutional circles.'

*

The huge expenditure on building connections and notoriety was supported by a lot of free publicity. SBF was not initially interested in the press, which fit with his character as a maverick founder who was intensely focused on the 'expected value' of every second of his time. What was the point of gassing with journalists and dealing with their half-baked questions? Plus, meeting new people plainly made SBF physically uncomfortable. 'Early on, Sam had no interest in PR,' said a close former employee. An early appearance on Bloomberg TV helped to start changing his mind. SBF came to see clearly that being a media personality opened exactly the doors he needed, with investors, regulators and politicians. The more interviews he gave, the better it got.

'He was so good at it naturally,' said the former employee. Most CEOs go through hours of media training before facing the press, and often put on a pretty dismal show. Without that kind of instruction, SBF intuitively mastered the role of celebrity chief executive. Rather than redirecting questions back to his talking points or trotting out industry consensus views and clichés that journalists loathe (personally, 'I don't have a crystal ball' is the one I hate the most), SBF was almost always ready to be interviewed and give an original – often controversial – take.

When I sat down with him in an early interview, he gave me a meta aside on his media philosophy, reflecting on how patently phoney many CEOs sound when they answer a question. 'You'll hear [them] and you're like, first of all, an hour went into crafting that answer. They used a word that no one has ever used in speech before, unless they're reading from a note card. It's too long of a word. And there's a simpler, easier word that 100 per cent of the time you would use,' he said. 'Second of all, like, everyone knows, that was inauthentic, right? Like, it just doesn't sound like it's a real answer. So like, already, there's no win from having done it.'

Legendary

SBF understood that the bullshit trade practised in so many corporate interviews is a pretty pointless, performative exercise. The point, he told me, is that 'I want to be in a position in which when there's something which is important and true, and I have no evidence for, that I can say it and people will take my statements seriously. It's incredibly important. And, like, in order to be in that position, I have to generally give straightforward, honest answers.'

Whether his answers were actually straightforward and honest is something US prosecutors, among others, would later decidedly question. However, he gave a masterful impression of it. The media largely failed to penetrate the illusion until it was too late. SBF was so smart, and so ready to be interesting, that it was easy for him to distract questioners from their lines of enquiry. 'Sam is very good at not answering the question,' said one senior FTX exec.

When SBF was crypto's golden boy, a little bit of obfuscation didn't stop him booking plenty of TV slots. SBF became a journalist's dream, an endlessly accessible, super-fluent CEO who put a face to crypto and captured the moment of wild financial excess. We ate up the colourful details, from his haircut to his hard-core ethics, and delighted in the intellectual contradiction of a man running an online casino while promising to change the world with his philanthropy.

*

Those charitable pledges were another key plank of how he built his platform, particularly when it came to winning over celebrities at a time when they are ever more concerned about signalling their virtue. The idea that this twenty-something crypto billionaire, who could literally throw himself a cocaine-fuelled yacht party full of supermodels every night if he wanted to, had instead decided to be a board-game-playing vegan who made earnest speeches about the importance of bug nets to prevent malaria was an irresistible draw. A pitch presentation prepared by FTX ended with the line: 'One percent of all net revenues are donated to the world's most effective charities, and many of our members have given substantially more.' Indeed, SBF's personal pledge was much more: giving away 99 per cent of what he earned. The language is also an interesting clue. FTX doesn't have 'employees', it has 'members'. Basking in the philanthropic aura, many people in the FTX orbit talked as if the company itself was basically a charity.

Charmed by SBF, the pop star Kate Perry posted to Instagram in February 2022: 'I'm quitting music and becoming an intern for FTX ok.' This promotion of FTX was tame by comparison to other celebrities' crypto shilling. In June 2021, Kim Kardashian posted a breathless promo for a token called Ethereum Max to her 225 million Instagram followers. Ethereum Max, which is not actually related to the real Ethereum, barely made a pretence of offering any new technology or value. But it did pay Kardashian $250,000 to hype it up – alongside deals with other stars. The token was a classic example of what crypto calls a 'pump and dump'. Its founders created an essentially worthless coin, and paid celebrities to sell it. As the public started buying, the founders sold their own stock of the coin at a profit. A week after Kardashian posted, the token had lost 70 per cent of its value. It never recovered. Kardashian paid $1.3 million to settle with the SEC over the case.

Legendary

Not every crypto scheme could recruit Kim K. But the same pattern was repeated thousands of times on a lesser or greater scale. Crypto's hype squad includes armies of dedicated influencers – some with millions of followers – as well as questionable websites masquerading as cryptocurrency news outlets. Token promoters could buy influence with a few thousand dollars paid to the right influencers, who themselves were frequently accused of profiting off insider information about the obscure coins that they promote. It's tricky to gauge the scale of this machine for rinsing gullible investors. The crypto analytics firm Chainalysis looked for tokens that lost most of their value shortly after launch as a sign of likely pump and dumps. Of around 40,000 crypto tokens launched in 2022 that gained a decent level of traction, a quarter lost 90 per cent of their value in the first week. Against this backdrop, FTX's use of celebrities to build an apparently squeaky-clean brand looked like innocence itself. 'They had a sterling social media reputation. Everyone was talking about Sam like he was a crypto messiah,' said an employee who joined FTX in early 2022, thanks in part to its positive reputation.

*

SBF's charitable pledges also helped SBF's image in Washington DC, as did another more direct set of donations. After giving millions to Joe Biden's presidential campaign, SBF was the number two backer of the Democrats in the 2022 midterms, after George Soros. Prosecutors charge that he spent more than $100 million on political donations. A key nexus for his political activities was the foundation led by his brother, Gabriel Bankman-Fried, dedicated to tackling an issue that was understandably top of the agenda in 2020 and 2021: stopping the next global pandemic. Their circle indulged in some out-there brainstorming. Extracts from a document sent to Gabe covered whether to buy the island nation of Nauru to build a 'bunker / shelter' in case of 'some event where 50%–99.99% of people die [to] ensure that most EAs [effective altruists] survive'. 'Probably there are other things it's useful to do with a sovereign country, too,' the paper noted. Behind the scenes, the FTX lobbying operation could be far more cynical than its public goals suggested. One consultant wrote to Nishad that 'you being the centre left face of our spending will mean you giving to a lot of woke shit for transactional purposes'.

Unaware of these private discussions, Washington welcomed the Bankman-Frieds. 'Ninety-nine per cent of [the pure political donations] was Sam, Nishad and Ryan Salame in concert and in coordination with Gabe Bankman-Fried and the Guarding Against Pandemics apparatus,' said someone close to FTX's Washington operation. The willingness to write big cheques, and the promise to write more, undoubtedly smoothed SBF's entry into the halls of power.

FTX US had a parallel lobbying operation, focused on changing American financial rules to let FTX offer its most lucrative derivatives products to the massive US market. 'Sam was spending time in DC to push on the regulatory agenda because of its importance to the company,' said the former FTX insider in Washington. For years, crypto companies had banged their head against the door in DC without much success. The industry's stance was often too combative. People like Alex Mashinsky talking about how regulators were in hock to big banks, out to get crypto, and bent on stifling innovation were not going to win friends.

SBF came to Washington ready to listen, but also ready to teach. FTX was ever ready to help 'educate' lawmakers about digital assets (a word that crypto people have shamelessly stolen for progressive discourse and which in this context means 'convince to agree with me'). He took dozens of meetings with senior regulators, members of Congress on key financial committees, and even senior White House officials. Soon, politicians were starting to call him, for public testimony and private chats, about how they could get a handle on crypto. With millions of Americans trading digital assets, lawmakers had realised they needed to catch up and were keen, even desperate, for a trusted expert who could help them. 'People thought he was brilliant and people thought they could learn from him and his successes in how to regulate the crypto industry,' the lobbyist told me.

SBF excelled in these private sessions, patient, charming and persuasive. 'One of the things that I marvelled at at the time is that the public version of SBF was the same version that I saw in those meetings. I think the lawmakers, just like the investors and others, were very impressed with him. He came off as very honest and earnest and sincere,' the DC insider said. 'He never seemed annoyed with the time he spent with these members, and as you can imagine some of them didn't ask the most thoughtful question . . . There was never a time when he would come out of the meeting and say, "Ah, what a bullshit person that congressman was."'

The apparent consistency between SBF in public and private added to the sense of authenticity that he knew played so well in the media. With his shorts and frizzy hair, SBF was an unconventional 'face of crypto'. But his undoubted strangeness was part of his charm. One story from the SBF legend has it that when an important potential lender turned up for a first meeting, SBF had accidentally fallen asleep on his beanbag. The lender apparently concluded he must be an honest partner. No fraudster would have dreamed of being caught napping. For á lot of people, it just didn't seem plausible that, if SBF's persona was an act, he would have chosen such a weird act. Surely someone trying to deceive them would have been more polished.

At the same time, SBF had an implicit understanding of how to speak the language of the US elite. He was born to it. He was educated at the top schools. His parents were respected professors. His mother was a major democratic organiser. Other crypto luminaries, like CZ or Mashinsky, tended to be outsiders. SBF was steeped in the culture of America's coastal elite. In the aftermath of the collapse, Arthur Hayes tellingly wrote that SBF was 'the right kind of white boy'.

'SBF played the game on the meta level, and traded social currency – hoodwinking the Western financial establishment and the crypto industry alike in the process,' Hayes wrote.

After the fact, SBF was straightforward with me about the edge his elite background gave him. 'I was way better situated than other non-American crypto exchange CEOs to break into that because I was American. I speak English. I can talk with American politicians. Whatever.'

There are a few instances where the pretence around SBF slipped. In the pitch presentation, FTX called itself 'the largest non-Chinese crypto exchange'. Although it is practically true that the larger exchanges would be harder for Americans to invest in, the xenophobic undertone is barely concealed. Perhaps the translation is: the largest crypto exchange you can trust.

Chatting via Twitter messages with Vox journalist Kelsey Piper late at night, shortly after FTX collapsed, SBF was even more unguarded. (He said he thought the conversation was a private chat with a 'friend'. She said they had 'very little interaction . . . outside an interview for Vox conducted eight months ago'.) The conversation is fascinating. 'You were really good at talking about ethics, for someone who kind of saw it all as a game of winners and losers,' Piper said. 'I had to be,' SBF replied. 'It's what reputations are made of, to some extent. I feel bad for those who get fucked by it . . . by this dumb game we woke westerners play where we say all the right shibboleths and so everyone likes us.'

But back in 2021, SBF was still playing this game like a master. Called to testify on Capitol Hill in front of the powerful House Financial Service Committee, he even ditched his trademark shorts. SBF turned up to the hearing looking like his aides had bought a suit at Walmart that morning and hustled their boss into the new clothes in the congressional waiting room. As SBF gave his customarily smooth answers to lawmakers' questions, people spotted that – under the table – his shoelaces were untied. It turned out that this was not the only untidy detail that the FTX founder would prefer to have remained unseen.

*

Hype Machine

A story circulated around the FTX staff in Nassau. By and large, people in the Bahamian capital were affectionate, even protective, towards SBF. Locals were charmed by his boyishness and excited about what one of the world's hottest tech companies could do for their island's economy. This was true of the young man who drove me across the island for a meeting with SBF. As we sped along the narrow, left-hand-drive roads in his maroon Honda, listening to Christian rock on the radio, he told me how he'd been an embalmer at a local undertakers until he'd been hired to work in logistics for FTX. What is Sam like as a boss? 'He's the best,' he said.

SBF himself normally did not use a driver. His battered Toyota Corolla was, like the shorts or the beanbag chair, one of the key props that defined his character as someone who didn't care about material possessions. He would regularly drive himself between his home and the FTX office, across a relatively desolate part of the island, past the scrubby trees and sunburned grass. Given SBF's notorious sleep schedule, he quite often took this route – always the same route – in the total silence of the small hours of the morning. Alone.

The story, which I heard from an ex-FTXer, started with a few employees going out to dinner. Groups of FTX staff were pretty easy to spot in Nassau. A server eyed the party and came over to the table. 'Do you work for FTX,' he asked. It turned out that one of the server's family worked as a cleaner at the FTX office. He said all the cleaners were anxious about SBF, driving the lonely roads in a predictable pattern at night. 'Someone is going to kidnap that little boy,' he said, according to my contact's retelling.

This episode added to worries that had been simmering about SBF's personal security as the amount of money held in FTX's digital vaults grew and grew. Other crypto CEOs had bodyguards. For anyone who has the reputation of being rich in crypto, there is a constant risk that thieves might threaten them into unlocking their wallets – or blackmail their company into doing the same. The CEO of one major custodian told me he makes a point of saying, as often as he can in public, that he doesn't even know the codes to access the company's assets.

SBF refused to take precautions. At the time, his stance – although it deeply worried some FTX staff – also had admirers. There was something almost messianic about his lack of concern for his own safety. Why waste time and money on something that would distract from FTX's mission to change the world? In retrospect, of course, it was unconscionably reckless. SBF didn't want security because it was awkward and inconvenient. It would annoy him. The risk was real, if still small, that he could be targeted. And it was not just a question of his personal safety. If SBF was in danger, the company would be put under enormous pressure to hand over billions of dollars' worth of their clients' money.

'There was a constant war, where I was trying not to have security guards and my employees were trying to make sure I had security guards,' SBF told me. The company was 'losing productivity' worrying about me, he said. 'When I would push back on this, rather than giving me arguments they would very quickly get emotional and pissy and defensive. There is a flavour-of-the-month nature to people's concerns. There would be, for a couple of months, something it was cool to be concerned about, and everyone at the company would be freaking out about it. It seemed to rotate somewhat at random. They weren't crazy things to be concerned about, but it seemed arbitrary. I was generally in the position of saying this new concern is dumb. I probably did that too much. I probably ended up in a pissy dismissive mood.'

I said I thought his refusal to take personal security seriously pointed to not being very inclined to worry about, or try to prevent, unlikely risks – even if the consequences could be severe. 'That is basically right,' he said. 'The risk with that is if you're not careful about which of the risks is a 1 in 20 or 1 in a million.'

That attitude and lack of caution was evident from the top to the bottom of FTX's operations. The cryptographic keys to digital assets come in two parts: the public key, which identifies the assets on the blockchain, and the private key, which lets you access them. Essentially the public key is the address that tells you where the house is. The private key opens the door. At big crypto companies, or for large amounts of money, owners often add additional security by requiring multiple separate keys to authorise access to their funds – like requiring two separate missile keys to launch the nuclear weapons on a submarine. Professionals also normally keep most of their assets in cold wallets, which are devices not connected to the internet. Because they are physically offline, cold wallets are much safer from hackers. Internet-accessible hot wallets are essential for doing business, like the pile of chips in front of the blackjack dealer in a casino. But you want most of the money to be downstairs in the vault.

In 2022, FTX said it kept only two days' worth of assets needed for trading in internet-connected hot wallets, while the rest were in cold storage, 'which means only a small proportion of assets held are exposed to the internet; the remaining assets are stored offline in air-gapped encrypted laptops, which are geographically distributed'. According to the team of bankruptcy experts now running FTX, who are in the process of snooping around and airing SBF's dirty laundry, these reassurances about security were strictly for show. FTX seemingly had no particular system for where it kept the keys to hundreds of millions or billions of dollars' worth of their clients' crypto. Some keys were stored, unencrypted, in relatively accessible online servers. Others were kept in commercial password manager software. Some were labelled simply 'use this' or 'do not use'.

Cyber security, according to these reports, was equally chaotic. Dozens of people had access to central wallets holding billions of crypto. FTX did not even effectively require all its employees to have two-factor authentication for its Google accounts or password managers, even though SBF recommended the measure to his Twitter followers. '90% of crypto security is making sure you've done the basics,' he tweeted. The whole enterprise relied overwhelmingly on a tiny number of core employees, who had built most of FTX's systems themselves, who knew where everything was and how to run the machine. 'If Nishad got hit by a bus, the whole company would be done. Same issue with Gary,' one former executive said.

Everything was controlled from the inner circle. It was understood inside the company that some of the people who nominally held important positions didn't really do those jobs. Of the company's official chief financial officer, a former employee said: 'I genuinely don't think she understood what was going on financially.' SBF was urged to staff up, to add professionals to handle cyber security, bookkeeping and risk management. In key roles like tech, finance and legal he was very slow to hire. 'Sam told me he would rather take the risk of something blowing up than having someone who was not right for the culture. He wants to find someone who is perfect. But I don't really understand his standard of perfect,' the former employee said.

'We also made hiring unnecessarily tough for ourselves by being located in the Bahamas which is sort of a random island that no one wants to go to,' said another former senior executive, who said FTX was moving so fast that it struggled to recruit new employees. Eventually, hiring was actually slowed down to allow time to integrate new arrivals. 'We wanted to stop growing in headcount, but we also recognised that things were falling apart. The app was getting slower. There was technical debt that was piling up. There were personnel issues. A lot of the hiring was blocked by Sam.'

Some of those personnel issues were focused inside the penthouse where SBF lived with his closest associates, and where decision-making really lay. Most of the inner circle were romantically entangled. SBF and Caroline had an on-again-off-again romance. Gary was in a long-term relationship with an employee. Nishad's girlfriend, Claire Watanabe, who oversaw people management and some marketing, was particularly unpopular, according to several former employees who felt she'd been promoted quickly. 'A lot of people internally were not very happy with that management arrangement,' said one. 'She came from nowhere, joined the company and became very important right away.'

Whether it was cyber security or personnel, the FTX culture was to breeze past these snags and inconsistencies in the headlong pursuit of growth. The ethos from Alameda's early days – don't worry too much about the mistakes unless you have to – was going strong. One former employee described their view of the management style: 'Anything that does break can pretty much be papered over by throwing money at it.' A lot of that money came from Alameda, which operated both as a trading firm and a sort of general purpose slush fund. The lines between SBF's personal fortune; Alameda, which he owned privately with Gary; and FTX, which had outside investors and handled client money, were blurred. FTX's new management say SBF 'operated with a near-total disregard for corporate formalities'. Spending across the companies would have made Louis XIV blush.

On arrival in the Bahamas, FTX spent a cool quarter of a billion dollars on 30 properties including its office and homes for employees, the equivalent of about 2 per cent of the country's 2022 GDP. The portfolio included a $30 million penthouse at the Albany, a 600-acre private compound home to some of the Bahamas' richest people. For those wishing to picture the scene, the James Bond film *Casino Royale* filmed some of its Bahamas sequences on the Albany beachfront. SBF's apartment was in a more modern part of the resort, which the Nassau elite considered slightly tacky. The five-bedroom apartment has an orchid-shaped plunge pool, wrap-around veranda and a view over the yachts in the Albany marina. SBF moved in with a posse of up to nine room-mates. They lived in the luxury apartment like it was the MIT frat house. The space was still decorated and furnished like it had been staged for a real estate agent's photo shoot, although someone had hung up a *Harry Potter* movie poster in the TV room, with its purple velvet walls and matching L-shaped sofa. The penthouse became the centre of SBF's court.

Alameda meanwhile invested huge sums in private companies and crypto ventures. After hanging out with Kives at the Super Bowl in 2022, for example, SBF negotiated a billion-dollar investment deal with his businesses. FTX's new management has launched a lawsuit to recover money from the deal. One part of the transaction included buying a stake in an investment company called MBK Capital from Kives and his business partner. The lawsuit claims that MBK's only asset was a 42 per cent stake in another company, K & Soda LLC, which serves as the distributor of 818 Tequila, the drinks brand promoted by Kendall Jenner – who is one of K & Soda's directors along with her mother, Kris. Corporate filings at the time put the value of those assets at just under $3 million. But SBF agreed to pay $214.5 million for a 38 per cent share of the company, overpaying by 200 times, the lawsuit claims. Kives has contested the lawsuit. His lawyers said that, overall, the assets SBF received from the deals 'were well worth the amounts invested and paid' and that any implication that Kives was 'complicit in SBF's wrongdoing has no basis in fact'.

The details of these transactions point to how cavalier SBF could be in his business decisions. The structure of the deal put owner-ship of the new investments in the hands of a company called SGN Albany, named for Sam, Gary, Nishad and the compound where they lived. Even though all the money came from Alameda, the trading firm only owned 8 per cent of SGN Albany while the three FTX founders personally owned the rest. So the deal effectively transferred hundreds of millions from Alameda to the three men.

Since SBF and Gary owned Alameda, perhaps they were enti-tled to make whatever deals they wanted to. But their management was often bizarre. SBF described Alameda in internal communications as 'hilariously beyond any threshold of any auditor being able to even get partially through an audit . . . Alameda is unauditable. I don't mean this in the sense of "a major accounting firm will have reservations about auditing it"; I mean this in the sense of "we are only able to ballpark what its balances are, let alone something like a comprehensive transaction history". We sometimes find $50 million of assets lying around that we had lost track of; such is life.' Even in this context, employees did raise concerns about whether SBF was making good decisions in his dealings with Kives and his businesses. But there was generally no stopping SBF from getting his way.

'There were a lot of "yes people" around,' said a former FTX staffer. Most FTX and Alameda employees had signed up because they admired SBF. He was one of the older figures in the company, respected to the point of worship. As FTX grew, and the gaps in how it was run became more glaring, there were few to challenge him. 'There were really, really massive vacuums of competence,' the staffer said.

'It was a mistake to build the company with people who thought of him as a superhero even from when he was in college,' they went on. 'At a certain point [SBF] believed the hype and he believed he could do more than he could do. He actually didn't have the professional expertise to make a lot of the decisions he was making . . . The move fast break things model was on hyperdrive.'

Speed is something venture capitalists tend to like. In November 2021, Sequoia's Bailhe said: 'I love how fast everyone at FTX moves . . . That is such a superpower. To move extremely quickly.

Not where you are not thinking about things. But where you are not overthinking things, not delaying things, not exploding things where they need 10,000 sign-offs for production, quality etc. Moving really fast is a superpower . . . that is something that I have learned at a different level from working with founders and everyone at FTX.'

The 'move fast and break things' motto, coined by Facebook's Mark Zuckerberg, had been pioneered by tech startups mostly working in social media. These companies got in plenty of trouble for issues like how they handled personal data or allowed misinformation. But in general, the consequences in the information business were less severe. John Carreyrou, the two-time Pulitzer Prize-winning reporter who played a key role in exposing fraud at Theranos when at the *Wall Street Journal*, observed that Holmes's company disastrously applied the 'fake it until you make it' culture of Silicon Valley tech companies to the realm of healthcare, where the stakes and the standards are higher. It's not uncommon for software CEOs' ambitions to run ahead of their company's capacity, to have chaotic bookkeeping, promise features that aren't quite ready or to release the app first and fix the bugs later. You really can't do that with products like Theranos's promised blood-testing machine.

A key part of what went wrong at FTX was that as the company grew to hold tens of billions, the huge weight of all that client money was resting on the same rickety structure. Even SBF now says this was a problem, even though he maintains the disaster at the company was an accident rather than fraud. He told me that the checks and procedures that would have caught the problems that ultimately sank FTX were probably a year away from being put in place. But he would not listen to the experts he tried to bring in to professionalise the operation. 'Every time we tried to bring adults into the room, they brought up dumb, irrelevant shit that distracted everyone . . . Had we had a risk management department, they may well have caught this way earlier. We probably should have had one . . . That is the risk of growing too quickly. I think that slowing down slightly from what we did would have been correct. Maybe 25 per cent slower.'

I'm not sure I agree that 25 per cent less growth is really only 'slightly' slower. And I certainly don't accept that FTX's demise was the result of innocent mistakes. But simply saying that fraud by SBF and his co-founders was the one and only reason that the company crashed is too simple an explanation. There were a hundred red flags that should have prompted SBF and those around him to slow things down. The responsibility of looking after billions of other people's dollars is not one you can shrug and walk away from.

There were people who saw these flags. At BlockFi, the lender which had made loans to SBF's companies, co-founder Flori Marquez wrote that she was worried about the risks posed by FTX's breakneck growth. 'I have questions of operational risk given how fast they scaled,' she said in private messages to CEO Zac Prince, in November 2021, a month after FTX had raised fresh money from investors.

Who should have pumped the brakes as it became clear that FTX was moving much too fast? The investors are high on the list, undoubted experts with decades of experience guiding the growth of young companies. One investor told me the structure of the deals with FTX limited their influence. 'FTX justified not giving any investor a board seat because each investor owned 1 per cent or less,' they said. 'While the dollars were large, every investor justified not taking a formal active role because it was a small cheque relative to their fund size.'

Investors did have a choice, of course. They could have walked away. One investor who passed on the opportunity to invest in FTX told me he just couldn't get comfortable with how the company was run, the structure and how much information it was offering. 'There was absolutely and positively no way,' he said. 'I didn't think it was a fraud. I just thought: we don't do deals like that. We don't do deals with companies set up like that.'

When FTX was apparently super-successful, things that now look like inexcusable laxity and incompetence could be seen as exemplary efficiency, which allowed the company to keep up its stunning profitability. In search of companies that are ever leaner and ever faster, venture capitalists seemed to have lost sight of the fact that there is such a thing as too fast – and some functions that don't fit well with the full-steam-ahead startup mentality. Would you drive your car across a suspension bridge built by a two-year-old startup? I wouldn't. The sloppy record keeping, shambolic management and tangle of personal and romantic relationships at FTX remind me more of a university debating society than a billion-dollar financial institution. These attributes were in plain sight, even if the alleged fraud was not. 'No two-year-old company could handle the scale of things that we were doing without opening itself up to the risk of a fuck-up,' SBF said.

*

Legendary

Adam Yedidia was nervous. He had always been more cautious than SBF, one of his best friends at MIT. Adam had tried out trading at Alameda for a few months in the early days. But he thought his friend's crypto dreams were crazy. He went back to finish his PhD. In 2021, SBF tried again to recruit him. By then, FTX was clearly on a rocket ride to astronomic success. Adam said yes.

Adam's relatively low-profile job as a senior computer developer for FTX belied his importance. He was the fifth key room-mate in the penthouse that SBF, Gary, Caroline and Nishad shared with their romantic partners. In the early summer of 2022, he'd be tasked with working on the exchange's systems for processing customers' bank transfers. And he noticed something odd.

Adam knew that Alameda sometimes handled these bank transactions. A key service that crypto exchanges provide is bridging customers' money between hard currency and the cryptoverse. Maintaining these links was a constant battle, because traditional financial institutions are extremely wary of handling flows of money in and out of crypto, particularly when it comes to large numbers of customers. It was hard for an exchange to get a bank account. Things were somewhat easier, however, for a private trading shop. Alameda already had bank accounts set up. So early on FTX told customers to send bank transfers to Alameda's accounts, and then credited the clients' FTX trading account with those funds. It was a simple enough workaround. Nor was it really a secret, since FTX had to tell customers where to wire the money. It was certainly a bit messy to have client money flowing to a technically separate company. The arrangement would have given any traditional compliance professional palpitations. But by crypto standards, this barely registered on the scale of shady practice.

What made Adam nervous in 2022 was when he noticed just how much money was involved. The two companies kept records of how much hard currency Alameda was holding for FTX customers, represented as a debt Alameda owed to FTX. When Adam found it, the number was $8 billion. 'It seemed like a lot of money,' Adam later said. 'I wanted to be certain that Alameda could repay that debt.'

Adam took SBF aside on the padel tennis courts in the Albany grounds. It was one of the few sports the FTX gang enjoyed. They sheltered from the sun in a little hut next to the courts. Adam asked about the debts. 'Are things okay?' In Adam's telling, SBF's response was cryptic.

'We were bulletproof last year but we're not bulletproof this year,' SBF said.

'How long until we're bulletproof again,' Adam asked.

SBF said it might take from six months to three years. He tried to reassure his friend. Adam says he didn't press for details. Perhaps he didn't want to know. If there was a problem, it was better to trust that Caroline and SBF would take care of it.

Adam wasn't the only person asking questions about the relationship between FTX and Alameda. Banks were suspicious that Alameda's accounts were being used for purposes far beyond the trading firm's own business. FTX and Alameda set up a second entity, called North Dimension, which took over handling some of the customer money and helped to obscure how the cash was really flowing. Eventually, FTX secured bank accounts in its own name – but even after this, some money was still deposited in an account controlled by Alameda.

Investors were also worried about the relationship between FTX and Alameda. But they focused on the conflicts of interest around Alameda trading on the exchange. Investors said FTX told them that Alameda was a totally separate operation. It's a little hard to understand how they took that seriously, given the historical and personal links between the two. SBF even sometimes communicated with investors using his @alameda-research.com email account.

Asked if potential investors had dug into FTX's banking arrangements, which might have led to the suspect handling of customer money, two people with direct knowledge of the diligence process told me that was not where investors focused. 'I don't recall it coming up,' said one. 'It is a very legitimate question now. I don't think it would have been a natural question that would have come up. There were a lot of these bank accounts that were opened for crypto exchanges,' they said. Even if the questions had been asked, they said, 'to really actually see money being taken away from customers, [you] would not only need to have the bank account [you] would need to have internal customer ledgers and Alameda's records . . . I think that was one of the key reasons why people, both investors and inside the company, didn't figure it out . . . You basically needed access to very confidential information. All of these scams are done with secrecy, with only a small number of people who could see the broad picture.'

The banking arrangements meant that from the start, customer money at FTX was never properly separated from Alameda. The tangle made the two companies not distant sister firms but financial conjoined twins. Ultimately, neither could survive without the other. When the new FTX management team produced a diagram with lines and arrows to show where customer money had gone, it looked more like spaghetti thrown against a wall. The dozens of overlapping routes and entities were impossible to follow.

Alameda owed lots more money than it should have to FTX. People also failed to grasp how much FTX owed its success to Alameda. FTX had arrived very late to the exchange market, and came from nowhere to become one of the leading players. It couldn't have done this without Alameda. What people want from a crypto exchange is to be able to trade, whenever they want in whatever asset they want. Because SBF owned Alameda, it would do things that purely commercially minded trading shops had no interest in doing. Exchanges are a bit like social media networks. You need a lot of people to participate to get the enterprise off the ground. There's no point going on to a social network when there's no one for you to connect with. In the early days, Alameda was a willing friend for every new FTX customer. Whatever you wanted to buy or sell on FTX, 24/7, Alameda was there to trade with you. At the start, SBF's own trading firm had been 50 per cent of all trading volume on FTX. It gave the exchange a huge and indispensable jump start. Alameda's share of trading declined over time to just 2 per cent, but it was still important to make sure that there was liquidity in the more obscure tokens where trading would otherwise be thin.

Alameda also stood ready to protect the exchange from a type of loss that had plagued crypto exchanges prior to FTX. The danger of running a derivatives exchange is that because you are letting your customer trade with borrowed money, there is always a chance that one of them will screw things up so badly that they create a loss that becomes the exchange's problem. If a trader runs a big losing bet and ends up in the red, and if the exchange's risk systems don't stop them in time, the trader can just walk away and leave the exchange holding the loss. Before FTX, crypto exchanges tended to deal with these losses by 'socialising' them. Everyone who made money would have their profits clipped to fill the gap. 'Clawbacks', as they were called, were a major hazard of early crypto derivatives trading.

One of the innovations FTX brought to bear was to have a list of professional trading firms act as 'backstops', who would take over big losing positions and sort them out – preventing clawbacks. Sometimes this could be a profitable activity for the backstop traders, who got certain incentives. But the system really only worked because Alameda was there as a backstop of last resort. SBF's ability to have his own trading firm sweep in and save the day, on several occasions saved the exchange from losses in the hundreds of millions, which would otherwise have blown a huge hole in its finances or have inflicted serious pain on its customers.

Alameda was the secret ingredient in FTX's meteoric success. Its role made SBF's claims to investors, and the world, that the two firms were really separate even less credible. These were not two independent companies that happened to be owned by the same guy. Alameda did all sorts of things to benefit FTX that no other trading firm, with purely commercial motives, would do. The two arms of SBF's enterprise always worked together.

But at the time when SBF was drumming up new investors for FTX, all the incentives were pointed against asking awkward questions. From July to January, FTX's valuation had risen from $18 to $32 billion. Its early investors were already looking at brilliant returns, and hoping for more. At 29, SBF was one of the youngest people ever to make so much money so quickly. By his 31st birthday, he was under arrest.

Accidentally

Towards the end of April 2022, SBF gave one of the most remarkable interviews in his short career as a media darling. Speaking to Bloomberg, he was asked by columnist Matt Levine to explain a practice called 'yield farming', that had become a trendy way of making money in the wilds of decentralised finance.

'Where do you start?' said SBF, as he launched into what he called a 'toy model' of yield farming. 'You start with a company that builds a box and in practice this box, they probably dress it up to look like a life-changing, you know, world-altering protocol that's gonna replace all the big banks in 38 days or whatever. Maybe for now actually ignore what it does or pretend it does literally nothing. It's just a box.'

What does the box do? You can deposit crypto tokens into the box. And you can take them out. The box also issues its own token. 'We'll call it, whatever, "X token",' said SBF. The token represents some sort of vague promise that anything good that comes out of the box – new products, tech or profits – will flow to holders of the X token. Then, the people in charge of the box decide to start giving away tokens as a reward for anyone who puts their crypto assets into the box. Suddenly, SBF said, X token has a market value. Let's say it would be worth $20 million.

'Wait, wait, wait, from like first principles, it should be zero,' Levine cut in. There's no good reason that a totally random crypto project with no actual new product that's giving away made up tokens should have any value at all, let alone $20 million.

'Uh, sure. Okay. Completely reasonable comments,' SBF replied breezily. 'In the world that we're in, if you do this, everyone's gonna be like, "Ooh, box token. Maybe it's cool. If you buy in box token," you know, that's gonna appear on Twitter and it'll have a $20 million market cap . . . I acknowledge that it's not totally clear that this thing should have market cap, but empirically I claim it would have market cap.'

SBF went on to the next step. Now that X token is worth some money, people who put their crypto into the box are getting an actual return on that 'investment', in the form of new X tokens. The payback can be pretty large, especially compared to your other options in a cheap money world where everyone is struggling for income. So investors start piling into the magical crypto box. 'And now all of a sudden everyone's like, wow, people just decide to put $200 million in the box. This is a pretty cool box, right? Like this is a valuable box as demonstrated by all the money that people have apparently decided should be in the box,' SBF said.

More money goes into the box. X tokens look more valuable. More profit incentive for people to put even more money in the

box. The cycle just goes up. And it gets better. Within decentralised finance, SBF explained, you can now take your X tokens and
put them up as collateral for a loan in crypto coins that are linked
to the dollar. So there is real cash to be made. 'It is sort of like real
monetisable stuff in some senses,' he said. Does it make any sense?
No. Can you do it? Yes. Is it happening right now? Also yes. But,
key question, when will it stop?

Surely at some point people will look at this set-up and say,
'Hold on just one minute . . .'? SBF acknowledged the possibility.
For now, though, the proof was in the profit. 'And you know, at
some point if the world never decides that we are wrong about this
in like a coordinated way . . . like, you're kind of the guy calling
and saying, no, this thing's actually worthless, but in what sense
are you right?' he said. SBF estimated there was $5 billion a year
of profit to be made from this kind of 'farming'. Levine was gob-
smacked, by the number and by the cynicism of SBF's tour of the
cryptosphere. 'You're just like, well, I'm in the Ponzi business and
it's pretty good,' he said.

I first listened to this interview a few days after it came out, pac-
ing up and down the short stretch of beach in front of my roadside,
budget hotel in the Bahamas. I had flown from London to visit the
court of SBF at the height of his powers. To coincide roughly with
its third birthday, FTX had thrown itself a massive party. I was
staying miles down the road from the centre of the action, as the
main hotel hosting FTX's conference had been overrun by 2,000
eager guests. (In any case, I think the *FT*'s travel department might
quite reasonably have baulked at the $600-a-night room rates at the
lavish Baha Mar resort.)

The crowd FTX attracted was a curious fusion of celebrity, high finance and flip-flop-wearing crypto bros. Goldman Sachs was there. So were executives from Ontario Teachers, representing my mother's pension money. A crowd of crypto developers had turned a darkened auditorium into a sort of skunkworks hackathon. Among them was a 14-year-old crypto prodigy who has more than 30 million Twitter followers. Walking down a hallway past the resort's luxury boutiques towards the casino, I passed Katy Perry without recognising her. She was heading, I later learned, to the VIP dinner hosted by SBF, joined by her partner Orlando Bloom.

While some of the A-listers stayed in the background, others were on stage. The agenda, which began with daily 'Sunrise Yoga', included One Direction singer Liam Payne interviewing German billionaire Christian Angermayer about psychedelics – a session entitled 'Elevating Crypto Consciousness'. Except that the pop star didn't turn up.

FTX used the conference to launch a *Vogue* magazine advertising campaign, featuring SBF and Gisele Bündchen, and promoting crypto as a philanthropic force. 'I'm in on crypto because I want to make the biggest global impact for good,' ran the slogan next to SBF, pictured in battered New Balance trainers, high white socks, shorts and a T-shirt, juxtaposed next to the lofty, elegant Bündchen. The unlikely duo were on stage in the Bahamas with Tom Brady for a session entitled 'Winning', which consisted of the three of them asking each other how wonderful it is to be as wonderful as they are, and sharing tips for being more wonderful.

The ultimate coup came the next day when SBF took to the stage again, this time with former president Bill Clinton and ex-UK prime minister Tony Blair for a conversation on how crypto could help people in developing economies access financial services. SBF and the two world leaders made every front page on the newspaper rack at the Bahamas supermarket. The international media was equally mesmerised. But, in some of the coverage, the over-the-top agenda and the all-night parties with celebrity DJs flown in had started to backfire. It was hard to watch all this and not think that the crypto bubble was near its peak.

In reality, the peak had already passed. Crypto prices were down 40 per cent from their autumn 2021 high. Like Wile E. Coyote in the Looney Tunes cartoons, crypto had run off the cliff, legs pumping wildly, but still hadn't looked down. In retrospect, the Bahamas conference was the last wild party of the crypto boom, the tequila shots at 3:00am that you regret the following morning. In a column I wrote about the event, I quoted a prediction from a venture capital partner that the vast majority of crypto companies would fail in the imminent downturn. As gloomy as that sounds, I did not know how bad the crash would be or how far the rot ran at FTX. Even as I interviewed SBF, on the weekend after the conference, sitting on the beachfront balcony of a restaurant in the Albany complex, crypto's momentum was running out. By the time the interview was published just a few weeks later, it had started to fall.

In retrospect, it looked as if SBF was toying with us, trolling the public, breaking the fourth wall of his own deception. His description of FOMOing investors bidding up the value of an essentially worthless crypto box appeared to be a stunningly brazen account of the game he himself was playing in hyping up the valuation of FTX. It was as if the legendary fraudster Bernie Madoff had given an interview, just before he was found out, saying: 'So, imagine you have this investment scheme where you, like, use money you get from new investors to pay profits to the previous investors. Just hypothetically.'

My view has always been that the 'box' interview has been slightly misunderstood. SBF loves to talk in exaggerated hypotheticals, like theoretical maths equations or philosophical thought experiments. FTX was not an empty box. It was a real company, with smart employees who were making quite a lot of money. A crash in crypto prices or a slowdown in trading should not have put FTX out of business. It would have made less money. But it wasn't doomed.

What SBF gave in the interview was an incisive and remarkably accurate description of what was going on in much of the rest of the crypto world by spring 2022. Using the promise of a bright new technological future to spin up tokens and endow them with millions in value, despite their being fundamentally worthless today; linking these hyper-inflated projects together in complex, self-referential financial structures; and doubling down by adding tottering piles of increasingly perilous borrowing. That is the essence of what was going on beneath crypto's glittering surface.

The problem for FTX was not that the company itself was an empty shell. It was the links with Alameda that dragged FTX down. Through Alameda, the exchange and its millions of customers were inextricably and secretly entangled with the over-extended market in crypto speculation. And as the crypto financial system fell apart through the spring and summer of 2022, SBF's empire was weakened to the point where, later in the year, a single storm could blow it away.

Accidentally

Plenty of people had warned that crypto didn't make sense, that it was an accident waiting to happen. But as SBF alluded to in his interview, in finance, being right at the wrong time does you no good. For two years, anyone who bet on crypto to fail had very likely lost their shirt. Against the reason and logic of sceptics, crypto backers could show a huge pile of profits as proof that their view of the world was correct.

So what changed in 2022? It's textbook economics. After starting to slow the flow of cheap money in autumn 2021, the Fed in March 2022 started raising interest rates, and then began selling off the bonds it had accumulated as part of its easy money spending spree. The world's most influential central bank in effect started un-printing dollars. The money pump was set to reverse. And it upended the economic gravity of crypto. Everything that had looked like a bright idea up until that moment suddenly started to seem awfully dangerous.

'Eventually the money printer stopped. The [Covid stimulus] cheques stopped coming. That leverage had to get unwound. It was hard to imagine an orderly way for that to happen,' one crypto entrepreneur told me. They had largely stayed on the sidelines during the height of the bubble, convinced it was sure to pop.

'You had a system with an insane amount of leverage . . . People were using assets that had a market cap value that wasn't real, borrowing against it and then looping around,' he went on. The crash was inevitable. 'It's like there was an avalanche. It doesn't matter what snowflake started the avalanche.'

*

As it happened, the snowflake that did start the avalanche was falling on the other side of the world. Do Kwon was in many respects a foul-mouthed alter ego to SBF. Another Ivy League prodigy, Kwon was raised in South Korea and studied computer science at Stanford University, where SBF's parents taught, before co-founding his crypto venture, Terraform Labs, in Singapore in 2018.

While SBF promoted veganism and worthy humanitarian causes, Kwon – who worked at Microsoft and Apple before going into crypto – delighted in slapping down his critics. When British economics writer Frances Coppola posted a long thread dissecting flaws in his Terra crypto project, Kwon replied, pithily: 'I don't debate the poor on Twitter, and sorry I don't have any change on me for her at the moment.'

Kwon's rudeness won him a devoted online following. Interest in alt-investments like crypto and meme stocks went along with a love of sticking it to the stuffy guardians of the traditional financial order. What did experts know that Do Kwon didn't? After all, they were poor and he was rich. On top of that, Terra offered its followers the chance to get rich themselves. As part of the ecosystem, investors could earn an apparently guaranteed nearly 20 per cent return.

One of the key features of the Terra crypto universe is that it is heinously complicated. In an analysis, published by the National Bureau of Economic Research, the authors wrote: 'The system's complexity also made it difficult even for insiders to accurately assess the build-up of risk.' At the heart of the story are three key components: Luna, the crypto token created by the project; TerraUSD, a stablecoin that was supposed to match the value of the US dollar; and Anchor, a borrowing and lending system that paid some lenders those very appealing 20 per cent returns. As SBF would have put it, it was a 'magic box'.

TerraUSD was different from other stablecoins. Its goal was still to match the value of the US dollar. But for Kwon and his followers, who called themselves 'Lunatics', major stablecoins like Tether, which promised to hold a stockpile of traditional assets to back up each digital dollar, were too reliant on old-world finance. They were total sell-outs. He preached a purer form of decentralisation. TerraUSD used a more radical tech solution to keep its value in line with the dollar. It relied on a blockchain smart contract that let any owner of TerraUSD swap the token for an equivalent amount of Luna at any time. Luna, like SBF's X token, essentially had value because people believed in the promise of the Terra ecosystem. In theory, the swap system would work because anytime the value of TerraUSD deviated from the value of the dollar, arbitrage traders would jump in to profit off the gap and their frenzy of swapping back and forth would eventually push the prices back into line. The design was supposed to work like those Coast Guard boats that are impossible to capsize. If the value of TerraUSD and Luna leaned too far either way, irrepressible buoyancy provided by profit incentives would set them back on an even keel.

Not everyone bought this notion. One of the Twitter criticisms from Coppola that prompted Kwon's disdainful reply was directed precisely at this supposedly foolproof system. 'Self-correction mechanisms that rely on financial incentives do not work when panicking humans are stampeding for the exit,' she said. The prescient comment, in July 2021, came in the aftermath of a near-death experience for Terra. A few months earlier, in May 2021, TerraUSD lost its link to the dollar and fell to around 90 cents. Within a few days, however, the price had recovered. Kwon touted the episode as a real-world stress test that his design had passed with flying colours, claiming the system had 'naturally heal[ed]'.

The Securities and Exchange Commission, which is now suing Do Kwon, says that this was a lie. In secret, Kwon had struck a deal with Jump Trading, a major Wall Street high-frequency trading firm with a strong interest in crypto, to bail out TerraUSD by buying up more than $62 million worth of the token and pushing the price back up. The lawsuit argues that the secret deal and Kwon's misleading publicity meant that, far from exposing the faults in the system, the May 2021 episode gave many investors false confidence and led them to pour more money into Terra for another 12 months. By that time, the total value of the Terra ecosystem reached $50 billion, with $1 billion of daily trading volume, making it the third-largest crypto network in the world behind Bitcoin and Ethereum. Key to that growth were those irresistible 20 per cent yields, paid to investors as a sort of promotional rate to encourage the use of TerraUSD. Only users who bought TerraUSD and then deposited it in Terra's own Anchor lending system received those top interest rates.

The deep-seated flaws in this supposedly decentralised constellation of ventures persisted. For one thing, it was obvious that Kwon and his associates were key central cogs in the machine, playing an outsized role in directing and promoting Terra. Another issue was that Anchor didn't actually earn enough income to fund the very generous rates, so they had to be subsidised by issuing new TerraUSD. As in the real world, money printing tends to devalue your currency, which put increasing strain on the Terra/Luna equalisation system. By spring 2022, the subsidy was running at $6 million a day. And so Terra decided to gradually decrease the rate to a level that would be set in line with the market and wouldn't require a subsidy.

By blinking in the face of hostile market forces and dropping the rate, Terra only added to the nerves of its followers. With the financial incentive set to reduce, investors started to pull out. As withdrawals escalated into full-on panic, the price of TerraUSD and Luna fell in tandem, meaning that neither token could act as ballast for the other as intended. Just a week after SBF's crypto party had concluded in Nassau, Terra began to wobble. By the end of the following week, the entire $50 billion edifice was essentially worthless. Analysts at CryptoCompare called it 'the largest destruction of wealth in this amount of time in a single project in crypto's history'.

In the aftermath, there have been efforts to blame some sinister outside force for driving the Terra ecosystem into the ground. Terraform Labs, which is fighting the SEC lawsuit, has suggested in court motions that Citadel Securities – a powerful US trading firm – was behind the collapse. Citadel vigorously denied the claim.

The loss was devastating for small investors who had trusted Terra, especially in Korea. Police increased patrols at a major bridge in Seoul to prevent suicides. Kwon spent almost a year moving from Singapore to the UAE and then to Serbia. On Twitter, he said he was 'not on the run' or anything similar.' In one reflective interview, he said he had been too 'carried away' with his 'shitposting' social media persona. He was arrested in March 2023 in Montenegro as he tried to take a private flight to Dubai, allegedly on a forged Costa Rican passport. Both the US and South Korea requested extradition.

*

Kwon's undoing was just the beginning. Terra was such a popular cash cow for the crypto industry that many of the biggest players in digital assets suffered from its demise. One of the first to show signs of pain was Three Arrows Capital, widely known as '3AC'. Its founders Su Zhu and Kyle Davies were another pair of migrants from the world of conventional finance. The two had studied together at the elite US boarding school Phillips Academy in Andover and then at Columbia University, and reportedly bonded over a sense of being out of place in the blue-blood atmosphere. Both went into trading, with jobs at major institutions including Credit Suisse and Deutsche Bank. Zhu, like Arthur Hayes, traded equity derivatives and started in finance in 2008. His whole team was laid off four months later.

Zhu and Davies founded their own hedge fund together in 2012. Hedge fund is a pretty grand name for their early operation, trading from their apartment. Like many later emigrants to crypto, they were currency traders at first, focusing on the wilder emerging economies before branching out into other assets, including stocks and later crypto. The firm pivoted to crypto trading around 2018, the same time that SBF was launching Alameda. By 2022, the fund had grown to several billion. The founders, now in their mid-thirties, commissioned a multi-million-dollar yacht and christened it 'Much Wow' – in a reference to Dogecoin. (The token is based on a meme involving a quizzical-looking Shiba Inu captioned with phrases in broken English – 'much wow', 'so dog', 'very coin').

It seems that the 3AC founders, like many others in crypto at that time, were starting to get high on their own supply. In a 2020 interview, Zhu had seemed sceptical, recalling the previous bubble. 'It is a little bit like 2017, in the late stages, where people know that it's just a money game or it's just a, I won't use the word Ponzi because I think it's loaded, but it's a game of . . . "what is the next meme, what is the next fashion?"' But soon he was selling a narrative of crypto's inevitable success.

Even the most devout crypto enthusiasts generally accept that theirs is a boom and bust business. Prices, attention and activity rise through a 'bull run' to reach a fever pitch of excitement, and then inevitably correct into a long period of languid trading and lacklustre interest known as a 'crypto winter'. Zhu became famous for a more radical idea. He called it the 'supercycle thesis'. He reasoned that so much new money was bound to flow into crypto, as everyone from major institutions to more individual traders saw the light, that the relentless buying pressure would keep pushing crypto prices up. The downturn would never come. In the heady days of crypto's prosperity, setting out confident targets for the future prices of cryptocurrencies on Twitter or in interviews became a running fad. There was plenty of competition for the title of most insanely optimistic price target. Zhu was a very strong contender with his prediction that the price of Bitcoin would rise from the mid-tens of thousands to north of a million dollars.

If you think that Bitcoin is almost certainly going to increase in value by at least 15 times – probably much more – then you'd really be crazy not to own as much Bitcoin as you can possibly afford. Same goes for other coins. This logic seems to have impressed itself on 3AC. Harkening back to 2019, early in the run-up in crypto prices, Zhu once tweeted: 'I know ppl who unironically say if someone had lent them $50k more back then they'd have $500m more now.' Apparently following that logic, the fund borrowed billions of dollars from more than two dozen lenders and loaded up on crypto investments. Among their bets was an investment in the Terra/Luna ecosystem valued at $600 million. When Do Kwon's empire went up in smoke, 3AC suffered grievous losses.

The old adage has it that if you owe the bank $100, you're in trouble, but if you owe the bank $100 million, they are in trouble. To take just one of its larger creditors, the lender Genesis, 3AC owed the bank 2,400 million dollars (that is, $2.4 billion). And the crypto banks, several of them, were definitely, definitely in trouble. 3AC's exposure to Terra/Luna was well known. Lenders almost immediately started to hit the panic button, demanding that the fund repay loans.

At this point, back in the newsroom, I recall the conversation turning to 'contagion'. Setting aside the 2011 pandemic thriller, in finance 'contagion' is about following the money – or more specifically, the lack of money. If someone has a problem, we ask who else has a problem because the first guy has a problem? Who else has been 'infected'? The more entangled and opaque a market is, the worse the contagion will be and the harder it is to predict. In crypto, the blight spread quickly and through several overlapping routes. Celsius was directly tied to 3AC as a lender, calling in $75 million of loans in late May, according to court documents.

Accidentally

But the two companies were also both investors in another abstruse corner of the crypto market, and it was this link that proved the more damaging.

*

This particular market opportunity had come about because of a software update. Ethereum, the second largest cryptocurrency network, had been working on a major change to the system that it uses to validate transactions on the blockchain (which they have since completed). The old system, called 'proof of work', was pioneered by Bitcoin and required energy-intensive 'mining', adding to the criticism of crypto's environmental impact. The idealistic Ethereum crew were eager to move to the new 'proof of stake' model, where the participants that validate new blockchain entries have to commit a big pile of Ether tokens as a sort of hostage for their trustworthiness. If the validators do a good job, they are rewarded with fees from the network. If they mess about, some of their pile of 'staked' Ether will be 'slashed' as a financial penalty, creating economic incentives to secure the blockchain.

By 2022, Ethereum was running a pilot version of the new 'proof of stake' system. There was decent income to be earned by committing assets to staking on the tester version of the new chain. But there was a catch. Any Ether committed to staking in the new system was locked up until after the upgrade was fully completed, and the timeline for that was unclear, depending on the intensely complicated technical efforts of Ethereum's numerous boffins. Still, staking your Ether looked like a good way to earn income in a crypto market where such opportunities were starting to dry up. And if you needed the money back sooner, people assumed that some other trader would be happy to swap some regular Ether for your staked Ether and earn the income themselves.

Not content with this modest income stream, traders used circular lending to stack debt on top of the staked Ether. In some decentralised lending markets, traders could use staked Ether as collateral to borrow regular Ether. If you then took your borrowed Ether and swapped it for even more staked Ether, you could add to your income stream. And there was nothing to stop people from repeating this trick over and over again. So what looked like large investments, paying hefty incomes, were often in reality just a daisy chain of borrowed money, all based on a much, much smaller initial outlay of cash that the traders actually owned.

Ethereum is a mainstream investment by crypto standards, much less risky than smaller and more obscure tokens. Traders mostly afforded staked Ether the same status. The assumption that staked Ether could be swapped for regular Ether held for a while, as long as the market was basically in good shape. The two tokens' prices had been aligned for almost a year. But as the crisis in crypto accelerated, too many people rushed for the exits and the staked Ether market dislocated. Suddenly, people didn't want to take the risk of having their money tied up in staked Ether until God knows when. Traders wanted their wealth to be in the safest and most easily saleable assets, or else – like 3AC – they needed cash urgently to pay back lenders or cover losses elsewhere.

Celsius, in its search for income, had put large sums into staking Ether. Its position was so large that it became impossible to shift.

Accidentally

The company ended up with around half a billion dollars of assets that it couldn't get its hands on. The breakdown in staked Ether heaped more anxiety on to the already panicky market.

*

Contagion continued to spread through another time-honoured avenue: fear. Far from the centre of the action, where the crypto elite watched the unfolding crisis on their multi-screen trading desks, a Philadelphia real estate broker named John made, for him, a series of fateful decisions. John, who I interviewed some months later and who asked me not to use his last name, was by crypto standards a veteran trader. Since 2018 he had regularly put modest sums into digital assets and patiently watched them rise and fall. My lasting impression of chatting with John is how overwhelmingly he seemed to embody a certain type of enthusiastic American capitalism. He was a smooth talker. For work, he cut deals in real estate. As a hobby, he traded crypto. But he described his approach to digital assets as 'diligent' and 'conservative'. He told me he 'didn't touch Defi'.

That changed in March 2022. The lure of the apparently guaranteed 20 per cent interest rate on TerraUSD was too strong for John to resist. He pulled together around $250,000 worth of Bitcoin and Ether to obtain a loan from Celsius, and used the borrowed money to invest in Terra/Luna. For a little more than a month, everything looked OK. Then, TerraUSD started to fall, from being worth close to a dollar to being worth close to nothing. Shaken, John became even more worried when he read rumours on Twitter that Celsius had also been dabbling in Terra and had suffered severe losses. Fearful that Celsius might collapse, he cobbled together money from the rest of his crypto portfolio to repay the loan he'd taken and get back the precious Bitcoin and Ether he had pledged.

John's story was repeated hundreds and thousands of times in different forms across the crypto industry in the spring of 2022. Traders, big and small, who had become a little too comfortable that the good times would last forever, were hit with losses and gripped by fear. One failure led to another. The rush of clients like John heading for the exit, combined with the massive sums frozen in staked Ether, left Celsius unable to honour clients' demands to pull their funds. Over the weekend of 11 and 12 June, John managed to get back some of the assets. But on Monday morning, with around $150,000 worth of John's crypto still stuck in a Celsius processing delay, the company announced it had frozen all withdrawals.

*

Executives across the industry describe those months as the 'holy shit' moment. People scrambled to reduce their risk-taking and pull in their horns. A lot of the risky lending had been funded by deposits from everyday customers like John, who now wanted their money back. There was a rush to get money out of crypto, with investors swapping stablecoins for hard cash to the tune of $10 billion in May and early June. Everyone asked for money back from everybody else. More bodies quickly floated to the surface. As Celsius and 3AC began to slide towards bankruptcy, it became clear that other major companies including BlockFi, Voyager and

Accidentally

Genesis were also in trouble because 3AC owed them vast amounts that they were unlikely to pay back. It was as if the 2008 financial crisis had struck crypto, but instead of being bailed out, most of the big banks were failing.

Lennix Lai, an executive at the exchange OKX, explained the metaphor to me in an interview at the time. Terra and Luna were like the subprime mortgages that caused the 2008 crash. It was something hyper-complicated that few people really understood in detail but which was packaged up to look like a lucrative and almost risk-free opportunity. It's not as if these products were a secret, or that their risks were unknown. It's just that they were not front and centre, and warnings about what could go wrong were drowned out by the clamour for profit.

As the crypto financial system rocked on its foundations, and many of its biggest institutions started to topple, SBF looked like a tower of strength. In 2008, governments and central banks stepped in to finally stop the spread of contagion and prevent more bankruptcies. SBF seemed to be filling the same role in crypto. From the outside, it appeared that Alameda had been smarter than other big crypto traders and had weathered the storm better. FTX should only have benefited from the chaos as the flurry of panicky trading generated more fees.

In mid-June, SBF threw a lifeline to Voyager, which had warned its losses on loans to 3AC could be more than $650 million. Through Alameda, SBF agreed to loan the struggling company up to $200 million in US dollars and 15,000 Bitcoin to help it weather the storm. A few days later, SBF intervened again. FTX offered a $250 million loan to backstop BlockFi. After hammering out the terms, the final deal announced in early July increased the maximum size of the loan to $400 million, and gave FTX the right to buy the company outright in the future. At the time, FTX thought it might pay as little as $150 million to acquire BlockFi. The company had been valued at $4 billion just a year before when it raised money from venture capital backers. Even as crypto's saviour, SBF drove a hard bargain.

BlockFi was the main, temporary beneficiary of SBF's bailouts. After Voyager ran through the maximum amount it could borrow in the short term, SBF let it go bankrupt. FTX held talks with Celsius about a bailout, but again decided it was better to let the company fail. 3AC was finally pushed into bankruptcy at the end of June. The crash had claimed several multi-billion-dollar companies, and inflicted tens of billions of losses on investors who saw their hard-earned money trapped in failed pseudo-banks or else go up in smoke.

Not everyone suffered. The 3AC founders, Davies and Zhu, who many blamed for setting off the crash, appeared untroubled. In a spectacular example of ill-judged PR, about a year after the event, they went on the record with David Yaffe-Bellany of the *New York Times*. He published a brilliant piece on how Davies flew to Bali to meditate and take magic mushrooms and Zhu took up surfing as the crypto markets melted down around them and cost investors billions. Neither showed any remorse. Pushed on that score, Davies replied: 'Remorse for what?'

Zhu was detained at Singapore airport in September 2023 and imprisoned for four months after the liquidators convinced a local court to order him and Davies to cooperate with them.

Accidentally

The liquidators said Davies's whereabouts were unknown at the time. When I contacted Zhu, prior to his detention, he blamed the bankruptcy liquidators of 3AC for spending too much money and taking too long, without paying creditors back.

SBF, however, emerged from the first act of the crypto crash with an even more glowing reputation. Anthony Scaramucci, known for his short stint as White House Communications Director for Donald Trump, is mostly a finance guy, hedge fund manager and promoter of one of the biggest industry conferences. He was close to SBF. As FTX swept in to rescue tottering crypto firms, 'the Mooch' compared SBF to the legendary Wall Street titan who gives his name to the bank JP Morgan. 'Sam Bankman-Fried is the new John Pierpont Morgan – he is bailing out cryptocurrency markets the way the original JP Morgan did after the crisis of 1907,' said Scaramucci, who had co-hosted FTX's Bahamas conference and would later receive an SBF bailout himself. Few suspected that SBF's apparent strength in bailing out floundering lenders actually betrayed his hidden weakness, and that an even more dramatic second act to the crypto crisis was taking shape behind the scenes.

*

Through the first half of 2022, FTX was only just getting settled in its Bahamas home base. New recruits and relocating employees flew to the island. Few had more than a couple of suitcases of personal belongings, after years of bouncing around the world and spending 12 hours a day in the office. For many, it was a difficult adjustment after cosmopolitan Hong Kong. To ease the transition, FTX arranged to fly in Amazon deliveries on chartered planes.

The social environment and dating pool for FTX staff was basically limited to their colleagues. They lived like college students in their multi-million-dollar waterfront apartments. Some of the new hires had come from the orbit of Big Tech, where years of privacy scandals and wrangling with regulators had eroded the feeling of being 'the good guys'. They relished working for FTX, which still felt like it had such positive momentum.

One of the new arrivals in the Bahamas was troubled by an obvious fact. Early on, FTX like other exchanges had created its own token. FTT, as the token was called, never really took off, like Binance's rival BNB coin. Still, with FTX's success, the price of FTT had risen from a few dollars per token to around $50 in early April 2022, down from a peak of nearly $80 at the top of the market in the previous autumn. FTX had said that a percentage of the money it made would go to buying back FTT and 'burning' the tokens, taking them out of circulation and increasing the value of the rest of the supply. In crypto, this practice worked a bit like stock buybacks, to link the company's performance to the token's value (although without giving token holders an ownership share in the business).

This new arrival at FTX Bahamas had watched the token over the previous months as they weighed up the decision to uproot their life and move to the island. They noticed how FTT responded to news about the company. The price action seemed to be driven by good or bad news about FTX on social media. The observation made them uneasy. 'I was wondering: what was stopping Twitter from murdering the company?' they said.

Accidentally

The answer should have been simple. In theory, FTT should be able to vanish back into the thin air from which it was created without any lasting harm to the company. But in reality, this was exactly the right question to be asking in the spring and summer of 2022. In the years since Alameda had spun off FTX, the trading firm's round-the-clock work ethic and 'don't worry about your mistakes' ethos had remained, but the nature of what it did had changed fundamentally. Under the surface, the incestuous relationship between FTX, FTT and Alameda had turned toxic, and the whole enterprise was drifting towards disaster.

Arbitrage, where Alameda started, is a clinical profit-spotting enterprise. See a gap. Exploit a gap. Profit. It should be as simple as that. But over time, Alameda had leaned further and further into more expansive bets on where the market would go. These investments were the risky moves that Tara Mac Aulay and the early Alameda dissenters had objected to. They became a major part of the business, partly because crypto arbitrage had become more competitive as big Wall Street shops got in on the fun. When I met Sam Trabucco on a shady lawn outside FTX's Bahamas conference, he complained about the increased competition. 'It's harder to make money in crypto than it used to be,' he told me. 'It's not easy to get to the timescales that you need to compete with traditional finance.'

Caroline appeared to allude to this pivot in Alameda's strategy in a March 2021 tweet, where she wrote about 'wasting time trying to trade back and forth for a few points of edge' when 'the way to really make money is figure out where the market is going to go up and get balls long before that.' Taking big bets on which cryptocurrencies would rise fundamentally changed how much risk Alameda was running.

In the days when Alameda looked like a money-making machine, its traders seemed to delight in telling everyone how amateur-ish their strategies actually were. When Trabucco stood down as Alameda co-CEO, he gave an interview about his trading record – and explained how he chose which crypto coins to bet on. 'What I think about the products doesn't even really matter. The thing that matters is what I think other people think about the products, if I'm just trying to price them . . . The more important thing is under-standing sentiment around these things . . . Internally people would always make fun of me for not understanding technology,' he said.

The host asked if Trabucco used sophisticated social media fil-tering and scraping to figure out which tokens would start trending. 'Yah, Twitter, it's not like scraping exactly,' Trabucco said. 'I have a smallish set of people whose opinions about this kind of thing I tend to trust. People on Twitter talk extremely openly about things, in a way where it is sort of just leaking information. Obviously that's true for people who don't have information as well, so it's important to understand who is worth listening to.'

In early 2021, Trabucco explained by way of an example, he – and much of the rest of the world – noticed that Elon Musk had started to tweet about Dogecoin, the joke cryptocurrency. Based on Elon's early tweets, Trabucco said he decided it was a good time to buy. 'Once he has done this twice, the probability that he is going to do it ten more times just sort of skyrockets,' he said. 'If he does keep tweeting about it, it just sort of seemed like it was going to 50x or something like that . . . It's pretty simple.'

Accidentally

The interviewer followed up. Maybe you can get in early when a coin is about to get popular, but how do you know when to sell? 'It's sort of all intuition,' said Trabucco. 'It's really just kind of guessing what is going to be the best time.' In the case of Dogecoin, Trabucco said he thought the coin was getting overhyped by the time Musk was due to appear on *Saturday Night Live*. The crypto internet expected Musk to send some signal of his support for Doge on national TV. Trabucco thought this dubious. 'It was not likely that the writers of *SNL* were going to pander to Elon's Doge agenda,' he said. He was right. Doge's price fell after the episode and never recovered. 'It ended up being a good read. But it's really all intuition and guessing how things are going to happen. It's not quantitative at all,' Trabucco reflected.

Most hedge fund CEOs do not base their trades on assumptions about the attitude of the *SNL* writers' room. Crypto is a different market, sure, and I think you probably have to allow for some hyperbole in the way Trabucco tells his war stories. But if even half of what he said is true, then some of Alameda's directional crypto bets were rank guesswork. Ellison, too, sometimes publicly acted the part of someone in way over their head. In one interview, she talked about how her trading strategies 'use a lot of elementary school math[s]' and that she didn't see much use for stop losses, a common risk management tool. She also joked on Twitter that there is 'nothing like regular amphetamine use to make you appreciate how dumb a lot of normal, non-medicated human experience is', apparently alluding to the study drug Adderall.

As long as people believed that Alameda was one of the best trading shops in crypto, the CEO's schtick seemed like harmless self-deprecation. In reality, their reckless, slipshod attitude was evident in private, too. In a June 2022 'portfolio summary' document unearthed by the bankruptcy team, Alameda was supposed to be modelling for the value of some of its crypto positions. Where the inputs to the model should go, someone wrote: 'come up with some numbers? idk.' By January 2022, Caroline sounded a little less confident in public. 'Stuff has just been pretty crazy. So I am spending a lot of my time I don't know, whatever, putting out fires or things like that,' she said, with a nervous laugh.

Alameda had piled up investments in a huge range of tokens and ventures. Starting in August 2021, it gradually invested more than $1 billion in a Bitcoin mining company with extensive operations in Kazakhstan – an investment that took SBF on a visit to meet the country's president in late 2021. It invested millions in funds run by close associates, such as Scaramucci's SkyBridge, and FTX's venture backers Sequoia and Paradigm. The internal list of these bets runs to nearly 500 items, including some absurdly tiny ones, such as $218 put into a startup called Snickerdoodle Labs that, according to its website, aims to let 'people own their data and lease it anonymously to brands in exchange for rewards'. The total cost of all these bets, according to Alameda's records, ran to more than $5 billion.

Its spending spree was financed with borrowed cash. For big lenders, they were VIP clients. And it was comforting for lenders to know that, if push came to shove, the trading shop would probably be backed up by FTX, a $40 billion company. Chaotic bookkeeping has made it hard to get a handle on the exact size of Alameda's tab. I have no doubt bankruptcy experts will be haggling over the accounting for years. SBF puts the peak of Alameda's borrowing spree at around $15 billion in loans, at the top of the market at the beginning of 2022.

Making things more perilous, for crucial spans of time, Alameda was not hedging its bets on crypto. Hedging (as in 'hedge fund') means taking steps to limit how bad it will be if your main bet goes wrong. If you're betting $10 on a coin toss coming up heads, you could hedge your bet by wagering another person $5 on tails. If you're right, you profit by $5. It's less than the $10 you would have won without the hedge, but if you're wrong, the loss is only $5, not $10. However, this sensible approach of reducing your profit to reduce risk ran against Alameda's extreme approach to trading. SBF kept urging Caroline to add hedges limiting their risk. She delayed.

Asked about how Alameda would weather the crypto downturn, Trabucco said: 'We're literally never putting enough money at risk at any given time where we would actually be in real trouble if things went south. That has always been Alameda's mindset.' Looking through Alameda's list of investments, it's true that only a few projects received very large amounts. The largesse was widely spread. The average investment ticket was just $10 million. So you could make the argument that Alameda was following standard venture capital practice. Even if some, or many, of those projects failed, none of the blow-ups should be big enough to hurt the firm. But if you zoom out from thinking about if this or that crypto project would be the winner, the key fact is that almost all of these ventures are one way or another linked to crypto. In total, Alameda's position by the start of 2022 was a multi-billion-dollar bet in favour of the future of crypto, financed mostly with borrowed money. They were what Caroline might have called 'balls long'.

Even SBF agrees it was a bad idea, in retrospect. He said the conviction they had formed that venture capital was '60 to 70 per cent bullshit' was crucial. It helped them to raise billions, but 'weirdly, it precipitated our downfall. We felt like we could do better. And we started doing it ourselves,' he said. 'Alameda made a bunch of . . . venture investments, but didn't hedge.'

'Alameda got really, irresponsibly leveraged long in the market,' he went on. 'A historically and implausibly large market crash followed.'

Alameda had reached a dangerous point. Jon de Wet, the crypto trading firm executive, also happens to be a former skydiving instructor. 'The most dangerous jumpers are males when they reach about 400 jumps,' he told me. 'It's the equivalent to having had your driving licence for about three years. You tend to underprice risk and overprice your skill levels.' The group of twenty-somethings running Alameda, who played with billions of dollars like you might buy a lottery ticket at a petrol station, had for around five years seen everything break their way. On top of their undoubted intellect and elite education, they had the confidence born of this long stretch when it was easy to make money, because the crypto market had been rising beneath their feet. 'They thought they could smart their way out of this,' he said. 'Immaturity, a lack of risk-taking experience in their life, meets huge amounts of capital and moral hazard. That is a recipe for disaster.'

*

Accidentally

FTX's Bahamas office was a line of single-storey, drab stucco buildings sitting in the middle of a vast car park. Staffers always called them 'huts', which made it sound like some colonial base in a distant jungle. It reminded me more of a strip mall in the North American suburbs.

On a mid-June morning, Caroline Ellison walked the short distance from the Alameda 'hut' to the building where SBF worked. Caroline is physically tiny – short, slight and stooping. The men who held almost every other senior position around her were hardly alpha males. But within the FTX kingdom, the guys had a sort of bravado. Even in the most stressful situations, Caroline kept her strangely deadpan style of speaking, with lots of 'likes' and valley-girl inflection. This morning, her message got an immediate reaction. 'Hey, guys, I am worried that Alameda might be close to bankruptcy,' she said.

In the early weeks of June, 3AC was reeling towards bankruptcy. Crypto markets were plunging. The shock had knocked so much value off Alameda's crypto assets that, Caroline thought, they were on the brink of owing more money than they had. The crypto lenders who had loaned Alameda billions could ask for repayment at any time. And there was no more money to pay them.

The key assets on Alameda's books fell into two buckets. One was its eclectic portfolio of crypto ventures, including random tokens and ownership stakes in crypto-focused companies. The other was what people called 'Sam coins'. These were crypto tokens of which SBF himself was a crucial backer. The most important was FTT, the token created by FTX. On the other side of Alameda's balance sheet were three big problems. It owed billions to crypto lenders,

233

usually loans in dollars, Bitcoin or Ether. It also had a large line of credit from FTX itself. But the last piece was the most important. The roughly $8 billion that FTX customers had, over time, deposited in Alameda's banks had not been kept sitting snugly in its accounts. The line on its books that said 'Don't forget, we owe $8 billion to FTX customers' was not just a matter of accounting – like having $1,000 on your credit card and $10,000 in your checking account. It was a real debt, which now looked like it could not be repaid. Alameda had spent the money.

Over the years, Alameda had dug the hole deeper and deeper. The first big item on its credit card had been the billions SBF wanted to buy Binance out of its ownership stake in FTX. Billion after billion in venture investments had also been put on the tab. But despite its spending spree, Alameda could tell itself it was solvent, mostly, because of the 'Sam coins' like FTT. As long as the market endowed FTT with value, Alameda treated it as a real asset that it could use. In particular, Alameda used FTT as collateral for billions of its borrowing and to justify that its overall finances remained positive. If this sounds crazy, that is because it is. If I have a notebook of 100 sheets of paper, and I write 'money' on every sheet, and then I sell the first sheet to someone for $1, does that mean the rest of the notebook is worth $99? And can I use those 99 paper dollars as security for a loan? The answer really should be no. But in practice, for Alameda and FTX, it was yes.

Alameda was not exactly blind to how bizarre its position was. The previous autumn, Caroline had created a model to analyse the risks of its situation, what would happen if there were a crypto crash and whether the firm could afford roughly $3 billion in new venture investments. The former Jane Street whizz-kids were all smart enough to know that if you tried to sell the other 99 sheets in your magic notebook, you would not get anything like $1 apiece. In a spreadsheet called 'NAV Minus Sam Coins', Caroline calculated that without these magic tokens, Alameda's net asset value was already negative $2.7 billion by September 2021. Her analysis reckoned that there was already a 30 per cent chance that Alameda would not be able to repay its loans in a crypto market downturn. If Alameda added $3 billion to its debt pile to make the investments SBF wanted, the chance of surviving a crash fell, to zero. They made the investments anyway.

In May, Caroline sent SBF one of her regular Google Docs with business updates from Alameda. The last bullet point, under the title 'worries/questions' was 'leverage: both actual leverage, and presenting on our balance sheet'. She was worried about how much Alameda had borrowed, and how it might look. SBF replied in a comment: 'yup, and could also get worse'.

A month later, it did. When Caroline walked over to the FTX hut in June, almost the exact scenario she had modelled months earlier was coming true. SBF didn't believe it. He thought Caroline's maths must be wrong. There was no way Alameda could be so close to bankruptcy. He ordered Nishad and Gary to help Caroline with a frantic reappraisal of the accounting. The key to whether or not Alameda was bust appeared to be how much it really owed to FTX. They compared the debts recorded in Alameda's systems to FTX's books.

In SBF's telling, it was a rare moment when he felt pretty much useless. 'For that three-hour period, I was very concerned,' he told me. 'I tried asking the devs and they gave me this look of, "Fuck off, we are trying to fix a serious problem. We don't have time to teach you how to code." . . . I was sort of sitting there fiddling around trying to decide if it would be more distracting or helpful to talk to them about it.'

It was Gary who cracked the problem. He recorded his conclusion in a spreadsheet, labelling it 'Gary's number'. Alameda owed FTX $11 billion. Caroline's data had been wrong by about $8 billion. That discrepancy – it came to be called 'the bug' – was an error in the system that processed FTX customer bank transfers to and from Alameda.

The mood in the FTX hut was relief, if not jubilation. Alameda's debts were $8 billion less than they thought. So it was nowhere close to bankrupt. Adam Yedidia was told to fix *the* bug. It was in doing so that he says he became worried by the giant debts Alameda still owed FTX, which led him to question SBF on the padel tennis courts. But as Adam worked away on the accounting systems, Alameda dug the hole deeper and deeper. Over the following weeks, as the crypto lenders tottered and demanded repayments, Alameda paid back billions in loans. It took the money from the only source it had left. FTX.

*

SBF always said he was bad at naming things. In September 2022, he wrote a Google Doc with the title: 'We came. We saw. We researched.' If the joke was not really funny, nor were the contents of his memo.

Accidentally

'I only started thinking about this today, and so haven't vetted it much yet. But: I think it might be time for Alameda Research to shut down. Honestly, it was probably time to do that a year ago,' SBF wrote.

He shared the document with Gary and Nishad. As they read, it was obvious why Caroline – Alameda's CEO – was not included. SBF was brutal. 'The fact that we didn't hedge as much as we should have alone cost more in EV [expected value] than all the money Alameda has ever made or ever will make, and that's the kind of critical mistake we're likely to make if I'm not actually running the show there. Caroline is not a natural leader, and probably never will be. She's also unhappy at Alameda, and is doing it because she thinks it's important. Alameda's culture has become mediocre at best.'

It was true that, as the market turned against their bets in 2022, things inside Alameda were starting to fray. Trabucco began pulling back from day-to-day operations. Sometimes he just wouldn't turn up to the office. By the time he officially quit in September, he said he'd been checked out for months. Publicly, he blamed burnout. He normally worked 30 to 40 days in a row, he said. The record was 136 days without a break. He said that he would spend more time on his boat, and writing crosswords. It turned out that the yacht was paid for with $2.5 million of company money, according to court documents. His departure left a gap. Trabucco was probably Alameda's most diehard trader. He revelled in the pressure of high stakes market swings. He called the terrifying 2020 Covid crash 'the best trading I have ever seen'. When SBF handed over the post of Alameda CEO, Trabucco was effectively put in charge of trading and risk management. Ellison ran the all-important tech side, plus people management and administration. SBF had less confidence in her as a risk manager.

Ellison was unhappy taking the full burden of running Alameda, as Trabucco backed away, colleagues said. In private notes, published by the *New York Times* she wrote: 'I have been feeling pretty unhappy and overwhelmed with my job . . . At the end of the day I can't wait to go home and turn off my phone and have a drink and get away from it all . . . Running Alameda doesn't feel like something I'm that comparatively advantaged at or well suited to do.'

The breakdown in Caroline and SBF's personal relationship added to the stress. After years of on-again-off-again romance, she and SBF split up in the spring of 2022, apparently for good. Relations between the pair were awkward. Sometimes, they were hardly speaking. It was hard to imagine Ellison unloading her anxieties about being saddled with Alameda's faltering portfolio, right after the break-up.

SBF had started to favour another trading firm, called Modulo. He invested several hundred million. 'To the extent that there is a niche for a trading firm, that firm should be Modulo. It has much stronger culture and leadership than Alameda,' he wrote in his memo. Modulo was also run by Jane Street alumni. It was not lost on people that one of Modulo's leaders also had a romantic past with SBF. In another memo, SBF had told the two firms to play nicely. 'SBF is aligned with Alameda plus Modulo and treats 1 dollar to any as the same even though ownership percentages aren't a hundred percent, and in the end I will make sure that each side is fairly acknowledged and treated for public goods created,' he wrote. (SBF was no stranger to talking about SBF in the third person.)

Accidentally

When the idea of shutting down Alameda was relayed to Caroline, by Nishad, she said the idea was not just bad, but impossible. She had logic on her side. Winding up Alameda wasn't a simple matter. The trading firm and FTX were, in fact, inextricably tied together. The trading firm was no longer half FTX's volume, but it was a big customer. More than that, it could be trusted to keep trades flowing on FTX no matter what.

Then, there were its debts. To close down Alameda, it would have to pay back all its debts. On top of the billions in customer dollars sent to Alameda bank accounts, the trading firm had also borrowed from FTX through more official channels. As a derivatives exchange, FTX lent money to its clients for leveraged trading. That lending was supposed to be managed through a sophisticated, automated system that would protect the exchange, and by extension its other clients, if one trader got into trouble.

Alameda broke all the rules. Other traders would be automatically liquidated if their trades started to go sour. Alameda would not. Other clients could not run negative balances in their accounts. Alameda could. And other borrowers had limits on their loans. Alameda did not, nor did it pay interest on some of its loans. The theoretical limit on Alameda's borrowing written manually into the code that ran FTX's systems was $65 billion. The sum is many times bigger than all the money FTX ever had, even if you took every penny of its clients' funds. It was a fatal violation of the risk controls whose virtues SBF had extolled as a model for the rest of the financial world, in congressional hearings and private meetings with top US regulators. One former FTX executive explained: 'The whole risk system was predicated on the idea that no client could create holes in the system because they would be liquidated before they got to zero.' The special treatment for Alameda was a giant hole in the system.

In his memo in September, SBF acknowledged the truth: 'The main downside here is that, given the amount that Alameda is doing, we can't really shut it down.' Caroline was more explicit. She said it was impossible. Alameda couldn't shut down because it couldn't repay what it owed to FTX. None of this is what SBF had told the world about the relationship between his two companies. Even Nishad was shocked by the stark statement on the financial bind. He demanded a meeting with SBF that night.

Nishad still looked up to his childhood friend's big brother. He was nervous to confront him, one on one. For privacy, they met on the penthouse balcony. It was evening, and the blue spotlight illuminated the vast terrace with views over the dark water. Nishad paced up and down one side of the terrace, while Sam sat back on one of the lounge chairs. The conversation was tense. Nishad was beside himself with anxiety about the scale of Alameda's debt. SBF agreed, it was worse than he would have liked. But Alameda had plenty of assets. And there were ways out. They could raise more money, make more money, and refill the gap. As long as no one found out.

*

Alameda's financial statements, however messy and incomplete, were not totally private. The company shared copies, at least, with its lenders. After the June crisis, Caroline had overhauled the balance sheets. The internal version she prepared had a couple of awkward items. One was $4.5 billion in 'related party loans', which covered money Alameda had lent to SBF and his inner circle to fund investments made in their names. Loans Alameda made show up on a balance sheet as 'assets' because in theory it was money people owed them. But if anyone had asked *who* Alameda lent those billions to, the answer *'me and a few of my friends'* would not have been reassuring. More awkward, on the other side of the ledger, was a nearly $10 billion debt labelled 'exchange borrows'. It would not have been hard for anyone to guess which exchange would have lent so much to Alameda.

Caroline tried to find a way to make statements look presentable. She tried seven different versions. The final one, number seven, was the one she sent out. This version eliminated the awkward 'related party loans' by essentially assuming the money SBF and the inner circle owed to Alameda would – and could – be used to pay off some of the exchange borrows. Adding together the negative and positive to make zero eliminated both numbers from the spreadsheet. For the rest of the borrowing from FTX, she just changed the label – lumping it together with other debts in an item simply labelled 'loans'.

Even with the most difficult-to-explain items removed, the balance sheet was explosive. Somehow, a few months later, one document ended up in the hands of a journalist named Ian Allison at the crypto news outlet CoinDesk. The story, published on 2 November 2022, was the crypto scoop of the year – probably the decade.

Of $14.6 billion in assets on Alameda's books by that point, nearly $6 billion was FTT. The trading firm's ledger counted billions more in tokens closely tied to SBF, which would likely fall in value if the crypto kingpin stumbled. Allison wrote that the financial statement 'shows Bankman-Fried's trading giant Alameda rests on a foundation largely made up of a coin that a sister company invented, not an independent asset like a fiat currency or another crypto. The situation adds to evidence that the ties between FTX and Alameda are unusually close.' Readers doing the maths in their head could reach an even starker conclusion. If FTT went away, Alameda would be next to bankrupt.

FTT's price slipped but didn't tumble. There was still faith in SBF. The CoinDesk story acknowledged that its snapshot of Alameda's finances could be incomplete. Maybe there were more assets somewhere else? Ellison played on this notion when she responded on Twitter a few days later. 'That specific balance sheet is for a subset of our corporate entities, we have > \$10b of assets that aren't reflected there,' she wrote. 'The balance sheet breaks out a few of our biggest long positions; we obviously have hedges that aren't listed. Given the tightening in the crypto credit space this year we've returned most of our loans by now.' Just over an hour later came an earth-shattering tweet. The tweet that, more than anything else, murdered the company. It came from a familiar source. CZ.

*

Over the previous summer, SBF had been trying to raise more money. The attitude to crypto in venture markets had changed sharply. 'No one believed the valuations from 2021,' said someone closely involved in the process. If FTX could raise more money, even if it didn't increase its valuation, it could try to prove that the company was still worth the full \$32 billion. Some of the deepest pools of capital in the world are in oil-rich countries in the Gulf. Sovereign wealth funds in countries like Saudi Arabia and the UAE each have hundreds of billions to invest, and in recent years have looked to spread their wealth around the world to reduce their reliance on the proceeds of selling fossil fuels. FTX executives debated before deciding to include the Gulf on their fundraising tour. It wasn't an ethical concern, but a worry about territory. This was Binance's home turf. CZ lived in Dubai and forged close links with the government. Would trespassing there anger their rival?

Relations with Binance were undoubtedly tense. Some FTX insiders think that events in Washington DC, rather than in the Middle East, were what made matters worse. They believe that CZ suspected SBF of bashing Binance in private meetings with top American lawmakers. The suspicion seems to have been well founded. Months earlier, Caroline had compiled a list she titled 'things Sam is freaking out about'. Fourth on the list was 'getting regulators to crack down on Binance'. It was a common topic in crypto circles that CZ rarely, if ever, set foot in the US. People surmised that CZ was afraid US authorities might pounce on him. But when SBF sarcastically tweeted in late October that he was 'excited to see [CZ] repping the industry in DC going forward! . . . uh, he is allowed to go to DC, right?' It seemed like a needless provocation.

The timing of the leak to CoinDesk, shortly after SBF's visit to the Gulf, has added to suspicions that Binance was plotting to weaken FTX. CZ himself tweeted, about FTX: 'We gave support before, but we won't pretend to make love after divorce. We are not against anyone. But we won't support people who lobby against other industry players behind their backs.' But Binance also maintains that it did not attack FTX. CZ says the fateful message he posted was in the spirit of transparency. Whatever the motives, the impact was immediate.

'As part of Binance's exit from FTX equity last year, Binance received roughly $2.1 billion USD equivalent in cash (BUSD and FTT). Due to recent revelations that have come to light, we have decided to liquidate any remaining FTT on our books,' CZ posted.

Binance was dumping FTT. Its remaining stock of the token amounted to around half a billion dollars' worth. That much selling would undoubtedly hurt the price. And now people knew that if the price fell too much, Alameda might be pushed underwater. CZ's message turned nervousness into fear. FTT started falling like a rock. Customers were demanding millions an hour back from the exchange.

Nishad wrote to SBF and Caroline: 'lots of withdrawals on ftx are queueing up'. $1.25 billion had been withdrawn in a day, and the requests were 'continuing so far at about 120m/hr'. Caroline replied, simply, ':('. SBF said: 'oof'.

They were getting questions, even from the FTX employees, about what was happening. Caroline messaged in the chat group about what to tell Ryan Salame, a long-time senior executive: 'Ryan is asking me if FTX can meet all withdrawals. What should I say?'

Everyone knew that Gary liked to work on his own peculiar schedule. Efforts had been made to stop calling him in on every problem, so that he could get more sleep. That night, Nishad knew it was time to make an exception. The systems that handled withdrawals were being overwhelmed. He knocked on Gary's door for help. It was all hands on deck.

*

Accidentally

Employees at the Bahamas headquarters were bracing themselves for a real hurricane blowing in off the Atlantic when the financial storm broke over them. It took many by surprise. At first, one staffer told me, 'In our mind, it was just another chatter in the crypto world and it is going to pass . . . The workers had no idea or even speculation . . . We all had our own savings on [the] site. No one rushed to take out their own money.' But by Monday, the day after CZ tweeted, the person said: 'There was a lingering feeling that things didn't feel right.'

Even top executives at the company were confused by the crisis that overtook them. Several people involved in the early crisis talks told me that SBF consistently talked about the problem as a 'liquidity' issue, meaning there wasn't enough free cash on hand to pay back all the customers who wanted their money. It would take time to free up enough money to honour its obligations, but FTX might be able to weather the storm. Some of the executives had to work out the real story for themselves, combing through the company's spreadsheets.

'It is just clear to me that the disconnection from reality is very, very intense. I think the disconnection was in Sam's mind,' said one senior executive, describing the atmosphere. 'It was strange to me that Caroline was on the [chat] thread. She was digging into any asset she could find on the Alameda side. It was almost as if Alameda was stepping in to empty its purse to help with this bank run.' As the hours went by, the situation clarified in their mind. 'The runway of dollars to pay back customers was going to zero. This is why Caroline is trying to fire-sale things and dump assets back into FTX.' Another executive described the revelation:

'It's not liquidity. It's fucking solvency. It's a big gaping hole in customer assets.'

FTX executives say SBF was never clear about what the problem was. 'The fact that we had a solvency crisis, no one ever announced that. Sam consistently portrayed it as a risk mismanagement issue. It was so vague that no one knew what was going on,' said one. 'He was very dialled in on solution, solution, solution,' said someone else who was with him at the time.

The solution, for SBF, was to raise more money fast. He placed calls to his friends in venture capital, to top private equity firms and to his biggest competitors in crypto. The ask rose from 'a couple of billion' to $4 billion and then $8 billion. The sooner he could raise capital, the sooner he could staunch the bleeding from FTX's accounts. A document circulated to would-be rescue investors read: 'FTX is raising roughly $6-10b of liquidity this week. We are very open to structures here, and can be flexible.' An accompanying spreadsheet of financials disclosed that customers had pulled $5 billion from FTX on the day of CZ's tweet, and that there was $8 billion missing because of a 'hidden, poorly internally labeled . . . account'.

'All of these are rough values, and could be slightly off,' SBF wrote at the top of the page. Further down, he said: 'There were many things I wish I could do differently than I did, but the largest are represented by these two things: the poorly labeled internal bank-related account, and the size of customer withdrawals during a run on the bank.'

Even with these hasty disclosures, the dash for cash divided opinion. One former FTX executive said SBF was 'clearly trying to raise money on false pretences . . . You can't have the sunk cost fallacy. It was like someone coming in, robbing a bank and saying: "Trust me, if you give me two more weeks I will pay you back with interest."' Another senior exec said: 'You can't fundraise to solve a crime. That is not an appropriate reaction to a crime scene.'

A third colleague, who also thought fundraising would only compound the fraud, believes SBF's moral compass was skewed by his beliefs as an effective altruist. His philosophy was based on utilitarianism ideas, the greatest good for the greatest number. Honesty would not be a moral absolute. 'He has to keep telling lies in order to do good. It's just his own EA philosophy,' the employee said. 'I think he lied. But the end goal was good.'

The fundraising drive failed. Investors would not write billion-dollar cheques on the basis of SBF's scribbled financials, as the company was clearly tipping into free fall. 'Nobody got anywhere close to wanting to [due] diligence this,' said a senior executive. 'They didn't want to touch it. Sam had been so non-traditional. The fundraising that did happen was kind of a miracle.'

By Tuesday, the money had run out and FTX stopped paying customers back. Caroline posted to the leadership chat group asking: 'Multiple people internally asking me whether they should continue to make statements to external parties like "Alameda is solvent". Should I suggest they stall instead? Just stall on responding to their messages? Or what?'

SBF was out of options. He called the final person in crypto who might have enough money to save FTX. When SBF contacted CZ, the Binance boss 'knew he was desperate', he later said. They hastily thrashed out a deal. Announcing the bargain on Twitter, SBF tried to rekindle the early bond between the two companies. 'Things have come full circle, and FTX.com's first, and last, investors are the same: we have come to an agreement on a strategic transaction with Binance for FTX.com (pending DD etc.),' he wrote.

It was mid-morning on Tuesday in the Bahamas. The exchange was shut down and customer funds frozen. The rank and file of FTX staff were in suspended animation, waiting for news from their leader. 'We had extreme faith in the company and Sam himself. We were all waiting for him to come online and tell us something,' one said. The update he finally posted on Slack, as news of the Binance deal broke, was far from reassuring. 'You might have completely reasonable questions for me, like "What exactly is the transaction?", and "What entities would it include?" Unfortunately I don't yet have a definitive answer for you,' SBF wrote. Later in the day, he held a video call with the whole company, appearing on screen at the office from his apartment at the Albany, a few miles away.

Far from steadying the troops, the call finally broke the ranks. 'The message was: "We're fucked. I fucked up,"' an employee recalled. 'People just started quitting and it became a domino effect,' said another. 'My direct manager quit. And his manager quit. I didn't even have someone to ask.'

Dan Friedberg was the first lawyer hired by SBF, on the rec-ommendation of his father Joe. Dan was decades older than most of the FTX crowd and held a wide-ranging role overseeing legal and regulatory issues, covered by various titles from 'general coun-sel' to 'chief compliance officer'. On Tuesday, news spread that he had quit. Dan disappeared with hardly a word. The fact that the company's top lawyer had taken off added to the mounting panic.

Accidentally

'If one of the dads of the company thinks that something is wrong enough to leave, then maybe there is something wrong,' a third FTXer recalled.

The deal with Binance felt like a betrayal. People had joined FTX because they wanted to be one of the 'good guys' in crypto. Now they were going to be pressed into service on the Binance pirate ship. There were no answers on whether FTX would remain independent, or on who would keep their jobs. The deal was really little better than a handshake. 'It was completely ambiguous. It meant nothing. It was not an agreement to do anything,' said an FTX executive who saw the three-page document. The staff working on making the deal a reality were soon suspicious of Binance's intentions. 'This doesn't feel like a sincere process, from minute one,' one said. (Binance said, 'This is false.')

*

Even at a crypto trading firm, video meetings were inescapable. Alameda had its weekly staff meeting every Wednesday night. Its Hong Kong office was as generic a space as you could imagine. The floor was covered in grey square tiles of carpet. The ceiling was grey square panels with fluorescent lights. Between the columns, for some reason painted lime green, were long rows of desks with six-screen workstations.

Caroline had been on holiday in Japan when the storm broke over FTX earlier in the week. She had flown to Hong Kong – the nearest office. On Wednesday night, she sat slouched on a beanbag chair in the middle of a ring of her handful of employees, most sitting on a large semi-circular sofa. Throughout the gruelling week, she had been pulled between misery and elation. The pressure cooker of concealing Alameda's financial secrets, and being stuck in close contact with SBF after their break-up, was starting to crack. She wrote to SBF on Signal:

'this is the best mood I've been in in like a year tbh'

SBF reacted to the message with a heart emoji.

'wow', he wrote. 'uh, congrats? because shit's exciting?'

'I just had an increasing dread of this day that was weighing on me for a long time,' Caroline replied, 'and now that it's actually happening it just feels great to get it over with one way or another.'

Ahead of the staff meeting, she previewed her message to Alameda: 'I'm thinking a vibe of "Alameda is probably going to wind down; if you don't want to stay or want to take some time off, no pressure, if you do want to help with stuff like making sure our lenders get repaid it's super appreciated,"' she wrote to FTX leadership in a group chat.

The meeting started along those lines. 'Okay, let's get started, I guess,' she began. 'We have a bunch of people. Yeah, I guess I'll just start by saying some stuff. And then you guys can feel free to ask questions. Um . . . Yeah.'

She began to explain how FTX had ended up selling itself to its deadly rival, Binance. 'I mean, the basic story here is that starting last year, Alameda was kind of borrowing a bunch of money via open-term loans and used that to make various illiquid investments . . . Then with crypto being down, the crash, the . . . like, credit crunch this year, most of Alameda's loans got called. And in order to, like, meet those loan recalls, we ended up, like, borrowing a bunch of funds on FTX which led to FTX having a shortfall in user funds. And so, with the . . . once there started being, like FUD about this and users started withdrawing funds, they kind of eventually were realising that they were unable to . . . not going to be able to meet, like, the continued withdrawal pressure. So we reached out to various people but ultimately like . . . Binance,' she ended with a nervous laugh.

The account was stunningly blatant. Alameda's staff listened in silence. The pings of message notifications sounded occasionally. A few minutes later, someone interrupted Caroline. Alameda's remote employees were having trouble finding the video link on Slack. One of the people in the room, who had joined the company just three days earlier, secretly recorded the hour-long meeting on his phone. People began to ask questions.

'Can you say how big the hole is or like . . . ?'

'Uh, I probably don't want to share the exact number,' Caroline responded, haltingly.

'Is it close to one bil or six bil?'

'Uh, the latter,' she laughed, again.

The news kept getting worse. Caroline explained that most of the debt-fuelled spending had happened in the second half of 2021, when crypto markets were surging to their peak. FTX, Alameda and the people managing their effectively joint venture portfolio didn't 'do a great job of accounting' or 'coordination', she said. She listed some of the biggest investments that had started to dig the hole. $2.1 billion to buy out Binance's stake in FTX. A billion on the Kazakhstan crypto miner. Half a billion to Anthropic, an AI venture. And $300 million to K5 'which is, like, people who talk to celebrities,' she said. 'We weren't really, like, aware of the extent to which we were ending up leveraged.'

'How was Alameda able to get, uh, all of those loans to make those venture investments?' someone asked. Caroline appeared amused by the question, laughing through her answer. 'I don't know. Did you ever read about, like, Celsius or Three Arrows or whatever? The crypto lending space was kind of wild for a long time. Just, people had a lot of money. [They] didn't really, like, read your balance sheet. Just, [they] lent you a lot of money.'

Someone asked if Alameda should make a public statement, so that people wouldn't assume that 'we just gambled the money away'. Caroline said it seemed like a bad idea. 'What kind of legal stuff is going to, like, come out of this? I imagine, like, that there are several people in a scary place, like potentially yourself, which I hope isn't the case?' someone else asked. Caroline was, understandably, nervous. 'Yah, I think, I feel like I don't have a very good detailed answer right now. We have hired a bunch of lawyers to start working on it.'

Christian Drappi was sitting a few seats away from Caroline. Handsome and stocky, he looked better suited to a football team than a crypto hedge fund. He began to ask some more pointed questions.

'Was there, like, a plan to eventually, pay . . . like . . . was there in the road map of, like, oh, when are we gonna actually, like, try to, like, pay this back and, like, make FTX, like, users not fucked?' Drappi asked.

'Basically, FTX was trying to raise in order to do this. But yeah, after the crash, no one wanted to invest and I don't know. I guess there's, like, a question of, like, should you try raising, like, a big . . .

like, a . . . you know, steeply, like, discounted valuation or would that, just, you know, make people freak out more or something. I don't know. Obviously, in retrospect, the plan of wait around for several months and, like . . . for the market environment to get better and then raise did not work out,' Caroline replied.

As the meeting went on, Drappi intervened several times pressing for more details. He asked if the loans were 'officially done' and 'collateralised' through the normal channels for customers borrowing on FTX, what was called the 'spot margin book'. 'It was . . . yeah, it was not through the normal spot margin,' Caroline answered.

'Oh. That seems pretty bad,' Drappi replied.

A few minutes later, he posed another question. 'Who else was, like, aware of this? I mean, I'm guessing you and Sam certainly were. Like, I'm guessing probably very few people.'

Caroline said many could possibly 'piece it together' looking at Alameda's records. Drappi was insistent. 'I mean, like, more, like, explicitly aware. As in told, like, this is what we're doing in terms of, like, meetings that were had. I'm sure, like, this wasn't just, like, a YOLO thing, right?' he said.

'Yeah, I mean, I guess I talked about it with, like, Sam, Nishad and Gary, I think,' Caroline said. There was a very long pause.

A faint voice from across the room asked, 'Who made the decision on using user deposits?'

Caroline hesitated for a second. 'Sam . . . I guess,' she said.

'When?'

'I think, like, FTX, uh, always allowed Alameda to borrow users' funds. As far as I know,' Caroline explained. The trading firm didn't have to post collateral, although it often did, in FTT.

'I think basically the structure was that Alameda could go negative in coins without needing to actually borrow them.'

Employees asked about whether they would still get their FTX equity? Was it worth anything? What about the money they themselves had stored with FTX? The answers were all bad. Others asked about CZ, his intentions and motives. Why had he attacked FTX only to save it? Would he follow through on the deal, giving them enough money to pay back customers? Caroline was sceptical. 'Didn't this all, like, start with, like, a tweet where Sam was, like, oh, CZ isn't allowed in the US or something?' she wondered aloud.

'Do you think that's actually what made him angry?' someone asked.

'I have no idea,' Caroline laughed.

Towards the end of the hour-long meeting, people in the room started to notice stories popping up on their phones. The media was reporting Binance was going to pull out of the deal with FTX. 'It's all over Twitter, in the last five minutes,' said one. 'Seems like FUD, nothing legit,' said another. Caroline brought the meeting to a close.

'More questions?' she asked.

'Motherfucker,' was the reply. A broken, matter-of-fact expletive. 'It was a fun place to work.'

Caroline's voice was breaking. People were in tears. Someone thanked Caroline for 'answering all these . . . like, I'm sure this is not that fun for you. But I certainly appreciate how open you're being.'

She brightened. 'Thanks. I mean, it was kind of fun. I don't know,' she said with a giggle.

'Oh, OK, then. Never mind.'

Accidentally

Caroline reported back in the leadership group chat: 'think it went well. people seem obv upset/scared but really happy to get some clarity and just generally spent a while chatting about it/had good vibes. though now I'm kinda worried that everyone is going to quit/take time off and I'm going to end up trying to unwind all our positions by myself.' She was right. Most of Alameda quit immediately.

*

FTX staff in the Bahamas saw the same string of press reports that had interrupted Caroline's meeting with Alameda. The news that Binance was likely to ditch the deal, citing a single unnamed source, smelled strongly of leaks from Binance to soften up the ground. In the chat group created between FTX and Binance executives to coordinate the deal, there was a very awkward silence. SBF finally wrote to CZ. 'Hey, we are still extremely excited to work on this with you guys. We are obviously seeing a lot of public pieces coming out claiming leaks, but we obviously don't know if that's real. We would love to get clarity from you guys on this, and we are willing to do anything to make this work.' His rival came back with a one-line response. 'Sam, we won't be able to continue this deal. Way too many issues. CZ'

The news shattered the temporary calm that had descended on the FTX 'war room' at the Albany. The search for 'solution, solution, solution' was back on. But for some of the remaining FTX leadership, there really was only one solution – to file the company for bankruptcy. This faction, led by US general counsel Ryne Miller, heaped pressure on SBF to bow to the inevitable. Miller and other FTX lawyers had already instructed FTX's Wall Street law firm, Sullivan & Cromwell (S&C), to start work on legal options, and to compile a shortlist of restructuring experts who could take over running FTX. 'Ryne Miller came in and said: "Sam, you're done. Get out. Let the experts take over,"' said one former executive. Hostility between those following Miller's lead and those still loyal to SBF grew. 'During the collapse, people were losing faith in [SBF]. People who used to kiss his ass started to be very mean to him,' said another employee.

SBF posted news that the Binance deal had collapsed in a Signal chat group among senior executives. 'Thank you . . . Who can turn off the websites? And who can identify, on chain, what exact assets we have for US?' Miller replied. Constance Wang, the chief operating officer, who had been leading the fundraising drive with SBF, cut in. 'Hi Ryne, I love you but I don't want to stop trying yet. I appreciate you letting me try everything I can and manage the situation to provide clarities and assurance to our users too. If nothing works I'd be happy to work with you on a proper wind down.'

Frantic efforts continued down these parallel tracks. By Thursday, the US lawyers had prepared documents for SBF to sign over control of the company to John Ray, the restructuring expert S&C had identified. Everyone understood that his first move would be to file for bankruptcy. At the Albany, the search for a financial saviour continued. But the group had started to fray. 'Nobody had gone through a disaster before so people were breaking psychologically,' said a person who was there. 'It was never more apparent to me how young all of them were than in the 72 hours period before bankruptcy. People who had not been sleeping, had not been eating, were taking the responsibility to customers incredibly seriously . . . It was just this haunting number of [millions of] customers who needed to be made whole.'

People began to slip away from the war room. One by one, SBF's closest lieutenants and oldest friends packed their bags and fled the scene. 'The founding team was disappearing,' said a senior executive. Adam had reassured SBF, his college friend, that he would stand with him. 'I love you. I am not going anywhere. Don't worry,' he texted SBF. The next day, he quit. The story Caroline told had spread from the Alameda all-hands meeting through the FTX team.

By late Thursday, only a handful of allies, including his parents and Gary Wang, remained. The drumbeat of demands for the US to give up control and accept bankruptcy kept coming. 'People [were] pinging him all the way up until 4:00am to sign this damn thing,' said a former executive. The company lawyers, the outside counsel, his own attorneys – everyone told SBF to sign the document. A few months later, in an interview for the *FT*, I asked him why he gave up. 'Just, everyone left,' he told me. 'I couldn't do it alone. And, if I'm alone, then maybe I'm wrong. I am pretty impervious to pressure, but at some point I started to feel like maybe I'm the one who's wrong here.'

*

SBF has become fixated on that decision to sign away his companies. In the hours and hours of conversations we have had since, he returns to that moment again and again. He claims he was close to securing a rescue with investors. And that the irrevocable move to file for bankruptcy closed off options that would have quickly seen all his customers and investors get their money back.

He is not entirely alone. Among the many former FTX staff I've spoken to, including some of its most senior executives, there are still different camps on the question of what was the right decision to take in the pressure cooker of the company's final days. Several agree with SBF that the US bankruptcy process is a disaster. The fact that Miller used to work for S&C, and the links between the law firm and John Ray, look to some like a cabal.

Before a key bankruptcy court hearing, to decide if S&C could continue to act as FTX's lawyers during the bankruptcy process, Dan Friedberg filed an unsolicited 17-page statement with the court, describing what he viewed as conflicts of interest and inappropriate conduct by S&C. Dan appeared on the courtroom Zoom call at the hearing but was not allowed to speak and disappeared. An FTX customer who objected to S&C's appointment called it 'the most flagrant attempt by a fox to guard a henhouse in recent memory'. Lawyers for the US Trustee, the government office that oversees bankruptcies, also objected. Four US senators wrote to the bankruptcy court judge questioning whether S&C could be trusted to investigate FTX's collapse. 'Significant questions about the firm's involvement in the operations of FTX remain unanswered,' the senators wrote. S&C says its past work for FTX was limited and that John Ray and the other law firms appointed to help with the bankruptcy could manage any conflicts. The bankruptcy judge rejected the senators' letter as 'inappropriate' and ruled that S&C could stay on as FTX's lawyers.

The costs of the bankruptcy have been eye-watering. Together, the lawyers and consultants unwinding FTX have already paid themselves more than $200 million. The bill is rising by millions a week. All this money comes out of the cash that will be available to ultimately pay back the millions of customers who are still owed billions of dollars. For some of the former crypto whizz-kids that ran FTX, who were accustomed to making up the rules as they went along, to coming up with creative solutions in the moment, it must be agony to watch their company being dragged through the turgid, expensive, by-the-book US bankruptcy process.

On the other side of the argument is the fact that FTX was, in the literal sense, bankrupt. SBF could not play Peter Pan forever. The world of financial magical thinking that he and his youthful followers briefly occupied, on their tropical island, had come into abrasive contact with reality. If the cost of unwinding the company is high, it is because FTX left behind an unfathomable mess. Based on his investigation, Ray has put the hole in FTX's customer accounts on the day it filed for bankruptcy at $8.7 billion. I also found it hard to see a realistic alternative to bankruptcy. SBF admits that he lacked the support to keep fighting. Even before he signed it away, FTX had effectively ceased to exist. Its staff had fled from what they increasingly feared was the scene of a crime.

SBF remained on the island in the days after the bankruptcy. At first, he was engaged in winding things up and handling a massive hack that raided more customer money. Pretty soon, Ray cut him off and would have nothing more to do with him. Caroline was long gone, and out of touch. Nishad had left the island. Gary stayed until his lawyers flew down to the Bahamas and made his legal situation painfully clear. He came out of his penthouse bedroom to tell SBF he was leaving, right away. SBF's parents remained. Someone who knows them said Joe Bankman and Barbara Fried could see no fault in their son. 'Certainly his parents never want to think of him being deficient in any capacity,' they said. 'I am very fond of them. But seeing the three of them together I can see where some of the damage was done in terms of Sam thinking he could do anything.' SBF maintains he was surprised when the police knocked on his door.

The four friends – Sam, Caroline, Gary and Nishad – were not in the same room again until their trial. By then, the trio of lieutenants had implicated their boss in what they now called a massive fraud.

*

As the drama of FTX's final week unfolded, I was in London working frantically to keep up with developments and understand what had happened. SBF and I had kept in touch since our first meeting in the Bahamas. Our conversations were sporadic, on WhatsApp or the occasional Google call. I was used to SBF always being available.

As the crisis at FTX accelerated on Monday, he was chatty. On Tuesday, he went quiet. I sent him messages every day but heard nothing until Saturday. I had fired off a list of 11 questions and requests for comment for a long story we were about to run. In point number 11, I asked him if the 'poorly labelled account' he had written about in the financial documents was in fact money passed from FTX to Alameda. He swiped the reply feature on my WhatsApp message, offering a response only to my final question. Had FTX handed $8 billion of client money to Alameda? SBF sent one word. 'Accidentally.'

Conclusion

SBF spent many of the breaks during his trial sitting alone at the defence table as the lawyers and spectators left the courtroom to get coffees and chat in the hallway. On the day he was due to testify, he stood up and took his seat on the witness stand early. An official told him to step down and wait to be called.

His decision to testify had been hotly anticipated. But by the time the moment came for him to speak in court, it seemed inevitable. SBF had watched weeks of character assassination by the government's witnesses, his former closest advisers and friends. He had always been able to talk his way out of trouble, to bend reality towards him with his words. For someone who lived to take chances, there was no way he would not make the final gamble of trying to convince at least one juror that he never intended to commit a crime.

The evidence the prosecutors had painstakingly laid out implied three broad theories of guilt. Like so many scandals, it was all about what SBF knew and when he knew it. The first line of attack was that FTX and Alameda had been a conspiracy from the very start. SBF had told investors, regulators, Congress and the public that Alameda was treated just like every other trader on FTX. 'Alameda is a liquidity provider on FTX but their account is just like everyone else's,' he wrote in a 2019 tweet, which prosecutors showed the jury over and over again. Gary, Nishad and others testified about how SBF had instructed them to build the special rules for Alameda into FTX's systems from the exchange's early days. And the prosecutors showed countless examples of how SBF has assured investors and customers that there was no special treatment, in order to win their trust and their money.

Confronted with his tweet, SBF told the court that his assurances about Alameda's account being 'just like everyone else's' had been in response to a specific question about whether Alameda had an advantage in speed over other traders. He also argued that some of the exemptions from normal procedures helped Alameda perform the various services it did for FTX. This was true, as far as it went. He claimed some haziness around whether he knew the details of Alameda's special treatment, suggesting that it was Gary and Nishad who had made the decision based on his vague instructions. But under cross-examination, he admitted he did know about 'distinct rules' for how Alameda traded on FTX, at least since 2020. Asked whether he had told his customers and investors this, he said, 'I don't think so,' and 'I'm not sure.'

His idea of honesty was odd to say the least. In SBF's mind, or so he appeared to argue, a married man could pick up a woman at a bar. He could seduce her. He could start a second family, with children, and live a double life. And if neither his wife nor his mistress ever asked him point blank, 'Do you have another woman?' then he wasn't being deceitful. In the courtroom, however, SBF's admission – that he had indeed known the truth about Alameda and had never seen fit to mention it – barely registered.

The tangled argument over Alameda's trading parameters was overshadowed by the gravity of the moment when, prosecutors argued, SBF had moved from dishonesty to embezzlement. Their second argument for his guilt centred on the frantic discussions at FTX headquarters in June 2022. SBF had seen the calculations of Alameda's massive debts to FTX. He would have known, prosecutors charged, by 'simple maths' that so much lending could only have meant raiding customers' money without their permission. But faced with the choice of defaulting on Alameda's loan repayments, he had decided to dig the hole deeper. Although 'borrowing' was the word everyone used in court, prosecutors said it was really 'theft'.

SBF claimed ignorance. He said that until October 2022, he thought Alameda's debt to FTX was a manageable $2 billion in its main trading account. He said he didn't know about the other $8 billion Alameda owed, which related to its handling of customer cash in bank accounts. 'I first remember having concrete conversations about this in particular in October of 2022. I was aware of some pieces of it before then, however,' SBF said. Over and over again, prosecutor Danielle Sassoon's relentless cross-examination hammered at the implausibility of SBF's position. In her mid-thirties, Sassoon looks a decade younger with a fresh face and crisp manner. She got a laugh in the courtroom when she confessed to the judge that she had mistakenly walked into the jury room one morning and was mocked by the jurors. But standing behind the lectern, she was anything but absent-minded. Hour after hour, she scarcely paused in her forensic, implacable questioning. She set traps for SBF where she knew she had evidence to contradict his answers. And she took every opportunity to subject his tortuous explanation of events to the common-sense test.

'You were CEO of FTX, right?' Sassoon asked SBF.

'Yes,' he replied.

'And you called the shots as the CEO, didn't you?' she asked.

'I called some of them,' SBF replied.

'And you're a pretty smart guy, right?' Sassoon continued. There was an objection. Ultimately, SBF answered. 'In many ways. Not in all ways.'

Quizzing him about the events in June, Sassoon pointed out that Alameda's bookkeeping errors around its debts to FTX had left it apparently bankrupt. SBF had been so worried that he delayed a trip to Washington DC. 'And it all came down to this $8 billion . . . you never got to the bottom of that?' she asked.

'They were still getting to the bottom of the details of it at that time, but no. I had the number two, three, four and five people at the company all each independently confirm to me that the new understanding was correct, and I trusted them,' SBF said.

Indulging SBF's explanation that he didn't know about the $8 billion, she asked:

'So it's your testimony that while you were CEO of Alameda, some unknown people spent $8 billion without your knowledge?'

'No, I don't think that was my testimony,' he replied. His manner throughout was that of the smartest kid in class, giving a

Conclusion

substitute teacher the minimum of respect. Later, SBF said, 'Funds were being deposited and withdrawn all over the place every day,' and that no 'clear single person' was responsible for the spending. 'Money is fungible anyway,' he added.

If these exchanges left anyone on the jury in doubt, the prosecutors clearly thought they had SBF trapped by their third theory of guilt, over what he had done in FTX's last days. On the Monday of the company's final week, SBF had sent a series of tweets, trying to reassure customers and stop the bleeding of funds flowing out of FTX. 'FTX is fine. Assets are fine,' he wrote. 'FTX has enough to cover all client holdings.'

Prosecutors introduced into evidence a document SBF had written the day before, calculating FTX's 'current status' and weighing up what to do next. 'We have roughly enough to process current withdrawals . . . We have another ~2-3b of liquidity this week . . . That would mean enough to process ~1/3 of remaining client assets,' he had written. How could SBF have written that, and the next day honestly claim that FTX had 'enough to cover all client holdings'?

'At the point where I posted it,' SBF told the court, 'Alameda still had a net asset value of roughly positive 10 billion. FTX had no holes on its balance sheet. And there had been no attack on the customer assets. And so my view at the time was that the exchange was OK and that there, you know, there was no . . . no hole in terms of assets.'

He explained that after he posted the tweet, on Monday night and into Tuesday morning, was when the value of FTT and the other coins closely associated with his empire finally collapsed. The billions worth of these tokens that Alameda held had been the key, he claimed, to its solvency in his eyes. 'That was the . . . crash that drove its net asset value from close to $10 billion to only a little bit above 0,' SBF said. Once FTT was removed from the equation, Alameda had a big hole in it. It could not pay back FTX. And FTX could not pay its customers.

His explanation cuts to the heart of what happened at FTX. Real dollars flowed in from venture investors, profits and customer deposits. Real dollars flowed out to SBF's own investments, to celebrity deals, real estate and lobbying. And the hole left by that spending was filled with 'Sam coins', the tokens like FTT that SBF himself had helped to create and endow with value. Within the warped world of the crypto bubble, the value of these tokens made the reality on SBF's spreadsheets look OK.

But to take that reality seriously is a huge leap. Could SBF have deluded himself into believing that these tokens had durable value? With his Wall Street background and obvious intelligence, did he really think FTT was a reliable asset to set against his hard-dollar obligation to his customers? On top of that, whether Alameda was solvent shouldn't have mattered to whether FTX could pay back its customers. No one trader on the exchange was ever supposed to be in a position where its failure could threaten the entire system. The money should have been just where FTX customers left it.

The implications of SBF's story were extraordinary. When Alameda and FTX spent billions more dollars than they made, SBF claimed he simply didn't quite know where the money was from and assumed it was all legitimate profits. To suppose SBF was telling the truth would mean that Gary, Caroline and Nishad had each learned the reality of Alameda's position before him, and not communicated it to their boss. It also almost certainly meant that they had lied on the

Conclusion

stand about how far SBF was aware of key documents, about what he had said in meetings and that he had made the crucial decisions.

There were few records of their private discussions. Their encrypted Signal chats were set to automatically delete. The closest thing to a clear statement of the conspiracy was a message Nishad sent to SBF in the final days about what to tell FTX staff to make them keep working. Nishad wrote: 'this is wildly selfish of me, but they may need to know that it wasn't a ton of people orchestrating it.' 'I think that's probably correct,' SBF had replied. In court, SBF explained it away. Nishad had been suicidal. SBF had simply tried to say what his friend wanted to hear.

The documentary evidence showed that incriminating documents and suspicious spreadsheets existed. Metadata from Google showed that SBF had, at least, opened some of them. But all the crucial questions – what the documents meant, how they had been understood and who had made decisions – the question of guilt and innocence lay in the conflicting testimony. The crux of the case was who to believe.

The jury appeared to have little difficulty. After a five-week trial, they reached their verdict in less than five hours. SBF stood and stared at them as the verdict was read. Guilty on all charges.

The only moment SBF had shown emotion in court was the day before, as both sides finished their closing arguments. For the first time, he looked behind him in the direction of his parents. He blinked rapidly, as if tears were coming to his eyes. Maybe that was the moment he knew it had all been lost. His final gamble had not paid off.

*

In his closing argument, Nick Roos, one of the lead prosecutors, had posed three questions to the jury about FTX's collapse: 'Where did the money go? What happened? Who is responsible?'

The answer to the first two questions is now pretty clear. The answer to number three is a little more complicated. SBF certainly bears a large share of the responsibility. Even if he still maintains his innocence of criminal charges, he is the first to admit it was, in a broader sense, his fault. A criminal trial is not really a fact-finding exercise. It is a guilt-finding exercise. You could sit through every day of the trial and come away with an incomplete understanding of what happened, and the lessons that should be learned.

If, for a moment, we think about SBF without worrying about guilt and innocence, how would we explain what happened? He is a person whose personality is hyper-polarised. He is uniquely, astonishingly good at some things – spotting opportunities, reasoning, speaking persuasively. He also has enormous blind spots, around social skills, awareness of his limits, management, thinking about downside risk and, obviously, integrity. SBF might be a robot assembled in a lab with the sole mission of going out and getting a big valuation for a tech startup in a hyped-up environment. He was also the last person you really wanted running a big financial company. Unfortunately, a person with this remarkable and odd combination of traits entered into the perfect economic and social context where he was enabled to raise all those billions of dollars.

If you now go back to thinking about who is guilty, the fault lies with the individual – for sure – but also with the context. SBF will pay a heavy price for what he did. The system that enabled him – both in cryptoland and in high finance – looks set to escape most of its share of the accountability.

It was worryingly easy for SBF to hack the financial system. It takes a village to create the conditions for a financial disaster on the scale of FTX. The irrationality of the crypto bubble, absent financial regulators and large parts of the media all played a part. SBF was a huge miss for the press. We largely failed to catch on before his scheme started collapsing under its own weight. Investors, who had the power and opportunity to spot the problems at FTX, did not sound the alarm or act to halt the company's growth by starving it of capital. Instead, they did the opposite – boosting FTX's resources and reputation to the scale where its failure was a multi-billion-dollar calamity. Venture capitalists showed an uncomfortable level of groupthink, a failure of scepticism and an unwillingness to upset the money-spinner as long as it was apparently making them rich. Some are battling lawsuits over their role in FTX.

In the model village of society, where doctors heal the sick; teachers educate the young; and butchers, bakers and candlestick makers look after food and lighting needs, where do investors fit in? The job is about looking after money that people don't need right now and growing it for the future. In a world where governments and corporations have increasingly pushed the financial responsibility for retirement on to individuals, this role has rarely been so important.

It's important to remember that when we talk about the investment world we are usually, in some part, talking about your money. The ultimate owners of all the assets being managed by investors includes plenty of ultra-rich individuals, plus insurance companies, sovereign wealth funds and charitable endowments. But pension funds are some of the world's biggest investors, managing around $50 trillion globally, not counting private pension savings. That money flows down from whatever provider or workplace scheme sends you your annual pension statement through various funds to businesses, assets and entrepreneurs who will hopefully generate some returns to help make sure that you don't have to work until you die. Fund managers who invested in FTX look after cash that belongs, in the end, to us.

As stewards of our money, they also wield huge power over which ideas get funded. Investors sometimes talk about themselves as 'asset allocators'. In a technical sense, that means choosing the right mix of different sorts of assets. But in a broader sense, a big part of what investors do is allocate money so that good ideas can be turned into reality. One way of assessing the consequences of investors' failure when it comes to FTX is to count their losses. Another side of that failure is the other ideas that might have benefited from those billions if investors hadn't been acting like ten-year-olds on a football pitch, all chasing after the ball and competing with each other for the privilege of cutting a cheque to SBF.

'I think the fact that we delegate so much of our innovation policy to venture capitalists who frankly don't have the incentives to solve long-term problems is very damaging,' said Hilary Allen, the law professor. 'None of the flak of any of this ever seems to reach them even though they are the ones who have orchestrated and profited from it.'

Before his trial, SBF and I talked about his dealings with these investors, and the question of whether FTX was rewarded for growing at a dangerous speed. He claimed he never lied to investors, or anyone else. But he told me: 'Were we as forthright as possible about the parameters that Alameda traded on? No, we were not ... I totally get the argument that we could have been more forthcoming.' He said there was a plausible argument that FTX grew too fast and that created too high a risk of a major failure. Reflecting on the likely impact of his failure on startup investors, he said: 'Maybe companies will settle for blowing up with less fanfare or growing less spectacularly. Maybe we just won't have really successful companies again.' If your model of a successful company is FTX, would that really be so bad?

*

What other lessons can be drawn from the crypto crash? It's hard to put one number to the scale of the financial fallout. The direct losses to investors and customers of bankrupt crypto firms are certainly north of $100 billion, hurting millions of people. There are billions more in losses for people who bought cryptocurrencies near the peak and saw their values plummet. A lot of people understood the risk they were taking and bought into crypto with money that they could afford to lose. There are, however, too many cases of people who risked too much and whose financial lives were ruined in the crash. Still, the harm is limited.

Equally, the losses suffered by big, 'smart money' funds in crypto are not going to do any lasting damage. A few hedge funds that went too deep into crypto have had to close. For bigger investors, like Ontario Teachers, a few million lost to a bad investment is little more than a bump in the road. My mum will not miss a cent from her pension when she retires. Temasek, the Singapore sovereign wealth fund, which invested in FTX, went further than most – at least in public – by saying it had cut the pay of executives involved in backing SBF, although an internal investigation found no misconduct. The reputational hit is more painful than the financial loss. Losing money in venture capital is factored in.

The wider economy also escaped serious harm from the implosion of the crypto bubble. Jon Cunliffe, the Deputy Governor of the Bank of England, is the man in charge of worrying about what central banks call 'financial stability'. In a 2021 speech, he pointed out that the scale of the subprime lending that triggered the 2008 financial crisis was just $1.2 trillion – quite a bit smaller than the peak size of the crypto market. The central bank analysed crypto's threat to financial stability not just in terms of its size, but also its interconnectedness with the real economy. Subprime mortgage lending was dangerous because every household and every bank in the country is pretty closely linked to the mortgage market by one route or another.

For now, the Bank of England sees crypto as only a future threat to financial stability. The main links between crypto and the real financial system were venture investments by major institutions, and banking deposits made by crypto companies with real banks. So few banks were willing to deal with crypto firms that those deposits were quite concentrated in a few institutions. When crypto crashed, it did create a problem for a handful of banks. But the contagion was small scale. Crypto would have to be bigger or more closely tied into the financial system to cause a real problem.

Conclusion

Still, when you think about the level of acceptance that crypto figures like SBF had gained in elite political and financial circles in 2022, and the serious discussion in government in Washington and London about encouraging crypto at the time, I don't think we were miles away from crypto becoming much more integrated with the financial system. Hopefully, the process would have involved tighter regulation that would have limited the risks. Still, it was all a little too close for comfort. One way of looking at the crypto crash in 2022 is that it was a near miss.

Regulators need to treat crypto enterprises like what they are, not what they claim to be. A company like Celsius, which to all intents and purposes acted like a bank, should not have been allowed to exist without being subject to the same scrutiny as traditional lenders. I am all for taking the arrival of new technology as a moment to assess whether the rules we have are good ones and fit for the modern world. That does not mean throwing the rule book out of the window, or letting self-interested crypto entrepreneurs argue that their technology is so special and precious that they should be allowed to write the rules for their own gain.

Hopefully, people will now be less easily dazzled by crypto's novelty. In the aftermath of the crash, crypto should face a healthier level of scepticism and a higher burden of proof that it can be useful for something other than illicit transactions and speculation on its own price movements. At least until the next boom arrives.

Many see the greatest potential for crypto in the developing world, where the adoption of digital payments technology using cheap and ubiquitous mobile phones has often been swift. Crypto is viewed as an alternative to the outrageous fees commonly charged by traditional money transfer services, particularly for workers who want to send money to relatives in another country. However, it's not clear that what people really want is crypto, so much as a solution to meet their financial needs. Use of 'crypto' can sometimes be a proxy for wanting to hold US dollars. People in countries with runaway inflation, looking to convert their wealth into the global reserve currency, may find it easier to access dollar-linked crypto tokens than real dollars. I'm far from convinced that adding volatile crypto assets like Bitcoin to the mix is better than other financial technology options, and some economists fear digital assets will only disrupt these economies.

One of the potential uses of crypto technology, where serious work is being done, is central bank digital currencies. In some parts of the world, CBDCs – as they are called – are already well under way. The concept is essentially a government-issued cryptocurrency. China has pioneered a 'digital renminbi'. This is the antithesis of crypto's original vision, as a means of payment free from government control. China's digital currency lets the state effortlessly track each and every transaction. The consequences for privacy are obvious and devastating. However, the potential benefits in speed and efficiency, and the ability to work around Western payment systems like SWIFT, has led to concern that China's digital currency could help its push to dethrone the dollar as the global means of payment.

In the West, where thinking about CBDCs is further behind, the vision is somewhat less dystopian. If you, like me, have recently had to send an international transfer or wait days for a transaction to come through, the potential benefits from digitising our currency

Conclusion

and payment system will be apparent. How to make this all work, and incorporate privacy protections, is a massive project that has only just begun. These fundamental issues around money and privacy will be difficult to work through at a time when trust in institutions and serious policy thinking in politics are at historic lows.

CBDCs represent a future for 'crypto' that seems increasingly more likely. Traditional institutions – governments, banks, corporations – will poach aspects of crypto technology but leave its founding ideology and the idea of decentralisation behind. There will always be some people that want to operate outside regulation. It's like with adult content and gambling. There are only a few payments companies that will touch it – and they can charge what they want. 'The client will pay,' said Julian Sawyer, the former exchange CEO who now runs Zodia, a crypto custody company backed by Standard Chartered Bank. 'The future is going to be about being regulated.'

This may well be the version of 'crypto' that finally reaches widespread use. Bitcoin, decentralised finance and some vestige of the offshore crypto economy will continue. It's difficult to see how they will bridge the gap into the mainstream.

*

For people like me, who grew up around the time of the 2008 financial crisis, it was easy to get the impression that the main thing that finance and investors do is ruin everything. The first time I heard that there was such a thing as a 'financial system' was when it had a crisis, and a bunch of my friends' parents lost their jobs. A lot of people have developed the suspicion that finance is a self-referential, corrupt and pointless game that helps the rich get richer and screws everybody else. There is plenty of evidence to support this suspicion, not least the 2008 crisis. I don't think it's the right conclusion. What I didn't think enough about when the 2008 crisis put a bunch of people I knew out of work is that everyone I knew, if their family owned their home, had bought it with a mortgage. The roof over our head relied on the financial system. The main thing the financial system should do is quietly conclude boring little productive transactions that let people buy houses, start businesses, hire people, put food on the table. Obviously, there are loads and loads of inequities baked into the system, far too many people are shut out of its benefits and there are countless examples of bad behaviour in finance where the results are not good for society or are actively bad for it. But we do rely on the financial system, and we all have an interest in making it better.

One way to think about the financial system is that it's a bit like the London Underground. If you think about it in the abstract, a system of underground trains that can move millions of people a day around a fairly small geographic area isn't something that humans need to live. Then again, once you have built the modern-day city of London on top of it, you do need the Tube for London to function. Finance isn't necessary for people in the same way as farmers or doctors are necessary. But the society we live in today, for better or for worse, does need the financial system to function.

The 2022 crypto crash is like a lab experiment for what happens if you do finance without any democratic guardrails or rules to look out for the little guy. It is also a symptom of the political forces that are disrupting other sectors of society. The 2008 crisis is widely blamed for contributing to the rise of political populism. We now live in a world of alternative facts, fake news, distrust of institutions and demagoguery. Crypto as it exists today is part of that legacy. A lot of the arguments in favour of crypto make much more sense if you don't fundamentally believe in the legitimacy of democratic governments to impose constraints on individual freedom. Crypto is alternative finance. It is financial populism. It is based fundamentally not just on hatred of the established elites and a desire to chuck them out. It also reflects a distrust of established sources of truth. If traditional finance experts take a look at crypto and implore you not to put your life savings anywhere near it, there is a certain strain in the crypto ideology that interprets that warning as an endorsement. That is not to say that all crypto people are on the hard right. Digital assets have a diverse and eccentric political appeal. The impulse to create a better, fairer financial system is a good one. But crypto, like political populism, is based on a hollow promise of something better, which it has spectacularly failed to provide.

Notes

EPIGRAPH

ix **The media requires**: 'Public Speaking (2010) Fran Lebowitz, Martin Scorsese', Juan Ronco, YouTube, https://www.youtube.com/watch?v=G46BVjjkDfA

ix **The purpose of democracy**: 'Michael Ignatieff: Fighting Orban's Global Conservative Cabal', *The Rest is Politics*, 3 July 2023.

PREFACE

xix **It felt unnatural**: Michael Lewis, *Going Infinite*.

INTRODUCTION

7 **15 per cent**: The Block and CoinGecko, https://www.theblock.co/data/decentralized-finance/dex-non-custodial/dex-to-cex-spot-trade-volume

8   **as a gamble**: Financial Conduct Authority Research Note: 'Cryptoassets consumer research 2023', June 2023, https://www.fca.org.uk/publication/research-notes/research-note-cryptoasset-consumer-research-2023-wave4.pdf

11   **3 per cent in 2020 to 13 per cent by June 2022**: Demographics of U.S. Household Crypto-Asset Use, JPMorgan Chase Institute, December 2022, https://www.jpmorganchase.com/institute/research/financial-markets/dynamics-demographics-us-household-crypto-asset-cryptocurrency-use

11   **5 million people**: FCA research note https://www.fca.org.uk/publication/research-notes/research-note-cryptoasset-consumer-research-2023-wave4.pdf

12   **ordinary fish**: Author's interview, August 2023.

12   **entirely speculative in nature**: https://twitter.com/jerallaire/status/1590112499721940992

14   **what happened in 2008**: Author's interview, September 2023.

A BUNCH OF DORKS

24   **marginal dollar matters**: SBF interviewed on the FTX podcast, June 2020.

24   **I failed**: Lunch with the FT: Sam Bankman-Fried, *Financial Times*, May 2022, by Joshua Oliver, https://www.ft.com/content/83bc681a-a0f9-43bb-b627-c6dacae4a0a3

25   **take-no-prisoners utilitarians**: 'Portrait of a 29-year-old billionaire: Can Sam Bankman-Fried make his risky crypto business work?', Yahoo Finance, August 2021, by Roger Parloff, https://uk.finance.yahoo.com/news/ftx-ceo-sam-bankman-fried-profile-085444366.html?guccounter=1&guce_referrer=aHR0cHM6Ly9tYWlsLmdvb2dsZS5jb20v&guce_

referrer_sig=AQAAAHiggFEkH9g4Zjc1SPQynmGxZ
MyZ0zwqhK28YqxHqfkq-HzKkejjVGt0igaRdzkIFUu
khq56zZrtiWee852LNuXfXN3-eQCT3FpllFVzuj1p7Y
9lyhKiXBgsy3BH7qEDelsLg5QAXQDGCa2V1A9E-
a9wgHZFmg2vgCNVYezRxU4U

25   **endeared him to me**: https://twitter.com/BrettHarrison88/
status/1614371358519042051?lang=en

25   **early to spot**: 'Jane Street: the top Wall Street firm "no one's heard
of"', *Financial Times*, January 2021, by Robin Wigglesworth
https://www.ft.com/content/81811f27-4a8f-4941-99b3-
2762cae76542

26   **intuitively right**: FTX podcast, June 2020.

28   **worry about it**: Lunch with the FT.

29   **to share**: Max Boonen interviewed on the FTX podcast,
September 2021.

31   **yearbook photo**: 'From Math Camp to Handcuffs: FTX's
Downfall Was an Arc of Brotherhood and Betrayal', Bloomberg,
February 2023, by Ava Benny-Morrison and Annie Massa,
https://www.bloomberg.com/news/features/2023-02-16/sam-
bankman-fried-s-old-friend-co-founder-gary-wang-is-key-to-
case-against-ftx

31   **just understands him**: Author's interview, anonymous
source.

31   **speak to humans**: Author's interview, anonymous source.

31   **brilliant beyond belief**: Nishad Singh, interviewed on the
FTX podcast, December 2020.

31   **an enigma**: Author's interview, anonymous source.

32   **hang out with**: Caroline Ellison interviewed on the FTX
podcast, July 2020.

32 **full-time**: FTX podcast interview.

34 **amount of value**: Sam Trabucco interviewed on the FTX podcast, June 2020.

35 **long socks**: FTX podcast interview.

37 **drain our accounts**: archived by the Satoshi Nakamoto Institute, February 2009, https://satoshi.nakamotoinstitute. org/posts/p2pfoundation/1/#selection-45.1-45.479

37 **libertarian viewpoint**: Email archived by the Satoshi Nakamoto Institute, November 2008, https://satoshi.nakamotoinstitute. org/emails/cryptography/12/

38 **been feeble**: Based on a face-to-face survey of 1,800 Salvadoran households. 'Are Cryptocurrencies Currencies? Bitcoin as Legal Tender in El Salvador', National Bureau of Economic Research working paper, April 2022, revised February 2023, by Fernando E. Alvarez, David Argente and Diana Van Patten, https://www.nber.org/papers/w29968

39 **exaggerated form**: 'An Investor's Guide to Crypto', September 2022, by Campbell R. Harvey, Tarek Abou Zeid, Teun Draaisma, Martin Luk, Henry Neville, Andre Rzym and Otto van Hemert, https://papers.ssrn.com/sol3/papers. cfm?abstract_id=4124576

45 **the 1960s**: 'A Brief History of the Internet', published by The Internet Society, 1997, by Barry M. Leiner, Vinton G. Cerf, David D. Clark, Robert E. Kahn, Leonard Kleinrock, Daniel C. Lynch, Jon Postel, Larry G. Roberts, Stephen Wolff, https:// www.internetsociety.org/internet/history-internet/brief-history- internet/

46 **pulls people in**: Nathaniel Whittemore, interviewed on the FTX podcast, August 2022.

Notes

47 **looked fake**: 'Crypto Wash Trading', National Bureau of Economic Research working paper, by Lin William Cong, Xi Li, Ke Tang and Yang Yang, December 2022, https://www. nber.org/system/files/working_papers/w30783/w30783.pdf

47 **massive scheme**: 'Is Bitcoin Really Un-Tethered?', October 2019, by John M. Griffin and Amin Shams, https://papers. ssrn.com/sol3/papers.cfm?abstract_id=3195066

48 **Tether and Bitfinex**: For more on Tether and Bitfinex, read Zeke Faux's book *Number Go Up*.

48 **interact with him**: 'Tether's CEO: from IT sales to calling the shots in crypto land', *Financial Times*, December 2021, by Kadhim Shubber, Ryan McMorrow and Siddharth Venkataramakrishnan, https://www.ft.com/content/4576f34f-fcd6-4bef-bef4-d4a7ad49c5fc

48 **in 2008**: 'Tether: the former plastic surgeon behind the crypto reserve currency', *Financial Times*, July 2021, by Kadhim Shubber and Siddharth Venkataramakrishnan, https://www. ft.com/content/4da3060c-8e1a-439f-a1d7-a6a4688ad6ca

49 **changed the story**:
- Commodity Future Trading Commission order, CFTC Docket No. 22-04, October 2021, pp. 4–7. https://www. cftc.gov/PressRoom/PressReleases/8450-21
- Tether: Statement on Tether's Settlement with the CFTC, October 2021, https://tether.to/en/statement-on-tethers-settlement-with-the-cftc/
- 'Anyone Seen Tether's Billions?', Bloomberg, October 2021, by Zeke Faux, https://www.bloomberg.com/news/features/2021-10-07/crypto-mystery-where-s-the-69-billion-backing-the-stablecoin-tether

49 **been resolved**: Tether: Statement on Tether's Settlement with the CFTC, October 2021, https://tether.to/en/statement-on-tethers-settlement-with-the-cftc/

49 **was a lie**: Statement by Letitia James, February 2021, https://ag.ny.gov/press-release/2021/attorney-general-james-ends-virtual-currency-trading-platform-bitfinexs-illegal

49 **no wrongdoing**: Tether: Tether and Bitfinex reach settlement with New York Attorney General's Office, February 2021, https://tether.to/en/tether-and-bitfinex-reach-settlement-with-new-york-attorney-generals-office

49 **half of Bitcoin's price / criminal investigation**: 'Bitcoin-Rigging Criminal Probe Focused on Tie to Tether', Bloomberg, November 2018, by Matt Robinson and Tom Schoenberg, https://www.bloomberg.com/news/articles/2018-11-20/bitcoin-rigging-criminal-probe-is-said-to-focus-on-tie-to-tether

49 **'flawed' and inaccurate**: Tether: Tether Response to Flawed Paper by Griffin and Shams, November 2019, https://tether.to/en/tether-response-to-flawed-paper-by-griffin-and-shams

50 **seem untrustworthy**: 'The Crypto Story', Bloomberg, October 2022, by Matt Levine, https://www.bloomberg.com/features/2022-the-crypto-story/

52 **nearly $20 billion**: 'Data from Autonomous Research reported in Crypto Bulls Pile Into ICOs at Record Pace Despite Bitcoin Rout', Bloomberg, August 2018, by Benjamin Robertson, https://www.bloomberg.com/news/articles/2018-08-02/crypto-bulls-pile-into-icos-at-record-pace-despite-bitcoin-rout

52 **all the coins**: Su Zhu interviewed on the FTX podcast, May 2022.

52 **ICOs were 'scams'**: Study by Satis Group, reported in '80% of ICOs Are Scams', Report, Investopedia News, April 2018, by Shobhit Seth, https://www.investopedia.com/news/80-icos-are-scams-report/

52 **$4 billion ICO**: SEC: 'SEC Orders Blockchain Company to Pay $24 Million Penalty for Unregistered ICO', September 2019, https://www.sec.gov/news/press-release/2019-202

52 **$18.5 million fine**: SEC: 'Telegram to Return $1.2 Billion to Investors and Pay $18.5 Million Penalty to Settle SEC Charges', June 2020, https://www.sec.gov/news/press-release/2020-146

53 **recalling this period:** Nishad FTX podcast interview.

53 **largely monetary**: Trabucco FTX podcast interview.

54 **didn't know anyone**: SBF on the FTX podcast, June 2020.

55 **enamoured of the craziness**: Nate Parke interviewed on the FTX podcast, January 2021.

56 **the growing anxiety:** 'Early Alameda Staffers Quit After Battling Sam Bankman-Fried Over Risk, Compliance Concerns', *Wall Street Journal*, November 2022, by Gregory Zuckerman, https://www.wsj.com/articles/early-alameda-staffers-quit-after-battling-sam-bankman-fried-over-risk-compliance-concerns-11669810723; 'Effective Altruist Leaders Were Repeatedly Warned About Sam Bankman-Fried Years Before FTX Collapsed', *Time* magazine, March 2023, by Charlotte Alter, https://time.com/6262810/sam-bankman-fried-effective-altruism-alameda-ftx/

56 **concerns over risk management:** https://twitter.com/tara_macaulay/status/1592985303262072834

57 **gruelling period**: SBF on the FTX podcast, September 2022.

58 **I am shocked:** https://twitter.com/tara_macaulay/status/1592985303262072834

PIRATE SHIP

60 **Binance office**: 'Binance Doesn't Have a Headquarters Because Bitcoin Doesn't, Says CEO', CoinDesk, May 2020, by Paddy Baker, https://www.coindesk.com/markets/2020/05/08/binance-doesnt-have-a-headquarters-because-bitcoin-doesnt-says-ceo/

60 **Chinese authorities**: 'Binance's Shanghai office shut down following visit by authorities, sources say', The Block, November 2019, by Celia Wan, https://www.theblock.co/post/47922/binances-shanghai-office-shut-down-following-police-raid-sources-say; and 'Setting the record straight on our Binance reporting', The Block, November 2019, by Frank Chaparro, https://www.theblock.co/post/48112/setting-the-record-straight-on-our-binance-reporting

61 **two years**: 'Setting the record straight', The Block, https://www.theblock.co/post/48112/setting-the-record-straight-on-our-binance-reporting

61 **sunshine view**: 'Can Crypto's Richest Man Stand the Cold?', Bloomberg, June 2022, by Justina Lee and Max Chafkin, https://www.bloomberg.com/news/features/2022-06-23/binance-bnb-ceo-moves-to-dubai-as-us-regulators-target-the-crypto-exchange

62 **Tiananmen Square massacre**: 'Who Is Guangying Chen, and Is Binance a "Chinese Company"?', Binance Blog, September 2022, by Changpeng Zhao (since deleted), https://www.binance.com/en/blog/from-cz/who-is-guangying-chen-and-is-binance-a-chinese-company-23863309313 19516973

62 **possibilities for me**: CZ blog, https://www.binance.com/en/blog/from-cz/who-is-guangying-chen-and-is-binance-a-chinese-company-23863309313 19516973

Notes

63   **one headline**: 'The Former McDonald's Cook Who Made $1 Billion In Less Than 7 Months', Entrepreneurs Handbook, January 2022, by Ash Jurberg, https://entrepreneurshandbook. co/the-former-mcdonalds-cook-who-made-1-billion-in-less-than-7-months-6f82f811c04a

63   **poker game**: 'From Burgers to Bitcoin Billions: How CZ Built a Leading Crypto Exchange in Just 180 Days', Binance Blog, November 2020 (since deleted), https://www.binance. com/en/blog/from-cz/from-burgers-to-bitcoin-billions-how-cz-built-a-leading-crypto-exchange-in-just-180-days-421499824684901276

63   *New York Times* **interview**: '"I Feel Conflicted": Crypto's Offshore Trading Moguls Talk Shop', *New York Times*, July 2021, by Eric Lipton and Ephrat Livni, https://web. archive.org/web/20211125054457/https://www.nytimes. com/2021/07/23/business/dealbook/binance-FTX-ceos. html

63–4 **trading ecosystem**: 'Okcoin Launches Algorithmic Tools for Bitcoin Trading', Contify.com, June 2014, Archived by Dow Jones.

64   **black hoodie**: 'From Zero To Crypto Billionaire In Under A Year: Meet The Founder Of Binance', Forbes.com, February 2018, by Pamela Ambler, https://www.forbes.com/ sites/pamelaambler/2018/02/07/changpeng-zhao-binance-exchange-crypto-cryptocurrency/

64   **very good business**: Author's interview, anonymous source.

65   **6,000-word blog**: 'CZ's Principles', Binance Blog, October 2022 (since deleted), https://www.binance.com/en/blog/from-cz/czs-principles-6343713009794494746

65 **effectively CFO**: 'Meet "Heina" Chen, The Secretive Executive Holding The Purse Strings At Binance', Forbes, June 2023, by John Hyatt, Giacomo Tognini, David Jeans and Sarah Emerson, https://www.forbes.com/sites/johnhyatt/2023/06/14/binance-sec-cz-guangying-chen/?sh=6adf428a2a94

65 **do something**: Author's interview, anonymous source.

66 **rare interview**: 'Crypto's Most Powerful Woman Speaks Out as Crisis Rocks Binance', Bloomberg, June 2023, by Muyao Shen and Justina Lee, https://www.bloomberg.com/news/features/2023-06-28/binance-co-founder-yi-he-on-crypto-regulation-and-changpeng-cz-zhao#xj4y7vzkg

66 **cost is high**: CZ's Principles blog.

69 **$60 billion**: Nansen, Binance Dashboard, https://portfolio.nansen.ai/dashboard/binance

69 **Crypto.com**: 'Trading teams at Crypto.com exchange raise conflict questions', Financial Times, June 2023, by Nikou Asgari, https://www.ft.com/content/b5d2bf4b-225c-4f30-9f1c-cbe8dc762fa8

70 **a speech**: Reflections on DeFi, digital currencies and regulation – speech by Jon Cunliffe, November 2022 https://www.bankofengland.co.uk/speech/2022/november/jon-cunliffe-keynote-speech-and-panel-at-warwick-conference-on-defi-digital-currencies

71 **full of rocks**: 'LME finds bags of stones instead of nickel in metal warehouse', Financial Times, March 2023, by Harry Dempsey, https://www.ft.com/content/a8c4d8d5-7c81-4c54-a90a-9f3f60d1bdd2

72 **$5.5 trillion**: 'The world's 100 largest banks', 2022, S&P Global Market Intelligence, https://www.spglobal.com/

marketintelligence/en/news-insights/latest-news-headlines/
the-world-s-100-largest-banks-2022-69651785

72   **$630 trillion**: 'Global balance sheet 2022: Enter volatility',
McKinsey, https://www.mckinsey.com/~/media/mckinsey/
business%20functions/strategy%20and%20corporate%20
finance/our%20insights/global%20balance%20sheet%20
2022%20enter%20volatility/global-balance-sheet-2022-
enter-volatility.pdf page 5.

72   **$34 trillion**: 'Cryptocurrency exchange Binance: 2022 volumes
so far similar to 2021's $34 trillion', Reuters, June 2022, by Sudip
Kar-Gupta, https://www.reuters.com/markets/us/cryptocurrency-
exchange-binance-2022-volumes-so-far-similar-2021s-34-
trillion-2022-06-16/

75–6 **99 per cent of people**: 'Only 1% of people can handle crypto
self-custody right now: Binance CEO', Cointelegraph,
December 2022, by Brayden Lindrea, https://cointelegraph.
com/news/only-1-of-people-can-handle-crypto-self-
custody-right-now-binance-ceo

76–7 **1 million customers / 80 per cent of Bitcoin transactions
/ The newspaper described**: 'Tracing a Bitcoin's Exchange's
Fall From the Top to Shutdown', *Wall Street Journal*, April
2014, by Takashi Mochizuki, Kathy Chu and Eleanor
Warnock, https://www.wsj.com/articles/SB1000142405270
23043112045795083005131399 2292

77   **Quadriga**:
   • 'The Story Behind QuadrigaCX and Gerald Cotten,
   Netflix's "Crypto King"', CoinDesk, May 2023, by Toby
   Bochan, https://www.coindesk.com/learn/the-story-behind-
   quadrigacx-and-gerald-cotten-netflixs-crypto-king/

- 'Quadriga bankruptcy: C\$190 million may have turned into digital dust', Norton Rose Fulbright, July 2019, https://www.nortonrosefulbright.com/en/knowledge/publications/168bc350/quadriga-bankruptcy
- 'Ponzi Schemes, Private Yachts, and a Missing \$250 Million in Crypto: The Strange Tale of Quadriga', *Vanity Fair*, November 2019, by Nathaniel Rich, https://www.vanityfair.com/news/2019/11/the-strange-tale-of-quadriga-gerald-cotten
- 'Quadriga CEO's widow speaks out over his death and the missing crypto millions', CBC News, January 2022, by Cassie Williams, https://www.cbc.ca/news/canada/nova-scotia/quadriga-widow-jennifer-roberston-gerald-cotten-1.6318955

77 **Ponzi scheme**: 'QuadrigaCX: A Review by Staff of the Ontario Securities Commission', April 2020 https://www.osc.ca/quadrigacxreport/index.html#executive-summary

78 **more popular today**: 'CZ on Centralization Vs. Decentralization', Binance Blog, October 2022 (since deleted), https://www.binance.com/en/blog/from-cz/cz-on-centralization-vs-decentralization-2022-4766586322749082372

78 **as a bridge**: CZ on Centralization blog, https://www.binance.com/en/blog/from-cz/cz-on-centralization-vs-decentralization-2022-4766586322749082372

79 **in the FT**: 'Crypto shrugs at US crackdown on illicit activity', *Financial Times*, January 2023, by Scott Chipolina, https://www.ft.com/content/5f608ff2-8178-428c-b8d8-ddeb4c5a60da

79 **out of five stars**: 'World's biggest darknet marketplace, Russia-linked Hydra Market, seized and shut down, DOJ says', CNBC, April 2022, by Dan Mangan, https://www.cnbc.com/

2022/04/05/darknet-hydra-market-site-seized-and-shut-down-doj-says.html

80 **hyping up crypto**: 'Binance says footballer Andrés Iniesta was paid for Twitter post', *Financial Times*, November 2021, by Joshua Oliver, Samuel Agini and Daniel Dombey, https://www.ft.com/content/64d4cfa6-e277-4a5b-a8b7-f7def5b82e00

80 **historical issues**: 'Crypto Giant Binance Expects to Pay Penalties to Resolve U.S. Investigations', *Wall Street Journal*, February 2023, by Dave Michaels, https://www.wsj.com/articles/crypto-giant-binance-expects-to-pay-penalties-to-resolve-u-s-investigations-f1e3c9d2

80 **some gaps**: 'Binance Says it Had Compliance "Gaps" and Is Continuing Talks With US Regulators', Bloomberg, February 2023, by Olga Kharif, https://www.bloomberg.com/news/articles/2023-02-16/binance-says-it-had-compliance-gaps-and-is-continuing-talks-with-us-regulators

81 **pirate ship**: Complaint in Commodity Futures Trading Commission v Changpeng Zhao, Binance Holdings Limited, Binance Holdings (IE) Limited, Binance (Services) Holdings Limited, and Samuel Lim, March 2023.

81 **President Emmanuel Macron**: 'Binance's warm welcome in France draws stark divide with UK', *Financial Times*, May 2022, by Scott Chipolina, Leila Abboud and Joshua Oliver, https://www.ft.com/content/141408bb-3833-43c5-853b-a68d4fdaa330

81 **land anywhere**: CFTC v Binance complaint.

81 **ring-fence accordingly**: Complaint in Securities and Exchange Commission v Binance Holdings Limited, BAM Trading Services Inc., BAM Management US Holdings Inc. and Changpeng Zhao, June 2023.

82   **act with impunity**: https://twitter.com/jerallaire/status/ 1590112499721940992

82   **follow the rules**: 'Uber ride-sharing service targeted as Toronto seeks injunction', CBC News, November 2014, https://www.cbc.ca/news/canada/toronto/uber-ride-sharing-service-targeted-as-toronto-seeks-injunction-1.2839309

83   **important thing**: Author's interview, August 2023.

83   **It's irrelevant**: Author's interview, anonymous source.

84   **the USA bro**: SEC v Binance complaint.

84   **circumvent sanctions**: CFTC v Binance complaint.

84–5 **sanction countries**: CFTC v Binance complaint, p. 35.

85   **future liabilities**: SEC v Binance complaint, pp. 30–32.

85   *Forbes* **first reported:** 'Leaked "Tai Chi" Document Reveals Binance's Elaborate Scheme To Evade Bitcoin Regulators', Forbes, October 2020, by Michael del Castillo, https://www. forbes.com/sites/michaeldelcastillo/2020/10/29/leaked-tai-chi-document-reveals-binances-elaborate-scheme-to-evade-bitcoin-regulators/?sh=66c9eac22a92

85   **grey zone**: United States v Binance Holdings Ltd., November 2023; and Speech by Attorney General Merrick B. Garland Announcing Binance and CEO Guilty Pleas to Federal Charges in $4B Resolution, November 2023, https:// www.justice.gov/opa/speech/attorney-general-merrick-b-garland-delivers-remarks-announcing-binance-and-ceo-guilty#:~:text=The%20Justice%20Department%20is%20 requiring,defendant%20in%20a%20criminal%20matter.

86   **explicitly stating it**: Enforcement Release: OFAC Settles with Binance Holdings, Ltd. for $968,618,825 Related to Apparent Violations of Multiple Sanctions Programs, November 2023,

https://ofac.treasury.gov/system/files/2023-11/20231121_binance.pdf

86   **creative means**: SEC v Binance complaint, p. 35.

87   **support biz**: SEC v Binance complaint, p. 35.

87   **here for crime**: CFTC v Binance complaint.

87   **money laundering**: CFTC v Binance complaint.

87   **cake for you**: Speech by AG Merrick Garland, https://www.justice.gov/opa/speech/attorney-general-merrick-b-garland-delivers-remarks-announcing-binance-and-ceo-guilty#:~:text=The%20Justice%20Department%20is%20requiring,defendant%20in%20a%20criminal%20matter.

88   **funds going astray**: Statement: 'SEC Files 13 Charges Against Binance Entities and Founder Changpeng Zhao', June 2023, https://www.sec.gov/news/press-release/2023-101

88   **SEC claimed**: SEC v Binance complaint.

88   **Yellen said**: Remarks by Secretary of the Treasury Janet L. Yellen at Press Conference Announcing New Treasury Action Against Illicit Finance, November 2023, https://home.treasury.gov/news/press-releases/jy1926

89   **CZ wrote**: https://twitter.com/cz_binance/status/1727063503125766367

CASINO

94   **Andrew Goodwin**: Letter from Andrew Goodwin to Judge John G. Koeltl, 2022.

94   **tens of billions**: 'BitMEX Volume Hits $11 Billion As Bitcoin Nears $14,000: Is Retail Demand Coming Back?', Forbes, June 2019, by Joseph Young, https://www.forbes.com/sites/youngjoseph/2019/06/26/bitmex-volume-hits-

11-billion-as-bitcoin-nears-14000-is-retail-demand-coming-back/?sh=b3c257f1f75a

95   **a joke**: 'The Original King of Crypto Is Back', *New York* magazine, February 2023, by Jen Wieczner, https://nymag.com/intelligencer/article/arthur-hayes-bitmex-crypto-interview.html

96   **his schooldays**: Letter from Della Britton to Judge John G. Koeltl, April 2022.

96   **dancing to bodybuilding**: 'Class act: An outstanding young Western New Yorker', Buffalo News, October 2007, Archived by Dow Jones.

96   **Deutsch Bank**: 'Hires/Promotions/Honors', Buffalo News, October 2007, Archived by Dow Jones.

97   **you generously**: 'Class act', Buffalo News.

97–8 **my home**: 'Comeback', Entrepreneurs Handbook, October 2022, by Arthur Hayes, https://entrepreneurshandbook.co/comeback-fda90ba90677

98   **'out of the box' attitude**: Letter from Neil Cameron Hosie to Judge John G. Koeltl, March 2022.

98   **His room-mate**: Goodwin letter.

98   **bottle rules**: 'The Denominator', Entrepreneurs Handbook, May 2023, by Arthur Hayes, https://entrepreneurshandbook.co/the-denominator-536a8de34bf0

98   **What the fuck**: Author's interview with Arthur Hayes, July 2023.

99   **secular decline**: BitMEX: 'A bitcoin journey from bags of cash to the Cheung Kong Center', Euromoney, July 2019, by Chris Wright, https://www.euromoney.com/article/b1g2tc52h6l10q/bitmex-a-bitcoin-journey-from-bags-of-cash-to-the-cheung-kong-center

Notes

100   **make money**: Author's interview, July 2023.

101   **ancient world**: 'A Short History of Derivative Security Markets', by Ernst Juerg Weber, The University of Western Australia, 2008, https://www.law.uwa.edu.au/__data/assets/pdf_file/0003/94260/08_10_Weber.pdf

101   **Great Salad Oil Swindle**: History of the CFTC, Commodity Futures Trading Commission, https://www.cftc.gov/About/HistoryoftheCFTC/history_precftc.html

103   **trading at the bank**: Recording of Arthur Hayes presentation about BitMEX, 2016, https://www.youtube.com/watch?v=Ljw9ulT2NHE&t=489s&ab_channel=Beyond10x

103   **No one came**: Hayes presentation.

104   **entertainment business**: 'Crypto Conference Shows Bitcoin Getting Whole Lot More Fun Again', Bloomberg, July 2019, by Joanna Ossinger, https://www.bloomberg.com/news/articles/2019-07-05/crypto-conference-shows-bitcoin-getting-whole-lot-more-fun-again

104   **45th-floor office**: 'US$600,000 monthly office rent at Cheung Kong Center is a breeze for digital currency exchange BitMEX', *South China Morning Post*, August 2018, by Pearl Liu, https://www.scmp.com/business/article/2160878/us600000-monthly-office-rent-breeze-digital-currency-exchange

104   **caring young man**: Hosie letter.

105   **said in 2019**: Euromoney, July 2019.

105   **8,500 per cent**: Euromoney, July 2019.

106   **trading volumes**: CryptoCompare Exchange Review, September 2023.

106   **more than $1 billion**: CFTC v Binance complaint.

106   **dominated by excess**: Author's interview.

106   **Mic drop, bitches!**: 'Comeback', Hayes, https://entrepre-neurshandbook.co/comeback-fda90ba90677

107   **exchange was a bank**: Euromoney, July 2019.

108   **risk of liquidation**: Nishad FTX podcast interview.

109   **30 times**: Statement: 'FCA confirms permanent restrictions on the sale of CFDs and CFD-like options to retail consumers', September 2019, https://www.fca.org.uk/news/press-releases/fca-confirms-permanent-restrictions-sale-cfds-and-cfd-options-retail-consumers

109–10 **significant scale**: Statement: 'FCA bans the sale of crypto-derivatives to retail consumers', October 2020, https://www.fca.org.uk/news/press-releases/fca-bans-sale-crypto-derivatives-retail-consumers

110   **be exhausting**: Author's interview.

111   **set up to fail**: Author's interview, anonymous source.

111   **$8.6 billion**: 'Bitcoin gyrates on fears of regulatory crackdown', *Financial Times*, May 2021, by Thomas Hale, Tabby Kinder and Philip Stafford, https://www.ft.com/content/c4c29bb3-c8ee-454c-a2dd-eac9f644007f

112–13 **lose money**: Author's interview, July 2023.

113   **fraction of a penny**: Euromoney, July 2019.

113   **doesn't matter if it's crypto**: Author's interview.

114   **Lord Satoshi**: Author's interview.

115   **changed their life**: Lunch with the FT, https://www.ft.com/content/83bc681a-a0f9-43bb-b627-c6dacae4a0a3

115   **in Brazil**: 'Day Trading for a Living?', June 2020, by Fernando Chague, Rodrigo De-Losso and Bruno Giovannetti, https://papers.ssrn.com/sol3/papers.cfm?abstract_id=3423101

Notes

115   **study in Taiwan**: 'The cross-section of speculator skill: Evidence from day trading', *Journal of Financial Markets*, March 2014, by Brad M. Barber, Yi-Tsung Lee, Yu-Jane Liu, Terrance Odean, https://www.sciencedirect.com/science/article/abs/pii/S1386418113000190

115   **chase rising prices**: 'Crypto shocks and retail losses', Bank for International Settlements Bulletin, February 2023, by Giulio Cornelli, Sebastian Doerr, Jon Frost and Leonardo Gambacorta, https://www.bis.org/publ/bisbull69.pdf

115–16   **Vegas casino**: Author's interview, anonymous source.

117   **investigating BitMEX**: 'U.S. Regulator Probing Crypto Exchange BitMEX Over Client Trades', Bloomberg, July 2019, by Benjamin Robertson and Gregor Stuart Hunter, https://www.bloomberg.com/news/articles/2019-07-19/u-s-regulator-probing-crypto-exchange-bitmex-over-client-trades?sref=tnuvvlQG

117   **No real name:** Letter from the United States Attorney Southern District of New York to Judge John G. Koeltl, May 2022.

117   **to do otherwise:** SDNY letter.

118   **derivatives markets**: Statement: 'CFTC Orders Bitcoin Options Trading Platform Operator and its CEO to Cease Illegally Offering Bitcoin Options and to Cease Operating a Facility for Trading or Processing of Swaps without Registering', September 2015, https://www.cftc.gov/PressRoom/PressReleases/7231-15

118   **a 'sham'**: SDNY letter.

118   **created their account**: SDNY letter.

118–19   **users per day**: SDNY letter.

119 **$11 billion / 85,000 American users**: Commodity Futures Trading Commission v HDR Global Trading Limited, 100x Holdings Limited, ABS Global Trading Limited, Shine Effort Inc Limited, HDR Global Services (Bermuda) Limited, Arthur Hayes, Ben Peter Delo, and Samuel Reed, October 2020.

119 **$200 million**: Statement: 'FinCEN Announces $100 Million Enforcement Action Against Unregistered Futures Commission Merchant BitMEX for Willful Violations of the Bank Secrecy Act', August 2021, https://www.fincen.gov/news/news-releases/fincen-announces-100-million-enforcement-action-against-unregistered-futures

119 **mood-altering substance(s)**: SDNY letter Govt. sentencing memo, pp. 2, 11 and 13.

119 **refusing to comply**: Author's interview, anonymous source.

VERY PONZI-LIKE

121 **Ask Mashinsky Anything**: Available on YouTube: https://www.youtube.com/watch?v=GyRO_W-utXs&ab_channel=CelsiusNetwork

122 **the machine**: Alex Mashinsky, 'Celsius founder feeling the heat', *Financial Times*, June 2022, by Joshua Oliver and Kadhim Shubber, https://www.ft.com/content/18b6fb80-44dd-40ed-b5ea-3f3bf2814c7d

122 **$1.8 billion**: Complaint in Securities And Exchange: Commission v Celsius Network Limited and Alexander 'Alex' Mashinsky, SEC Celsius para. 273.

123 **full speed ahead**: 'Damn the Torpedoes, Full Speed Ahead', Celsius Blog, June 2022, https://celsiusnetwork.medium.com/damn-the-torpedoes-full-speed-ahead-4123847832af

Notes

124   **soothe our community**: Final Report of Shoba Pillay, Examiner, in Re. Celsius Network LLC, United States Bankruptcy Court Southern District of New York, January 2023.

124   **business case**: Examiner report.

124   **Waterfall report**: Examiner report.

124–5   **$428 million**: Examiner report.

125   **$8 million / US prosecutors now allege**: Indictment, United States v Alexander Mashinsky and Roni Cohen-Pavone, July 2023.

125   **easily get at him**: Author's interview, July 2021.

125   **New York's Attorney General**: Statement: 'Attorney General James Sues Former CEO of Celsius Cryptocurrency Platform for Defrauding Investors', January 2023, https://ag.ny.gov/press-release/2023/attorney-general-james-sues-former-ceo-celsius-cryptocurrency-platform-defrauding

125   **Federal Trade Commission**: Statement: 'FTC Reaches Settlement with Crypto Platform Celsius Network; Charges Former Executives with Duping Consumers into Transferring Cryptocurrency into their Platform and then Squandering Billions in User Deposits', July 2023, https://www.ftc.gov/news-events/news/press-releases/2023/07/ftc-reaches-settlement-crypto-platform-celsius-network-charges-former-executives-duping-consumers

125   **the CFTC**: Statement: 'CFTC Charges Alexander Mashinsky and Celsius Network, LLC with Fraud and Material Misrepresentations in Massive Commodity Pool Scheme Involving Digital Asset Commodities', July 2023, https://www.cftc.gov/PressRoom/PressReleases/8749-

23#:~:text=The%20complaint%20alleges%20that%20 from,digital%20asset%2Dbased%20finance%20platform.

126   **the SEC**: Statement: 'SEC Charges Celsius Network Limited and Founder Alex Mashinsky with Fraud and Unregistered Offer and Sale of Securities', July 2023, https://www.sec.gov/news/press-release/2023-133

126   **arrested and charged**: Statement: 'Celsius Founder And Former Chief Revenue Officer Charged In Connection With Multibillion-Dollar Fraud And Market Manipulation Schemes', July 2023, https://www.justice. gov/usao-sdny/pr/celsius-founder-and-former-chief- revenue-officer-charged-connection-multibillion

126   **external events**: Defendant's Memorandum Of Law In Support Of Motion To Dismiss Complaint, In The People Of The State Of New York By Letitia James, Attorney General Of The State Of New York Against Alex Mashinsky, May 2023.

126   **thrived under capitalism**: Alex Mashinsky personal website, https://mashinsky.com/about

126–7   **moved to the United States**: *Financial Times*, June 2022, https://www.ft.com/content/18b6fb80-44dd-40ed-b5ea- 3f3bf2814c7d

127   **maverick investor and entrepreneur**: Mashinsky personal website, https://mashinsky.com/failed-ventures

127   **inventors of VoIP**: Mashinsky personal website, https:// www.mashinsky.com/about

127   **are exaggerated**: 'Celsius's 18% Yields on Crypto Are Tempting—and Drawing Scrutiny', Bloomberg, January 2022, by Zeke Faux and Joe Light, https://www.

bloomberg.com/news/articles/2022-01-27/celsius-s-18-yields-on-crypto-are-tempting-and-drawing-scrutiny

128   **permission from AT&T**: Author's interview, July 2021.

128   **coming into things**: Author's interview, anonymous source.

128   **first significant loan**: Max Boonen interviewed on the FTX podcast, September 2021.

130   **savings in a bank**: Celsius Network White Paper, https://celsius.network/static/celsius-whitepaper.pdf p. 4.

130   **$50 million**: Declaration of Alex Mashinsky, Chief Executive Officer of Celsius Network LLC, United States Bankruptcy Court Southern District of New York, in Re Celsius Network LLC, July 2022,

130   **$200 million**: Mashinsky declaration.

131   **$10 billion**: Mashinsky declaration.

131   **half a million customers**: Complaint in Securities And Exchange Commission v Celsius Network Limited and Alexander 'Alex' Mashinsky, July 2023.

131   **deliver it to you**: Mashinsky indictment.

131   **8.5 per cent**: ICE BofA US High Yield Index Effective Yield, St Louis Federal Reserve, https://fred.stlouisfed.org/series/BAMLH0A0HYM2EY

132   **$1.36 billion**: Examiner report.

132   **investing customer assets**: Examiner report.

132–3   **Celsius lost**: SEC Celsius complaint.

133   **very Ponzi-like**: Examiner report.

133   **bought extra CEL tactically**: Mashinsky indictment.

133   **invisible hand**: Mashinsky indictment.

134   **$42 million**: Mashinsky indictment. The bankruptcy court examiner puts that number at $69 million. I use the more conservative figure.

134   **insider sales**: 'Inside Celsius: how one of crypto's biggest lenders ground to a halt', *Financial Times*, July 2023, by Kadhim Shubber and Joshua Oliver, https://www.ft.com/content/4fa06516-119b-4722-946b-944e38b02f45

135   **they would cope**: Author's interview, anonymous source.

135   **any of this got out**: Mashinsky indictment.

135   **very very bad look**: Examiner report.

135   **we cannot say that**: Mashinsky indictment.

135   **cryptocurrency mining**: Examiner report.

136   **holy grail**: 'North America's first bitcoin ETF captures flurry of trading on debut', *Financial Times*, February 2021, by Joshua Oliver, https://www.ft.com/content/d4c6bc33-97d9-4cef-82db-e8c0c1e6fc20

137   **under control**: Mashinsky indictment.

137   **very cringeworthy**: Author's interview, anonymous source.

138   **wrote those cheques**: 'Crypto lender Celsius Network raises $400m as regulatory pressure grows', *Financial Times*, October 2021, by Kadhim Shubber and Joshua Oliver, https://www.ft.com/content/b47c9499-f4a6-46f4-991b-e8f7f20d49e2

138   **Prime Trust**: 'Custodian Prime Trust Cuts Ties With Crypto Lender Celsius', CoinDesk, by Ian Allison, June 2021, https://www.coindesk.com/business/2021/06/24/custodian-prime-trust-cuts-ties-with-crypto-lender-celsius/

138   **$4 million**: Author's interview, anonymous source.

Notes

138–9   **document prepared by WestCap**: Document obtained from an anonymous source. I have confirmed its authenticity with independent sources.

139   **guarantee of success**: 'Canadian pension giant writes off $150mn Celsius investment', *Financial Times*, August 2022, by Scott Chipolina and Josephine Cumbo, https://www.ft.com/content/67048159-82aa-4e96-bfb3-f1764f632375; and 'Quebec's Caisse Writes Off Celsius, Saying Bet Was "Too Soon"', Bloomberg, August 2022, by Mathieu Dion, https://www.bloomberg.com/news/articles/2022-08-17/quebec-s-cdpq-writes-off-celsius-as-ceo-says-fund-was-too-soon

141   **the arrangement**: Examiner report.

141   **$105 million**: Examiner report.

141   **$230 billion**: 'Crypto feels the shockwaves from its own "credit crisis"', *Financial Times*, June 2022, by Joshua Oliver, Scott Chipolina and Kadhim Shubber, https://www.ft.com/content/032b95dc-7feb-4a2d-8eac-c71235643c07

143   **absolutely ludicrous**: Author's interview, anonymous source.

143   **pretty detailed look**: 'FCA leaves crypto firms in limbo as registration deadline looms', *Financial Times*, March 2022, by Joshua Oliver and Laura Noonan, https://www.ft.com/content/e2294ba4-3249-4272-91c4-0aee44e3368e

143   **rejection was private**: Examiner report.

143–4   **'regulatory uncertainty'**: Celsius Community Update, 23 June 2021. https://celsiusnetwork.medium.com/celsius-community-update-june-23-2021-a28fca899091

144   **Celsius's rival BlockFi**: 'Regulators in three US states close in on BlockFi's cryptocurrency accounts', *Financial*

Times, July 2021, by Gary Silverman and Miles Kruppa, https://www.ft.com/content/3d6c19d4-4848-4c0e-8112-5cff52dd1cbd

145   **6 per cent**: WestCap investment memo.

146   **Genesis / DCG / Gemini**: Statement: 'Attorney General James Sues Cryptocurrency Companies Gemini, Genesis, and DCG for Defrauding Investors', October 2023, https://ag.ny.gov/press-release/2023/attorney-general-james-sues-cryptocurrency-companies-gemini-genesis-and-dcg

146   **Voyager's former CEO**: Statement: 'CFTC Charges Former Chief Executive Officer of Digital Asset Platform with Fraud in Massive Commodity Pool Scheme', October 2023, https://www.cftc.gov/PressRoom/PressReleases/8805-23

148   **yesterday in Bahamas**: Examiner report.

148   **$6.5 billion**: 'The 2018 Meeting That Kicked off a Lending Relationship Between Alameda and Genesis', *Wall Street Journal*, January 2023, by Vicky Ge Huang and Caitlin Ostroff, https://www.wsj.com/livecoverage/stock-market-news-today-01-19-2023/card/the-2018-meeting-that-kicked-off-a-lending-relationship-between-alameda-and-genesis-7dzw1fYOFJUQqxDRt2IY

148–9   **One early investor**: Author's interview, anonymous source.

149–50   **A senior executive**: Author's interview, anonymous source.

150   **Molly White**: https://blog.mollywhite.net/celsius-letters/

150   **how to fix it**: Letter to Judge Martin Glenn, 3 August 2022.

150   **allowed to happen**: Letter to Judge Martin Glenn, 26 August 2022.

150   **good safe investment**: Letter to Judge Martin Glenn, 26 July 2022.

Notes

LEGENDARY

154 **NBC News**: 'Home of Miami Heat Officially Renamed as FTX Arena', NBC News Miami, June 2021, https://www.nbcmiami.com/news/sports/miami-heat/home-of-miami-heat-officially-renamed-as-ftx-arena/2466627/

154 **the biggest yet**: Available on YouTube, https://www.youtube.com/watch?v=buz89qQds0U&t=0s&ab_channel=BitcoinMagazine

154 **superspreader event**: 'Bitcoin conference attendees report testing positive for Covid after returning from Miami', CNBC, June 2021, by MacKenzie Sigalos, https://www.cnbc.com/2021/06/10/bitcoin-2021-attendees-report-covid-cases-after-returning-from-miami.html

155 **Michelle Bailhe**: Now Michelle Fradin. I will use her name at the time.

155 **bring your A-game**: Michelle Bailhe interviewed on the FTX podcast, November 2021.

156 **turned a profit**: This of course depends on which profit measure you prefer. 'Uber makes first operating profit after racking up $31.5bn of losses', *Financial Times*, August 2023, by Richard Waters.

156 **published by Sequoia itself**: 'Sam Bankman-Fried Has a Savior Complex—And Maybe You Should Too', sequoiacap.com, September 2022, by Adam Fisher (since deleted), https://web.archive.org/web/20221109230422/https://www.sequoiacap.com/article/sam-bankman-fried-spotlight/

157 **stays in work mode**: https://twitter.com/SBF_FTX/status/1357123557122187265

157 **it's not normal people**: Author's interview, anonymous source.

161 **unusually cheap**: Official Bank Rate history, Bank of England, https://www.bankofengland.co.uk/boeapps/database/Bank-Rate.asp

162 **Office for Budget Responsibility**: Coronavirus and the flow of funds, March 2021, https://obr.uk/box/coronavirus-and-the-flow-of-funds/#:~:text=While%20the%20net%20lending%20of,(by%20%C2%A3123%20billion).

162 **New Economics Foundation**: '99.5% Of Government Covid Debt Has Been Matched By So Called Bank Of England "Money Printing"', October 2021, https://neweconomics.org/2021/10/99-5-of-government-covid-debt-has-been-matched-by-so-called-bank-of-england-money-printing

164 **2,700 per cent**: 'Almost 900,000 accounts traded GameStop at peak of meme stock craze', *Financial Times*, October 2021, by Madison Darbyshire, https://www.ft.com/content/df758a2a-6caf-4d5f-ab70-bb5815922b91

165 **$1.7 trillion**: 'The end of the party looms for markets high on stimulus', *Financial Times*, February 2021, by Ruchir Sharma, https://www.ft.com/content/ed6f883f-eaaa-4dfc-85cc-e7d79251c89b

165 **$10 trillion**: Data from CryptoCompare.

165 **a fifth of US dollars**: *Financial Times*, Ruchir Sharma, https://www.ft.com/content/ed6f883f-eaaa-4dfc-85cc-e7d79251c89b

166 **most money on record**: McKinsey Global Private Markets Review 2023, https://www.mckinsey.com/industries/private-equity-and-principal-investors/our-insights/mckinseys-private-markets-annual-review

Notes

166   **made $3 billion**: 'With WhatsApp deal, Sequoia Capital burnishes reputation', Reuters, February 2014, by Sarah McBride, https://www.reuters.com/article/us-whatsapp-facebook-sequoia-idUSBREA1K04720140221

166   **around $1 billion**: Data from Crunchbase and PitchBook, https://news.crunchbase.com/health-wellness-biotech/theranos-elizabeth-holmes-trial-investors-board/; https://pitchbook.com/news/articles/Theranos-guilty-verdict-startups-venture-capital-silicon-valley

167   **burn $150 million**: 'The strangest and most alarming things in WeWork's IPO filing', CNBC News, August 2019, by Annie Palmer, https://www.cnbc.com/2019/08/17/wework-ipo-filing-strangest-and-most-alarming-things.html

167   **world's consciousness**: 'The beginning of a new story', WeWork.com, by Adam Neumann, January 2019, https://www.wework.com/newsroom/wecompany

167   **more than $1 billion**: 'WeWork Chairman Says Consulting Deal With Adam Neumann No Longer in Place', *Wall Street Journal*, October 2020, by Rolfe Winkler, https://www.wsj.com/articles/softbank-backs-out-of-consulting-deal-with-wework-co-founder-adam-neumann-11603136659

168   **$33 billion**: '2021: Crypto VC's Biggest Year Ever', Galaxy Digital Research, by Alex Thorn, January 2022.

168   **$2.2 billion**: Galaxy Digital Research, January 2022; Statement: 'Crypto Fund III, a16z', June 2021, https://a16zcrypto.com/posts/announcement/crypto-fund-iii/

169   **egregious example**: Author's interview, anonymous source.

169   **investors rely on them**: Author's interview, anonymous source.

170 **we were misled**: Alfred Lin interviewed by Connie Loizos, January 2023, available on YouTube: https://www.youtube.com/watch?v=Gf-d-Hrx6_A&ab_channel=ConnieLoizos

170 **hard fucking thing**: Author's interview, anonymous source.

170 **stealing customer funds**: Author's interview, anonymous source.

171 **five days or less**: Bailhe on the FTX podcast.

172 **early 2022:** Alfred Lin interviewed by Connie Loizos, January 2023, available on YouTube: https://www.youtube.com/watch?v=Gf-d-Hrx6_A&ab_channel=ConnieLoizos

174 **taking pictures**: Government Exhibit (GX) 1451, United States Of America v Samuel Bankman-Fried.

175 **Super Bowl or something**: Nathaniel Whittemore on the FTX podcast, August 2022.

175 **his wedding**: 'Larry David Officiates Agent Ari Emanuel's Wedding Attended By Elon Musk, Diddy & More', *Hollywood Life*, May 2022, by Erin Silvia; WME's Ari Emanuel Married By LD, TMZ, May 2022, https://www.tmz.com/2022/05/29/ari-emanuel-wme-wedding-marries-st-tropez-larry-david/

175 **supermodel Gisele Bündchen**: 'How FTX built its network of stars', *Financial Times*, February 2023 https://ig.ft.com/ftx-shareholders/

176 **get that validation**: Sina Nader interviewed on the FTX podcast, August 2022.

176 **$10 million**: GX 343.

176 **college football teammate**: Nader on the FTX podcast.

177 **cleanest brand in crypto**: Complaint in Securities And Exchange Commission v Caroline Ellison And Zixiao 'Gary' Wang, December 2022.

Notes

177–8 **Cambrian explosion**: Whittemore on the FTX podcast.

178 **$1.13 billion**: GX 343.

178 **laundry list of celebrities**: GX 42.

178–9 **electoral politics**: GX 42.

179 **surprised and dismayed**: Motion To Dismiss Plaintiffs' Complaint In Alameda Research Ltd (And Others) v Michael Kives (And Others), September 2023.

180 **no interest in PR**: Author's interview, anonymous source.

181 **not answering the question**: Author's interview, anonymous source.

182 **intern for FTX**: https://www.instagram.com/p/CZ5Qw2-vVoW/?img_index=1

182 **Ethereum Max**: 'Kim Kardashian, Floyd Mayweather and a crypto token's wild ride', *Financial Times*, January 2022, by Joshua Oliver and Madison Darbyshire, https://www.ft.com/content/a6dd4d6f-6a86-48cc-992c-f8a32c64fdd7; 'Kim Kardashian to pay $1.3mn to settle crypto charges', *Financial Times*, October 2022, by Stefania Palma, https://www.ft.com/content/9a2d66be-4598-401a-b5c5-750640bb1b82; Statement: 'SEC Charges Kim Kardashian for Unlawfully Touting Crypto Security', October 2022, https://www.sec.gov/news/press-release/2022-183

183 **a quarter lost 90 per cent**: '24% of New Tokens Launched in 2022 Bear On-Chain Characteristics of Pump and Dump Schemes', Chainalysis Research, February 2023, https://www.chainalysis.com/blog/2022-crypto-pump-and-dump-schemes/

183   **crypto messiah**: Author's interview, anonymous source.

183   **giving millions**: 'A Crypto Emperor's Vision: No Pants, His Rules', *New York Times*, May 2022, by David Yaffe-Bellany, https://www.nytimes.com/2022/05/14/business/sam-bankman-fried-ftx-crypto.html

183   **2022 midterms**: 'Sam Bankman-Fried's fall cuts off big source of funds for US Democrats', *Financial Times*, November 2022, by Stefania Palma, Courtney Weaver and Caitlin Gilbert, https://www.ft.com/content/428c7800-c72d-4c59-9940-4376fea6e263

183   **$100 million**: 'Bankman-Fried used $100 mln in stolen FTX funds for political donations, US says', Reuters, August 2023, by Luc Cohen, https://www.reuters.com/legal/bankman-fried-used-customer-funds-100-mln-us-political-donations-prosecutors-say-2023-08-14/

184   **Nauru**: Complaint in Ftx Trading Ltd (And Others) Against Samuel Bankman-Fried (And Others), July 2023.

184   **woke shit**: GX 477.

184   **Ninety-nine per cent**: Author's interview, anonymous source.

185   **White House officials**: 'Bankman-Fried Met With White House Aides on Crypto Policy Before FTX Collapse', Bloomberg, December 2022, by Josh Wingrove and Allyson Versprille, https://www.bloomberg.com/news/articles/2022-12-29/bankman-fried-met-white-house-aides-in-pre-collapse-crypto-push; 'White House Claims Meetings Between SBF and Senior Biden Officials Were About Pandemic', Decrypt, January 2023, by Sander Lutz, https://decrypt.co/118319/white-house-claims-meetings-between-sbf-and-senior-biden-officials-were-about-pandemic

Notes

185   **thought he was brilliant**: Author's interview, anonymous source.

186   **asleep on his beanbag**: 'The 2018 Meeting That Kicked off a Lending Relationship Between Alameda and Genesis', *Wall Street Journal*, January 2023, by Vicky Ge Huang and Caitlin Ostroff, https://www.wsj.com/livecoverage/stock-market-news-today-01-19-2023/card/the-2018-meeting-that-kicked-off-a-lending-relationship-between-alameda-and-genesis-7dzw1fYOFJUQqxDRt2IY

186   **right kind of white boy**: 'White Boy', Entrepreneurs Handbook, November 2022, by Arthur Hayes https://entrepreneurshandbook.co/white-boy-b12c33484a2e

187   **a 'friend'**: https://twitter.com/SBF_FTX/status/1593014934207881218

187   **eight months ago**: https://twitter.com/KelseyTuoc/status/1593031254076977152

187   **right shibboleths**: 'Sam Bankman-Fried tries to explain himself', Vox, November 2022, by Kelsey Piper, https://www.vox.com/future-perfect/23462333/sam-bankman-fried-ftx-cryptocurrency-effective-altruism-crypto-bahamas-philanthropy

190–91   **geographically distributed**: First Interim Report of John J. Ray III to the Independent Directors, April 2023.

191   **the basics**: https://twitter.com/sbf_ftx/status/1172060173604515840

191   **hit by a bus**: Ray, First Report.

191   **going on financially**: Author's interview, anonymous source.

192   **standard of perfect**: Author's interview, anonymous source.

192   **blocked by Sam**: Author's interview, anonymous source.

192   **very important right away**: Author's interview, anonymous source.

193   **throwing money at it**: Author's interview, anonymous source.

193   **corporate formalities**: Complaint In Alameda Research Ltd (And Others) v Michael Kives (And Others), June 2023.

193   **quarter of a billion dollars**: Second Interim Report of John J. Ray III to the Independent Directors, June 2023.

193   **country's 2022 GDP**: https://www.bahamas.gov.bs/wps/wcm/connect/6bf34cf8-9ff0-498e-8801-8af29a7ae550/PRESS+RELEASE+Annual+GDP+2022-Media.pdf?MOD=AJPERES

194   **owned the rest**: Alameda v Kives complaint.

194   **to the three men**: Alameda v Kives complaint.

195   **such is life**: Ray, First Report.

195   **raise concerns**: Alameda v Kives complaint.

195   **vacuums of competence**: Author's interview, anonymous source.

195–6   **everyone at FTX**: Bailhe on the FTX podcast.

196   **fake it until you make it**: *Bad Blood*, epilogue, by John Carreyrou.

197   **operational risk**: 'Preliminary Report Addressing Question Posed By The Official Committee Of Unsecured Creditors: Why Did BlockFi Fail?', July 2023.

198   **fuck-up**: Author's interview.

Notes

200　**Adam says**: Adam Yedidia testimony in USA v SBF.

201　**@alameda-research.com email**: GX 320.

ACCIDENTALLY

205　**Speaking to Bloomberg**: Transcript: 'Sam Bankman-Fried and Matt Levine on How to Make Money in Crypto', Bloomberg, April 2022, https://www.bloomberg.com/news/articles/2022-04-25/odd-lots-full-transcript-sam-bankman-fried-and-matt-levine-on-crypto?leadSource=uverify%20wall#xj4y7vzkg

212　**Do Kwon**: '$40bn crypto collapse turns South Korea against the "Lunatic" leader', *Financial Times*, May 2022, by Christian Davies and Song Jung-a, https://www.ft.com/content/c46f767c-c8e3-47cf-b0a3-46d3b84498c3

212　**going into crypto**: 'How Do Kwon Went From Crypto King to Fugitive to Jail', Bloomberg, October 2022, by Sangmi Cha and Sidhartha Shukla, https://www.bloomberg.com/news/articles/2022-10-17/how-onetime-crypto-titan-do-kwon-became-a-fugitive-quicktake; 'How a Trash-Talking Crypto Founder Caused a $40 Billion Crash', *New York Times*, May 2022, by David Yaffe-Bellany and Erin Griffith, https://www.nytimes.com/2022/05/18/technology/terra-luna-cryptocurrency-do-kwon.html?referringSource=articleShare

212　**debate the poor**: https://twitter.com/stablekwon/status/1410491186196795398?lang=en

212　**build-up of risk**: 'Anatomy of a Run: The Terra Luna Crash', National Bureau of Economic Research working paper, April 2023, by Jiageng Liu, Igor Makarov and Antoinette Schoar.

213 **stampeding for the exit**: https://twitter.com/Frances_Coppola/status/1410485529607643136

214 **naturally heal[ed]**: Complaint in Securities and Exchange Commission v Terraform Labs PTE Ltd and Do Hyeong Kwon, February 2023.

214 **Jump Trading**: SEC v Kwon complaint; 'Jump Trading Did Secret Deal to Prop Up TerraUSD Stablecoin, SEC Says', *Wall Street Journal*, May 2023, by Alexander Osipovich, https://www.wsj.com/articles/jump-trading-did-secret-deal-to-prop-up-terrausd-stablecoin-sec-says-11335951

214 **largest crypto network**: NBER Terra paper.

215 **$6 million a day**: NBER Terra paper.

215 **require a subsidy**: NBER Terra paper; 'Anchor Protocol Will Readjust Interest Rates Each Month, ANC Falls by 5%', CoinDesk, March 2022, by Shaurya Malwa, https://www.coindesk.com/markets/2022/03/25/anchor-protocol-will-readjust-interest-rates-each-month-anc-falls-by-5/

215 **destruction of wealth**: 'Exploring UST's Fall From Grace', CryptoCompare research, May 2022, https://ccdata.io/reports/exploring-usts-fall-from-grace

215 **Citadel Securities**: 'Terra Says Citadel Securities Caused UST Stablecoin Depeg', Decrypt, October 2023, by Andrew Asmakov, https://decrypt.co/201342/terraform-labs-alleges-citadel-securities-behind-may-2022-ust-stablecoin-depeg-event

215 **prevent suicides**: '$40bn crypto collapse turns South Korea against the "Lunatic" leader', *Financial Times*, May 2022, by Christian Davies and Song Jung-a, https://www.ft.com/content/c46f767c-c8e3-47cf-b0a3-46d3b84498c3

215   **'not on the run'**: https://twitter.com/stablekwon/status/1571197156907679745

215   **'carried away'**: 'Do Kwon of Terra: "It Was Never Really About Money or Fame or Success"', Unchained Crypto, October 2022, https://www.youtube.com/watch?v=RgYSJVC7Ps8&t=1066s

215–16 **forged Costa Rican passport**: 'Do Kwon Sentenced to 4 Months Jail in Montenegro Document Forgery Case', CoinDesk, June 2023, by Sandali Handagama, https://www.coindesk.com/policy/2023/06/19/do-kwon-sentenced-to-4-months-jail-in-montenegro-document-forgery-case/

216   **blue-blood atmosphere**: 'The Crypto Geniuses Who Vaporized a Trillion Dollars', *New York* magazine, August 2022, by Jen Wieczner, https://nymag.com/intelligencer/article/three-arrows-capital-kyle-davies-su-zhu-crash.html

216   **laid off**: Su Zhu interviewed on the FTX podcast, September 2020.

216   **from their apartment**: 'Ex-High School Classmates Are Among the World's Largest Crypto Holders', Bloomberg, May 2021, by Simon Hunt and Tom Maloney, https://www.bloomberg.com/news/articles/2021-05-25/ex-credit-suisse-traders-amass-billions-of-dollars-of-crypto?utm_medium=cpc_social&utm_source=twitter_&utm_campaign=bofu_content_0_subpagevisits&utm_content=0602cryptoholders

216   **several billion**: Affidavit of Russell Crumpler, liquidator of Three Arrows Capital Ltd, July 2022.

216   **Much Wow**: Foreign Representatives' Notice Of Filing Of 2 December 2022 Hearing Presentation, In Re Three Arrows Capital, Ltd, United States Bankruptcy Court Southern District Of New York, December 2022.

217   **next fashion**: Zhu on the FTX podcast, September 2020.

217   **his prediction**: 'Their Crypto Company Collapsed. They Went to Bali', *New York Times*, June 2023, by David Yaffe-Bellany, https://www.nytimes.com/2023/06/09/technology/three-arrows-cryto-bali.html#:~:text=Zhu%20were%20managing%20billions%20of,Bitcoin%20north%20of%20%241%20million.

218   **$500m more now**: https://twitter.com/zhusu/status/1453202115464028161

218   **two dozen lenders**: First Affidavit Of Kyle Livingston Davies, In The Matter Of Three Arrows Capital Ltd, June 2022.

218   **$600 million**: Davies affidavit.

218   **$2.4 billion**: Davies affidavit; 'Genesis Lent $2.4 Billion to Hedge Fund Three Arrows Capital', *Wall Street Journal*, July 2022, by Justin Baer, Caitlin Ostroff and Vicky Ge Huang, https://www.wsj.com/articles/genesis-lent-2-4-billion-to-hedge-fund-three-arrows-capital-11658170583

218   **$75 million**: Davies affidavit.

220   **traders actually owned**: 'On-Chain Forensics: Demystifying stETH's "De-peg"', Nansen Research, June 2022, https://www.nansen.ai/research/on-chain-forensics-demystifying-steth-depeg#steth-leverage-strategy

220   **prices had been aligned**: Nansen Research, June 2022, https://www.nansen.ai/research/on-chain-forensics-demystifying-steth-depeg#steth-leverage-strategy

Notes

221 **half a billion**: Declaration Of Alex Mashinsky, Chief Executive Officer Of Celsius Network LLC, United States Bankruptcy Court Southern District Of New York, In Re Celsius Network LLC, July 2022.

222 **$10 billion**: 'The Great DeFi Deleveraging', Glassnode Research, June 2022. https://insights.glassnode.com/the-great-defi-deleveraging/

223 **$650 million**: 'Voyager Digital shares crash after warning of Three Arrows crypto loss', *Financial Times*, June 2022, by Kadhim Shubber, https://www.ft.com/content/d75801c9-b9dd-4f90-b012-6948cca680d0

223 **SBF agreed to loan**: Statement: 'Voyager Digital Signs Term Sheet for US$200 Million and 15,000 BTC Revolving Line of Credit with Alameda Research', June 2022 (available in Web Archive), https://web.archive.org/web/20230531044648/https://www.investvoyager.com/pressreleases/voyager-digital-signs-term-sheet-for-ususd200-million-and-15-000-btc-revolving-line-of-credit-with-alameda-research

223 **$250 million**: Statement: 'BlockFi Signs a Landmark Term Sheet with FTX to Provide a $250 Million Credit Facility', June 2022, https://www.prnewswire.com/news-releases/blockfi-signs-a-landmark-term-sheet-with-ftx-to-provide-a-250-million-credit-facility-301572011.html

224 **$400 million**: 'FTX agrees deal with option to buy BlockFi for up to $240mn', *Financial Times*, July 2022, by Hannah Murphy and Joshua Oliver, https://www.ft.com/content/fa95d027-8afd-43f1-b9b1-ee8c204435c7

224 **let it go bankrupt**: 'Voyager Digital files for bankruptcy protection as crypto crisis deepens', *Financial Times*, July 2022, by Joshua Oliver, https://www.ft.com/content/0b5b68d9-85f1-47ce-a9f7-34252e4fe2ce

224 **end of June**: 'Crypto hedge fund Three Arrows files for US bankruptcy', *Financial Times*, July 2022, by Scott Chipolina and Adam Samson, https://www.ft.com/content/8e4538cc-e8c5-4cc2-9448-053074f72f67

224 **ill-judged PR**: 'Their Crypto Company Collapsed. They Went to Bali', *New York Times*, June 2023, by David Yaffe-Bellany, https://www.nytimes.com/2023/06/09/technology/three-arrows-cryto-bali.html#:~:text=Zhu%20were%20managing%20billions%20of,Bitcoin%20north%20of%20%241%20million.

225 **Davies whereabouts**: 'Three Arrows co-founder sent to prison in Singapore, says liquidator', *Financial Times*, September 2023, by Nikou Asgari, https://www.ft.com/content/2bc70649-d025-440f-ad56-d92998c5f695

225 **new John Pierpont Morgan**: 'FTX Ventures buys 30% stake in Scaramucci's SkyBridge Capital', *Financial Times*, September 2022, by Ortenca Aliaj and Joshua Oliver, https://www.ft.com/content/2767017b-ce15-4e88-9176-337a0d924fb8

226 **murdering the company**: Author's interview, anonymous source.

227 **get balls long**: https://twitter.com/carolinecapital/status/1368528742889390088

228 **understanding technology**: Sam Trabucco interviewed on the FTX podcast, September 2022.

Notes

229   **elementary school math[s]**: Caroline Ellison interviewed by El Momento, May 2022, https://www.youtube.com/watch?v=Qd2enI4RvXU&ab_channel=ElMomento

229   **non-medicated human experience**: https://twitter.com/carolinecapital/status/1379036346300305408?lang=en

230   **numbers? idk**: Ray, First Report.

230   **pretty crazy**: FTX podcast, January 2022.

230   **country's president**: 'Sam Bankman-Fried's Supersized Bet: $1 Billion for a Bitcoin Miner on the Kazakh Steppe', *Wall Street Journal*, January 2023, by Eliot Brown and Yuliya Chernova, https://www.wsj.com/articles/inside-sam-bankman-frieds-1-billion-bet-on-a-bitcoin-miner-on-the-kazakh-steppe-11673453716

230   **Sequoia and Paradigm**: 'Bankman-Fried invested in venture capital backers of his FTX exchange', *Financial Times*, November 2022, by Kadhim Shubber, Arash Massoudi and Tabby Kinder, https://www.ft.com/content/993942cb-1a7e-4689-9d9d-8434d4a74cc5

230   **internal list**: Records obtained by the *Financial Times*, https://www.ft.com/content/aaa4a42c-efcc-4c60-9dc6-ba6cccb599e6

231   **$15 billion**: Author's interview.

231   **Alameda's mindset**: FTX podcast, September 2022.

233   **close to bankruptcy**: This phrasing is as SBF remembered it in our interview. Caroline and other witnesses all agree on the substance of what she said.

234–5   **created a model**: GX 36 and Caroline Ellison's testimony in USA v SBF.

235   '**worries/questions**': GX 49A and Caroline Ellison's testimony in USA v SBF.

236   **Gary's number**: GX 50F.

236   **his memo**: GX 18.

237   **$2.5 million**: Notice Regarding the Debtors' Schedules and Statements, in Re FTX Trading Ltd, July 2023.

237   '**the best trading**': FTX podcast, September 2022.

238   **well suited to do**: 'Inside the Private Writings of Caroline Ellison, Star Witness in the FTX Case', *New York Times*, July 2023, by David Yaffe-Bellany and Matthew Goldstein, https://www.nytimes.com/2023/07/20/technology/ftx-caroline-ellison-bankman-fried.html

239   **pay interest**: Complaint in Securities And Exchange Commission v Samuel Bankman-Fried, December 2022.

239–40 **got to zero**: Author's interview, anonymous source.

240   **balance sheets**: GX 44.

242   **unusually close**: 'Divisions in Sam Bankman-Fried's Crypto Empire Blur on His Trading Titan Alameda's Balance Sheet', CoinDesk, November 2022, by Ian Allison, https://www.coindesk.com/business/2022/11/02/divisions-in-sam-bankman-frieds-crypto-empire-blur-on-his-trading-titan-alamedas-balance-sheet/

242   **>$10b of assets**: https://twitter.com/carolinecapital/status/1589264377433456641

242   **believed the valuations**: Author's interview, anonymous source.

243   **crack down on Binance**: GX 25B.

243   **allowed to go to DC**: SBF Twitter, October 2022.

243   **won't support people**: https://twitter.com/cz_binance/status/1589374530413215744?lang=en

244   **FTT on our books**: https://twitter.com/cz_binance/status/1589283421704290306?lang=en

244   **'120m/hr'**: GX 1621.

244   **should I say**: GX 1621.

244   **hands on deck**: Gary Wang testimony in USA v SBF.

245   **didn't feel right**: Author's interview, anonymous source.

245   **dump assets back**: Author's interview, anonymous source.

246   **big gaping hole**: Author's interview, anonymous source.

246   **risk mismanagement issue**: Author's interview, anonymous source.

246   **solution, solution, solution**: Author's interview, anonymous source.

246   **can be flexible**: Documents obtained by the *Financial Times*.

246–7   **robbing a bank**: Author's interview, anonymous source.

247   **EA philosophy**: Author's interview, anonymous source.

247   **kind of a miracle**: Author's interview, anonymous source.

247   **stall on responding**: GX 412.

248   **transaction with Binance**: https://twitter.com/SBF_FTX/status/1590012124864348160?lang=en

248   **tell us something**: Author's interview, anonymous source.

248   **We're fucked**: Author's interview, anonymous source.

248   **domino effect**: Author's interview, anonymous source.

249   **something wrong**: Author's interview, anonymous source.

249   **from minute one**: Author's interview, anonymous source.

250   **one way or another**: GX 480D.

250   **super appreciated**: GX 414.

251 **secretly recorded**: Extracts from an audio recording were played in court at SBF's trial. The full recording was published by Jacob Shamsian and Katie Balevic of Business Insider, https://www.businessinsider.com/alameda-all-hands-meeting-caroline-ellison-shut-down-audio-2023-10

256 **Sam, you're done**: Author's interview, anonymous source.

256 **kiss his ass**: Author's interview, anonymous source.

256–7 **breaking psychologically**: Author's interview, anonymous source.

257 **was disappearing**: Author's interview, anonymous source.

257 **I love you**: Testimony of Adam Yedidia in USA v SBF.

257 **sign this damn thing**: Author's interview, anonymous source.

259 **$8.7 billion**: Ray, Second Report.

260 **could do anything**: Author's interview, anonymous source.

CONCLUSION

262 **like everyone else's**: https://twitter.com/SBF_FTX/status/1156696100729806849

265 **remaining client assets**: GX 21.

267 **probably correct**: GX 480C.

270 **$50 trillion**: 'Global Pension Assets Study – 2023', Thinking Ahead Institute, https://www.thinkingaheadinstitute.org/research-papers/global-pension-assets-study-2023/#:~:text=The%20Global%20Pension%20Assets%20Study,the%20GDP%20of%20these%20economies.

270 **profited from it**: Author's interview, September 2023.

272 **Temasek**: 'Our Chairman's Statement on FTX Internal Review', Temasek, May 2023, https://www.temasek.com.sg/en/news-and-resources/news-room/statements/2023/our-chairman-statement-on-ftx-internal-review

272 **2021 speech**: 'Is "crypto" a financial stability risk? – speech by Jon Cunliffe', October 2021, https://www.bankofengland.co.uk/speech/2021/october/jon-cunliffe-swifts-sibos-2021

272 **future threat**: 'Financial Stability in Focus: Cryptoassets and decentralised finance', Bank of England, March 2022, https://www.bankofengland.co.uk/financial-stability-in-focus/2022/march-2022

273 **developing world**: 'Cryptocurrencies: developing countries provide fertile ground', *Financial Times*, September 2021, by Jonathan Wheatley and Adrienne Klasa, https://www.ft.com/content/1ea829ed-5dde-4f6e-be11-99392bdc0788; 'China capitalises on US sanctions in fight to dethrone dollar', *Financial Times*, August 2023, by Michael Stott and James Kynge, https://www.ft.com/content/3888bdba-d0d6-49a1-9e78-4d07ce458f42

274 **economists fear**: 'Crypto risks "destabilising" emerging markets, says senior IMF official', *Financial Times*, January 2022, by Chris Flood, https://www.ft.com/content/45ca2229-485e-4043-b709-deda943e9ddb

274 **digital renminbi**: 'Virtual control: the agenda behind China's new digital currency', *Financial Times*, February 2021, by James Kynge in Hong Kong and Sun Yu, https://www.ft.com/content/7511809e-827e-4526-81ad-ae83f405f623

274 **global means of payment**: 'China capitalises on US sanctions in fight to dethrone dollar', *Financial Times*, August 2023,

by Michael Stott and James Kynge, https://www.ft.com/content/3888bdba-d0d6-49a1-9e78-4d07ce458f42

276   **millions of people a day**: What we do, Transport for London, https://tfl.gov.uk/corporate/about-tfl/what-we-do#:~:text=London%20Underground%2C%20better%20known%20as,trains%20whizzing%20around%20the%20Capital.

Acknowledgements

My first thanks must be to all my sources for this book, both named and anonymous. So many people – insiders, bystanders and experts – were generous with their time and knowledge. Some took risks to speak to me and tell the truth. This book would not exist without you all.

I am profoundly grateful to my colleagues at the *Financial Times*. Our reporting on FTX and the crypto crash was a vast global team effort by many brilliant journalists, too numerous to name. I'd like to particularly acknowledge reporters Kadhim Shubber, Nikou Asgari, Scott Chipolina, Sujeet Indap and Antoine Gara – as well as Joe Miller, my courthouse ally. Special thanks to Akila Quinio, without whom this book might not have been possible.

I was fortunate to have many talented editors, including Katie Martin, Phil Stafford, David Crow, Jessica Dye, Geoff Dyer, Alice Fishburn, Jonathan Derbyshire, Matt Garahan, Peter Spiegel,

Tom Braithwaite and above all Adam Samson. Thanks to Brooke Masters for all her wise advice. My brilliant boss Harriet Agnew kept me on course. Alec Russell, Lorien Kite and Horatia Harrod at *FT Weekend* took a chance sending me on my first adventure to the court of SBF. Matt Vella at the *FT Magazine* commissioned and shaped the article that led to this book. Nigel Hanson indefatigably kept us on the right side of the law. The sub-editors, picture editors, graphics team and others who produce the *FT* every day are the unsung heroes of the newsroom.

I owe a special debt to Lionel Barber for his mentorship and for giving me my first big break; to Sally Kennedy and the former assistants' club for their good comradeship; and to Roula Khalaf and Patrick Jenkins for their constant support and guidance.

I also want to acknowledge my journalistic colleagues at other titles. I spent much of the past three years cursing your names when you got some scoop I wish I had written. But ultimately, public interest journalism is a team sport, and I have benefited enormously from having such excellent competitors. Among many, many talented rivals, I'd like to acknowledge Zeke Faux, Tom Wilson, Angus Berwick, David Yaffe-Bellany, Caitlin Ostroff, Alexander Osipovich and Teddy Scheifler.

I was fortunate in the brilliant team that helped me to take this book from the first germ of an idea to publication. Thank you to Jonny Geller, Ciara Finan and the team at Curtis Brown. Caitlin Allen was an eagle-eyed fact-checker and provided many helpful comments on the draft. Rik Ubhi and Tim Whiting at Bonnier took a chance on a first-time author, and have been thoughtful, encouraging, deft editors throughout. My thanks also to James Lilford, Ian

Acknowledgements

Greensill, Robert Sharman and everyone at Bonnier who helped to make it happen.

Many dear friends provided support along the way. Particular thanks to David Jeans, Eliot Brown and Joe, who provided invaluable advice on authorship. Rob Smith and Kadhim read parts of the early drafts. Jez Newton, Ali Witt and Alex Marshall were generous hosts in New York. Marty Katz has been a great supporter of this story and, with Laura Trachuk, was the first to celebrate the book. Madison Darbyshire has been a true friend and ally since the beginning. Eve Kraicer is wise in all things, especially books.

Finally, above all, I would not have got anywhere without my family. To Caroline, Phil and Steve; to Matt and Dave; and to Mum: thank you for everything. Cheddar the cat provided crucial moral support. And to Daniel, my strength and stay, all my love.

Index

Index

Index

Index

Index